The Wreck Hunter

The Wreck Hunter

Battle of Britain & The Blitz

To: Tom.
18/3/24

MELODY FOREMAN

FRONTLINE
BOOKS

THE WRECK HUNTER
Battle of Britain & The Blitz

Published in 2019 and reprinted in 2023 by Frontline Books,
an imprint of Pen & Sword Books Ltd,
47 Church Street, Barnsley, S. Yorkshire, S70 2AS

www.frontline-books.com

ISBN: 9-781-39902-175-3

CIP data records for this title are available from the British Library

For more information on our books, please visit
www.frontline-books.com, email info@frontline-books.com
or write to us at the above address.

Typeset in 10.5/13 pt Palatino
by Aura Technology and Software Services, India
Printed and bound by CPI Group (UK) Ltd, Croydon, CR0 4YY

Pen & Sword Books Ltd incorporates the imprints of Pen & Sword
Archaeology, Atlas, Aviation, Battleground, Discovery,
Family History, History, Maritime, Military, Naval, Politics,
Social History, Transport, True Crime, Claymore Press,
Frontline Books, Praetorian Press,
Seaforth Publishing and White Owl

For a complete list of Pen and Sword titles please contact
PEN & SWORD LTD
47 Church Street, Barnsley, South Yorkshire, S70 2AS, England
E-mail: enquiries@pen-and-sword.co.uk

Or

PEN AND SWORD BOOKS
1950 Lawrence Rd, Havertown, PA 19083, USA
E-mail: Uspen-and-sword@casematepublishers.com

Contents

Foreword

HAVING got to know many of 'The Few' during my role over the decades as a committee member of the Battle of Britain Monument in London, I was delighted to be asked to write a foreword to *The Wreck Hunter*.

My name was suggested to the author by the awesome Alix Kent, daughter of the late, great Group Captain Johnny 'Kentowski' Kent, DFC*, AFC, Virtuti Militari. I had experienced the pleasure of assisting Alix during her research into the RAF career of her courageous father and as this book is dedicated to his memory, on account of him being a hero much lauded by community aviation archaeologist Terry Parsons, our connections tied in perfectly.

At the time of writing (August 2017) it has just been announced that the wreck of USS *Indianapolis*, sunk in 1945, has been found 18,000ft down in the Pacific after a multimillion dollar search. Artefacts from the Titanic draw huge crowds whenever they are put on display. This human desire to seek out tangible objects linked to great events is obviously deep-seated.

Anyone interested in our military history would expect, given that we have fought just about every other country on earth at some time or other, that such relics would be found beyond these shores. However, in 1940 a truly pivotal conflict, the Battle of Britain, was fought above the cities and countryside of the UK itself and the resulting debris, from both sides, fell directly below the scene of combat.

Having fallen many thousands of feet, it follows that these objects, especially aircraft complete with engines, would be buried to a considerable depth.

In the immediate post-war era, with the country war-weary, rationing still in place and with exceptionally hard winters, there can't have been much appetite for literally raking up the detritus of war. However, the rapid escalation of aviation archaeology in the 1970s and 1980s shows that this interest was only dormant.

Probably the first person known to have embarked on researching and executing 'digs' is Terry Parsons who, fired by spending his childhood years (he was three years old in 1940) close to Biggin Hill, started the ball rolling in the early 1960s.

This book documents a selection of his most interesting (though they all are) excavations over the years and the personalities, living and dead, that were drawn in.

What comes out, and it is crucial that this is understood by the considerable number of people hostile to such undertakings, is that the control columns, the stopped watches, the still-functioning parachutes, the tickets for long-ago shows and the bent machine guns are not the ultimate goal, but a bridge to the young men of all nationalities who all too often met their end alongside them.

Edward McManus
Historian and Committee Member
Battle of Britain Monument London
bbm.org.uk

Introduction

WHY write another book about the Battle of Britain when there are already acres of very good ones out there? Why attempt to examine again the rightfully mythological status of the greatest aerial conflict the world has ever known? And what can be gained by applying long-gone meanings to contemporary situations?

I mulled over questions like these for some while when I was first asked to write *The Wreck Hunter* and soon I realised here really was a new and independent story which had to be told.

I'd argue the life and work of community aviation archaeologist Terry Parsons provides us with the kind of answers which add rare and important layers to the early foundations of historical facts which engineered the nostalgic notions of life in Britain in 1940. There is a genuine claim his recovery of artefacts from the Battle of Britain and the ensuing 'Blitz' is indeed archaeology. And I'd like to think the social context further endorses this fact.

So, within these pages sits one man's unique and passionate tale of discovery; driven, characterised and motivated not only by the monumental events which took place in the skies over south-east Britain in 1940 and after, but a lifelong sense of duty to preserve the memory of 'The Few' and 'The Many'.

Terry's childhood memories are as vivid to him today as much else in his 80-year-old life. Such recollections from seventy-seven years ago have resounded firm and resonant in the heart and mind of a man totally nourished in the inherited British DNA of struggle and survival. Of course, in 1940 this islander warrior-spirit of a generation was at its height. The Conservative politicians, led by Winston Churchill, enjoyed their chance to espouse policies which challenged the traditional class divide when it came to war. Didn't everyone want freedom? Rich and poor? Weren't we in it together? Conservatives? Labour? Liberals?

I'd argue this assumed fortitude during times of struggle goes way back to the days when the ancient people of Britain expected to fight to the death in a bid to prevent invaders storming in from across the Channel.

British people got used to taking defensive action. Think about the victories over the mighty Spanish Armada in 1588 – a time when the British success at naval warfare seized the fabric of military energies among islanders. Let's not forget the Battle of Waterloo of 1815 when 25,000 British men led by the Duke of Wellington took up arms with Anglo-Allied forces (totalling 118,000) to defeat Napoleon – Emperor of France – in his bid to seize power throughout Europe.

Wellington, obviously proud of the coalition victory, noted:

> 'I had occupied that post [Hougoumont] with a detachment from General Byng's brigade of Guards, which was in position in its rear; and it was some time under the command of Lieutenant-Colonel MacDonald, and afterwards of Colonel Home; and I am happy to add that it was maintained, throughout the day, with the utmost gallantry by these brave troops, notwithstanding the repeated efforts of large bodies of the enemy to obtain possession of it.'

The First World War demanded just as much, and even more 'gallantry and bravery' from the people of Great Britain. Once again, the right to defend homes and lives from the threat of invasion was called to the fore. Four years of total misery in the trenches of France and Belgium, and the battles in the sky and on the sea resulted in the death of millions. Still, Britain remained free of foreign tyrants. Victory in battle had become the ultimate framework of every British life.

When the Second World War broke out on 3 September 1939, whilst people in Britain were shocked it was 'happening all over again', as islanders they acclimatized to the fight as had generations before them. 'We never had much choice but to do so and to gird our loins against Hitler,' explained pioneer aviation archaeologist Terry Parsons.

There was a stoicism among the British. The desire to protect the island was all, and why should anyone else try and take it? This attitude of collective inherited justification turned into a readiness to beat off and keep out any foe. It was in the nature of the generation living in the Britain of 1940. The people of Britain had got used to invaders 'chancing their arm' in a bid to take over our leafy lanes, ancient oak trees, peaceful meadows, blue skies and hop fields. The British of the time embraced this myth in the hope that any social hardship characterised by parts of the country suffering the brutalities of intensive industry would one day after the war be transformed again into the alleged beautiful and rural country cottages and leafy panorama of the south.

This war was a visual experience, with photographs and films showing the British conquering all forms of heartbreak with a cup of tea, a Woodbine cigarette and a song from (Dame) Vera Lynn. Troubles, as in the First World War, were being 'packed up in old kit bags' and people 'kept smiling through'. The newspapers, although monitored by Winston Churchill's government, incorporated the need for morale-boosting photographs and information to sit alongside any deadly facts. Robust propaganda films of wartime like *The Canterbury Tale* and *One of Our Aircraft is Missing* and *49thParallel* (all by the legendary Michael Powell and Emeric Pressburger) helped explain a war that was ripping the heart out of Europe. The British were portrayed as the good guys, always one step ahead of the Nazis. These sinister and often quirky films which fed the audience's appetite for danger, always highlight how we got through it; but at what cost?

Terry Parsons was a schoolboy during the Battle of Britain. He was the youngest of the young, enveloped in what became known as the People's War. Patriotism was high, lives were lost and sometimes found, all for the sake of England's meadows and blue skies. 'And did those feet in ancient times, walk upon England's mountains green...,' goes the old hymn he sung each morning at assembly before class.

Dogfights between the RAF and the Luftwaffe were even fought on bright summer days in 1940. No season was exempt from hosting death, and then to die during a British summer... Well, that's the stuff the knights of old were made of! The glories of medieval valour sat strong and steadfast, and are arguably still used today as a reason by penny-pinching governments who aren't overly keen on supporting the recovery of remains of dead aircrews which have been deemed long ago as 'missing in action', and yet in some corner of some faraway field they lie alone where they fell among the wreckage of their chariot of the sky.

In 1940, BBC radio journalist Charles Gardner sat on the White Cliffs of Dover on the Kent coast, enthusiastically commentating on RAF and Luftwaffe aircraft as they swooped and swirled in a deadly Danse Macabre with the clouds. Some criticised him for his ebullient descriptions of the battles and reprimanded him for turning them into sports reports! Others praised Gardner for his approach to the reality. Death and destruction was about the truth of it – as a journalist, he was under pressure to tune his reportage to what he saw and what the British people had been led to believe by the government.

'I just want everything to be lovely,' snivels the character of Norman, who appears as the personal assistant in Ronald Harwood's exceptional play, *The Dresser*, about a wartime repertory theatre company and its struggle to present Shakespeare to audiences across a bombed-out Britain.

'Tsk. But things AREN'T lovely, Norman,' chides the stoic stage manager, Madge. 'I've got a show to run,' she growls. The narrative layers within this play and its belligerent characters, especially that of 'Sir', the actor/manager, make a fine representation of the British fighting spirit brought on by the difficult experiences endured during the Second World War. Madge's derision of Norman's hand-wringing behaviour about Sir's impending insanity says it all. 'Stiff upper lip... High and mighty,' retorts the sensitive, camp Norman in a brandy-fuelled outburst at Madge.

Shakespeare's plays examining wars, victories and defeats were used to educate and inspire wartime audiences.

Despite efforts from Number 10 to use optimistic newspaper stories to hide reality from those on the Home Front, within the armed forces and the enemy, the truth remained that people DID talk among themselves. And it was from out of those conversations the collective communities bound together and got on with the struggle and the survival. It was in this world, where 'everyone looked out for each other', the young Terry Parsons evolved.

In 1940 his heroes and role models were far off, high in the skies above, fighting a foe who had ambitions to threaten everything around him. In those days people perceived Britain as a strong power with a reputation to uphold. But there was kindness, too – an aspect of humanity not given much credence by the Nazis of Hitler's Germany.

Photographs of the wavy-haired and moustachioed young aircrews of the RAF show them smiling, but look closely and they have the eyes of the old who have seen and known darkness. And these dapper chaps in their uniforms were barely twelve years older than little Terry Parsons, and yet by fate of birth, it fell on their generation to serve and protect the traditions which ensured a country retained its status as unconquered and unbeaten. That's quite a burden; a responsibility that crushes the stem of youth and ages a spirit. The Battle of Britain is a time now long gone but I'd argue it was something well beyond nostalgia which drove Terry to spend his life looking for and finding the aircraft of both Britain and Germany, as it led to the discovery of aircrew who had lived and died in the name of honour and valour. Such a passion – and out of the wreckage of such chariots of the sky grew the roots for a new form of archaeology and social history.

Although in the early 1960s, when Terry found the wreckage of his first Hurricane, it was regarded as little more than a 'hobby'. Unconsciously of course, he was laying the foundations of early community archaeology, which was an important step on the road towards the artefacts of the Battle of Britain finally becoming embraced as important visceral and tangible evidence of a major part of the nation's military history.

In the English Heritage document *Military Aircraft Sites: Archaeological Guidance on their Significance and Future Management,* written in 2002 by the Head of National and Rural Environmental Advice Department, Vince Holyoak BA PhD MCIfA, he states:

'Belonging to a period still well within living memory, crash sites have significance for remembrance, commemoration, their cultural value as historic artefacts and the information they contain about both the circumstances of the loss and the aircraft itself. Crash sites may, on occasion, also contain human remains, giving them additional value and status as sacred sites and war graves.'

Dr Holyoak's interest in crash sites of the Second World War began in 1980 when he was 12 years old. He was given a copy of the encyclopaedic *Battle of Britain: Then and Now* by Winston Ramsey and became hooked on aviation history. Ten years later, aged 22, he was dismayed to find that his bid to write his PhD thesis on the archaeology of Battle of Britain crash sites had been turned down, as the subject matter was not regarded as 'real' archaeology. Instead, he had to settle on a topic on prehistory but his research into his first choice of quality study never wavered.

Since 1990 he is, however, pleased to report there has been progress and finally, aviation crash sites of the Second World War have entered into the archaeology mainstream. English Heritage has set standards, and specific procedures are in place in a bid to archive RAF and Luftwaffe wreckages of the Battle of Britain and the Blitz.

Dr Holyoak wrote: 'There were thousands of crash sites from the Battle of Britain and the Blitz but all of them should be considered of historic significance and the information they contain should not be destroyed or removed without adequate record.'

The English Heritage criteria for the selection of important sites are exacting.

1. The crash site includes components of an aircraft of which very few or no known complete examples survive. Examples of the commonplace may also be considered of importance where they survive well and meeting one or two of the other criteria.
2. The remains are well preserved, and may include key components such as engines, fuselage sections, main planes, undercarriage units and gun turrets. Those crash sites for which individual airframe identities (serial numbers) have been established will be of particular interest.
3. The aircraft was associated with significant raids, campaigns or notable individuals.
4. There is potential for display or interpretation as historic features within the landscape (for example as upland crash site memorials) or for restoration and display of the crashed aircraft as a rare example of its type.

In general terms, sites meeting any three of these criteria are sufficiently rare in England to be considered of national importance.

When Terry Parsons took his first steps into the brave new world of aviation archaeology in the early 1960s, it was a case of locating the site of a crashed aircraft, seeking permission from the landowner to dig it, and carrying out a little research into the pilot and aircrew. The discovery of artefacts was a plentiful experience.

However, as interest in the recovery and excavation of Second World War aircraft grew and small private museums began to evolve, especially in the south-east, where most wreckage could be located, the question over the discovery of human remains sparked a host of uncomfortable questions.

It became evident that Britain, unlike any other country, had never had a policy in place to recover fallen aircrews. And so, more often than not, the lifeless bodies of our young heroes of the sky would remain in the sunken cockpits of their aircraft and during the war, the term 'missing in action' was the only information sent to grieving families – many of whom never ever really knew what had happened to their loved ones.

There are stories of remains belonging to 'missing' pilots being discovered by determined parents who spoke to eyewitnesses about aerial combat and crashes of a particular squadron, then they proceeded to track down the aircraft wreckage and ultimately organise a decent burial.

By the 1970s, aircraft excavation had taken on a new seriousness. While most recovery groups tried hard to only seek out the 'unoccupied' wrecks, there were times when remains were disturbed. Disreputable characters would then fill the soil back in over the wreckage and keep quiet about who or what they'd found. Contacting the authorities could prove a tiresome business if trophy hunting had become the main purpose of any dig. Incidents of the remains of pilots and aircrew being found for a second time on another, later dig have been recorded and inquests were rightfully carried out.

In 1979 Terry was part of the team that found the wreckage of Hurricane P3049, which had crashed on 7 September 1940 and embedded itself 40-feet deep into marshland at Elmley on the Isle of Sheppey, Kent. The remains of 24-year-old Flight Lieutenant Hugh Beresford were still in the cockpit. He was buried at Brookwood Military Cemetery in Surrey on 16 November 1979 with full military honours. His sister was relieved to at last know the truth about what had happened to her 'missing' brother. Sadly, their parents went to their own graves still grieving and never knowing the whereabouts of their long-lost son.

By 1986, the new Protection of Military Remains Act came into force and since then, permission and a licence to dig must be granted by the Ministry of Defence with the full co-operation of English Heritage. In recent years, Operational Nightingale has been set up by the Ministry of Defence. This is a group of disabled ex-military service personnel who have professional archaeological, forensic and technical skills. In 2015 Operational Nightingale led by Richard Osgood joined forces with Stephen Macaulay and a team from Oxford Archaeology East with English Heritage's Dr Vince Holyoak to dig the wreckage of a Spitfire in Holm Fen, Cambridgeshire. It had been flown by 20-year-old Pilot Officer Harold Penketh, who died in 1940 when a training exercise in the aircraft went wrong and it plummeted into the ground to a depth of 30 feet.

During the dig, a small piece of bone was discovered at the scene. The remains of Pilot Officer Penketh were later cremated, and with the permission of his cousins, the ashes have been interred at St Peter's Church in West Blatchington.

For community archaeologists like Terry Parsons, there is now a three-month wait while specialists at the MoD consider applications to dig and check out any research offered about both RAF and Luftwaffe crash sites. Licences will not be granted if human remains are still with the wreckage.

There have been incidences though, where some community archaeologists were supported by the families of dead pilots and aircrew, who want to recover the aircraft and remains of a loved one, even though the MoD insists the 'missing in action' classification must not change. Those archaeologists, including Mark Kirby, who have bravely insisted they must do the right thing by our heroes and join with grieving families in demanding a full military burial for them, deserve a full salute. Men like Mark have often found themselves in court, but to date no one has been imprisoned for taking a moral stance.

Compassionate and forward-thinking magistrates have and do throw the cases out of court, and the essence of common law and moral decency have overruled the diktat of the MoD. It is stories like this that help to prove aircraft wreckage from the Battle of Britain and the Blitz should be regarded as an important archaeological specialism. There are whole realms of research to be undertaken, which provides us with information just as revealing and just as vital as that learned about the Prehistoric, Saxon and Roman eras. I will conclude with a quote from Dr Vince Holyoak of English Heritage, who told me: 'I once found a helmet dating back to 600 AD and the metal had been welded in places! That's amazing, as we still don't know how this was achieved in those days. The same goes for the Battle of Britain Hurricane, which had certain metal rivets welded specifically onto parts of the aircraft, and just exactly how this was done has not been studied or precisely revealed. The archaeology of such technology is an area in much need of research.' The reasons to recover crashed aircraft of the Battle of Britain number in their hundreds – a fact Terry Parsons has known for almost eighty years.

Melody Foreman
January, 2023

STOP PRESS: In recent days I was delighted to discover Battle of Britain Hurricane pilot Sgt Herbert Black was honoured in his hometown of Ibstock in Leicestershire.

A special green plaque sponsored by the city council has been placed on the wall of The Waggon and Horses public house in Curzon Street, Ibstock, Leicestershire to serve as a permanent reminder of the local hero who died after an aerial dogfight with the Luftwaffe over the skies of east Kent in 1940.

Sgt Black (featured in Chapter 7 of this book) was nominated in 2022 by the pupils and staff at his former school - Dixie Grammar School in Market Bosworth. A piece of his Hurricane is already on show at the school and his name appears on a plaque here alongside that of a former classmate - John Reed of the famous 617 Dambusters squadron.

Chapter 1

THE FIRST WRECK HUNTERS

THE excavation and recovery of remains of crashed military aircraft began just after the First World War with historically important debris from up to 185 different varieties scattered across the lands of Europe.

Twisted and charred lumps of metal, canvas and wood were often all that was left of, say, a British fighter like the S.E.5a, the Sopwith Camel or the Airco DH.9 bomber. Think, too, of the German aircraft which bit the dust with Royal Flying Corps and RAF bullets having ruptured their engines... Fokker Eindeckers, Gotha bombers and Siemens-Schuckerts. As each aircraft came down, so each mangled mess left another sad and brutal chapter of military history.

The Allies' aircraft were used for reconnaissance at first and were sent out over no man's land to photograph the enemy trenches and gun batteries. Research reveals that the information they flew back with and reported to the military high command of the time was ignored, and thousands of troops were still under strict orders to run over the top, only to be slaughtered needlessly. Despite the aircrews being easy targets and at great risk from enemy gun batteries on the ground, flying was outrageously not perceived as proper soldiering. Army commanders had disregard for pilots, who they called 'flyboys', and their value to the war effort was not taken seriously until at least early 1916. It's alarming to acknowledge the immense number of lives which could have been saved if only the intelligence gathered by pilots had been used to correctly direct those battalions on the ground. The endeavours of those risking all to fly over the German trenches were ignored and written off as chatter and nonsense supplied by 'flyboys'.

More often than not, once hit, the aircraft took its crew with it, and the fear of being burned alive gripped most men at the controls in the cockpit, many who were still in their late teens. Some, including the famous British fighter ace Major Mick Mannock VC, DSO**, MC* (1897 – 1918), carried a pistol to quickly end their lives in case of such horror. Mannock's fears were confirmed when his S.E.5a fighter was shot down in flames. Witnesses claim that his body was free of bullet holes when it was recovered not far from the wreckage, as if he had jumped, and he was later buried as an 'unknown airman' at a Commonwealth War Grave in Laventie in the Pas-de-Calais, France. Officially Major Mick Mannock is missing to this day, although many leading historians are convinced it is his remains beneath the headstone at Laventie.

So why didn't aircrews wear parachutes? Parachutes had been invented just before the start of the conflict but were deemed impractical and too heavy for the aircraft, and the harnesses were still in development stage. The Royal Flying Corps (which became the RAF in 1918) forbade the use of parachutes. It appears the British authorities believed aircraft were valuable and pricey military instruments which could not and should not be abandoned at the first sign of a problem. It was considered by the top brass, who were often army generals who didn't fly, that aircrew would jump out of the cockpit at the slightest hint of engine failure or threat of attack. On the other hand, the Germans did allow the use of parachutes by the early summer of 1918, when they realised that many experienced airmen were being lost day after day. More often than not the parachutes of 1918 failed to open when deployed and were known to get tangled and wrapped around the aircraft, but the number of aircrew from Europe who could have been saved by the use of a decent parachute during the 1914 – 1918 conflict reaches the tens of thousands.

It is not hard to imagine the vast quantities of human remains and aircraft debris which needed to be respectfully discovered. Along with the wreckage come the stories of the pilots, navigators and gunners who once manned the aircraft. Exactly how many men and aircraft from the First World War were never found and are missing to this day is a question which has remained unanswered for more than a hundred years.

A little more than two decades after the end of this war came the start of the next conflict in Europe, and once again, airborne winged chariots representing the latest in modern military technologies were flown by warriors of the sky.

Britain had invented fighter aircraft like the Hurricane and Spitfire, the multi-purpose Beaufighter and Gladiator, and bombers like the Blenheim, Wellington and Lancaster. Men of the Royal Air Force would roar across the British Isles and the Channel to fight off the invading German Luftwaffe flying high in speedy Me 109s, Me 110s, deadly Stukas, Dornier Do 17s and Heinkel He 111s.

It was inevitable that many RAF aircraft, which had often been delivered to the airfields straight from the factories and maintenance units by the hardy Air Transport Auxiliary ferry pilots, would come to grief as the aerial conflict intensified. As the Luftwaffe flew victorious during the Battle of France in early 1940, their determination to cross the Channel and beat the RAF out of the skies of Britain knew no bounds, either. They were in for a surprise as dogfights, desperate and bloody until the end, raged almost daily over the South East during the Battle of Britain in 1940. The RAF refused to give in and casualties were high.

Terry Parsons, who was later to become a pioneer in the field of aviation recovery and archaeology, recalled:

'As a youngster in 1940, and for the rest of the war, I noted how one by one the aircraft fell from the sky, sometimes tearing downwards up to 500mph in flames, sometimes making to crash land with a devastating crunch, and other moments they were force-landed by RAF and Luftwaffe pilots frantically wondering if it was their final goodbye.

'For the aircraft now a sorry mess embedded in hedgerows, fields, streets, homes and gardens, it was a time for the civilian and arguably original wreck-hunters to spring into action. These local men were salvage operatives who owned or had access to large, heavy duty trucks which could carry weighty pieces of battered aircraft to a scrapyard ready for smelting.

'These workers, who were often untrained and were required to work with basic equipment in trying circumstances and bad weather, would be commissioned by the Air Ministry to assist the RAF in the removal of debris. The salvage kit consisted of buckets, spades, cutting gear and a lorry with a flatbed trailer. Whilst they did what they could, I remember occasions watching them remove just the debris on the top of the ground. Sometimes if the lorry was already loaded too high they would throw a large piece of Me 109, Dornier, or even Hurricane over the hedge. Lots of pieces were found in the bushes and trees, too.

'The salvage chaps did their best I guess, with the time and resources they had, but I don't think they did that much digging to be honest. When I started digging in 1963, I certainly never came across any pre-dug sites. I think in the 1940s it was customary that the salvage crews just filled in any holes with top soil...and if it was time for lunch then they'd make for the local pub for a pie and a pint. It could be a case of what the eye doesn't see, the heart doesn't grieve over!

'I recall one day I was riding on the bus towards Westerham and I saw a Spitfire make a crash landing in a field. As soon as the aircraft ground to a halt, the pilot undid his harness and jumped onto the wing and slid down it to land on his two feet. He started walking away leaving the Spitfire complete even though the engine was smoking. Next day I looked at the site where the Spitfire had landed and it had been removed.

'I do know of times the salvage chaps and the RAF Maintenance Units never made it to a crash site. Remember – they just didn't have the resources to get to every wreck. I recall in the late 1950s how the tail of an Me 109 was still sticking out of a field near Westerham, Kent. Nobody had been near it until I got permission from the farmer a few years later to dig it.'

Records show that between September 1940 and March 1941 eighty recovery jobs were carried out by one recovery company from Brighton run by a Mr Arthur Nicholls. This would usually follow on from a detailed examination of the wreckage and the site by the RAF. Specialists from the RAF Maintenance Units would recover what parts could be repaired and restored as replacements for other aircraft. An RAF Queen Mary trailer would arrive to remove whole aircraft which could have useful spares. Of course, the experts from RAF test bases like Farnborough would be keen to assess Luftwaffe wrecks for any equipment which revealed advances in German aviation technology. Photographs of downed aircraft of 1940 often reveal members of the Home Guard standing to attention next to crash sites to warn off anyone keen to snaffle a souvenir or two. When a Dornier Do 17 came down in woods near Kilndown, Sussex on 15 September 1940, it was again a job for the Home Guard to keep watch. Sometime after this German aircraft hit the ground, its bombs went off, killing William Waters of the 23rd (Hawkhurst) Battalion, Kent Home Guard in the blast.

Tragic events like this, however, failed to prevent the determined collector from taking a chance to raid a downed aircraft for artefacts. Personal items belonging to the pilot and aircrew were at a premium and the main prize was any German insignia that could be carved off the fuselage or tail. The swastika removed from an Me 109, Me 110, a Stuka, Dornier or Heinkel was high currency for the collector even in those days when the war promised a deluge of crashed aircraft in the south-east of England every day! Decades later, in the 21st century, this type of artefact from the Battle of Britain and similar items from the era remain historical and arguably archaeological hot property.

In 1940 and during the war many such artefacts representing another RAF victory against the Nazis were often illegally removed by those opportunistic locals who reached the aircraft within a few minutes, or even seconds of it hitting the ground. Emblems of the Luftwaffe and various items from downed RAF aircraft were hidden in attics for decades until they appeared in collections in today's museums. Craftily, their acquisition was always very cloak and dagger and done 'on the nod' and often 'on the hoof'.

These days it is interesting to raise the controversial question of ownership when it comes to those wartime artefacts removed from military aircraft – fighting and bombing machines which, after all, had been financed by the taxpayers living in each country during the war. For example, should exhibits only be on show in government-funded official museums with a duty of care and security, as stipulated by a specific policy on such artefacts? And what of the personal items belonging to the aircrews? One hopes they were returned to any man taken prisoner of war, or if discovered decades later during digs, every attempt was made to return them to families.

One story of human salvation came about via the meticulous archive kept by the previously mentioned salvage company operator, Mr Arthur Nicholls. His work showed how the diligence of his teams helped to identify any aircraft and aircrew reported as 'missing in action'.

Author and aviation historian Andy Saunders refers to Mr Nicholls' steadfast archive when he writes:

'In relation to the loss of a Spitfire Mk I X4278 the Ministry of Defence and Commonwealth War Graves Commission was finally able to place a named headstone on the grave of Pilot Officer John Wintringham Cutts of No. 222 Squadron who had been killed when he was shot down by a Messerschmitt Bf109 over Maidstone at 13.30 hours on 4 September 1940.

For some reason, the casualty recovered from Spitfire X4278 had not been identified and was buried in 1940 as an "unknown airman" at Bell Road Cemetery, Sittingbourne, Kent, but a report in the archives of A V Nicholls & Co. identified the serial number of the Spitfire in which 20-year-old Pilot Officer Cutts had been lost and, thereby, provided a definite link to the grave of the previously unidentified pilot who had been recovered from that wreck and buried during the Battle of Britain.'

Spitfire X4278 had crashed and burned out on Amberfield Farm, Chart Sutton, Kent. The crash site was dug in 1972 and no human remains were found. Then in 1999 a search of Mr Nicholls' records led to the identity of the 'missing' airman.

It was not unusual for the wartime wreck hunters to discover human remains in or near a crash site. The men of No.49 Maintenance Unit, which was based at RAF Faygate near Horsham in West Sussex, were responsible for clearing the main Battle of Britain counties of Kent, Sussex, Surrey and Hampshire. They were often faced with this sad experience but took it in their stride as all was part of the job. They worked alongside a parent crew from RAF Tangmere, who received orders from No.43 Maintenance Group based at Cowley, near Oxford. It was No.43 that heard directly from the Air Ministry if an aircraft was sighted falling from the sky or was 'missing'. The '49-ers' were then scrambled into action.

Leading Aircraftman Cook arrived at a crash site one day and recalled finding a boot in the wreckage of a German aircraft, and as he pulled, he discovered to his horror that the foot was still in it. The alarmed Cook reported how he 'found a spot by a tree where the sun was shining and buried it there.' No doubt such swift, spontaneous actions and decisions were carried out on many dismembered remains. Busy salvage teams facing wreck after wreck after wreck on a daily basis knew the rules of the day very well. For a burial to be official then, at least eight pounds of human parts had to be placed in a coffin.

Of course, as grisly and upsetting as it is, the finding of human remains in and around wartime crash sites is not unheard of, as Terry Parsons discusses later in this book.

During the war, however, Britain benefited from captured Luftwaffe aircraft which had landed in one piece during a forced landing. Its German pilot and aircrew were often made prisoners of war. Many German aircraft were transported around the country as morale boosters for anyone wishing to pay a sixpence to take a look at such an exhibit. All the money raised went towards popular local Spitfire Funds, which had been devised by the Minister of Aircraft Production, Lord Beaverbrook in a bid to encourage communities in villages, towns and cities to finance new Spitfires in their name.

Even the young HRH Princess Elizabeth, who would become HM The Queen, paid her sixpence to visit a German Me 109 on display at Windsor Castle. It is also reported that she sat in the cockpit of the fallen Nazi fighting machine that attracted a healthy crowd of visitors every day.

As for the men of No.49 MU though, the deadly events of the Battle of Britain especially led them to five or six messy crash sites a day, where nothing was left of anything resembling a cockpit or pilot's seat! Of course, there was little publicity about the RAF aircraft which crashed; it was forbidden to take photographs of these stricken defenders of the British Isles. Public morale had to be protected and preserved at all times. As far as the press was to be concerned, the RAF were winning the war in the skies. Full stop. To further endorse this propaganda, images of downed Luftwaffe aircraft were plentiful for obvious reasons and often made the front pages of local and national newspapers. Patriotic editors wanted desperately to show readers just how Britain's noble RAF and Fleet Air Arm refused to let the Luftwaffe bully them into defeat.

In reality, RAF Faygate (also known as No.1 Salvage Centre) was turning into an ever-increasing graveyard full of sad heaps of aircraft wreckage representing both friends and foe.

Today many enthusiasts travel to a crash site in the hopes of finding a piece of stray metal as a souvenir of the world's greatest ever aerial conflict, and who can blame them? But what do they discover, seventy-plus years after the Battle of Britain and the Blitz? Nothing but neat, sheltered housing developments with foundations buried deep, along with any neighbouring discarded and fragmented victims of long-gone aerial combat. It's no surprise. The years roll by, and it's a common story of disappearance for many of the archaeologically important areas of Britain once crucial to the war effort.

That's why it's all the more important to reveal the story of a quiet man with a good heart, who in the 1960s set out to preserve the memory of 'The Few' of the Battle of Britain and the boys of the Blitz by finding their aircraft. And rightfully in doing so, he became a pioneer of aviation recovery – a genuine wreck hunter. His name is Terry Parsons and unknowingly, with every spadeful of earth he ever dug, he was creating a brave new world of aviation archaeology long before most of today's historians had even heard of the Battle of Britain. Softly, kindly and stoically, he ploughed on with his passion, helping and advising many young men keen to join various excavations. Some of these teenage enthusiasts mentored by Terry in the 1970s and early 1980s now have successful businesses and professional work linked to military aircraft of the Second World War, including Steve Vizard of Airframe Assemblies and Andy Saunders, historian and author of various books. Terry's friends who accompanied him on many digs over the years include Tony Graves (London Air Museum and aviation historian)

Ed Francis, Mark Kirby, Stevie Hall, Gordon Ramsey, Tony Parslow, Philippa Hodgkiss, and Geoff Nutkins.

Terry is keen to pay a huge tribute to those with hearts of gold who over the decades supplied and drove the diggers and cranes during each dig. 'Without these guys, we'd never have recovered half of what we did. Sometimes the aircraft were buried tens of feet down. We were talking much more than spadework!! Only the big machinery could do the job and prepare the way for us to examine the site in detail and recover the artefacts', he told me.

In the more than six decades until now, Terry has compiled a lengthy dig list of 900 aircraft in his 'Aviation Archaeology Logbook' – three-quarters of the aircraft he found had taken part in the Battle of Britain. All of them were flown by loyal, heroic aircrews, many of whom didn't make it, during a war which ripped the heart out of Europe and shaped the lives of many generations yet to be born.

Terry's story had to be told.

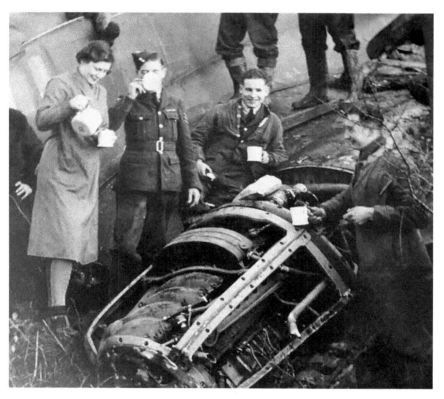

Personnel from an RAF recovery team enjoy a break before they make plans to have the wreckage of this Luftwaffe aircraft taken away.

Above left: Flying Officer John Wintringham Cutts, who shared in the destruction of a He 111 on 30 August 1940. F/O Cutts was shot down and killed on 4 September 1940. See page 78.

Above right: The wreckage of a Heinkel He 111 before its removal by RAF recovery teams and local haulage contractors.

A crew from No. 49 Maintenance Unit, based at RAF Faygate, strike a pose next to the wreckage of a Junkers Ju 87 before it is taken from the scene. (Courtesy of the Andy Saunders Collection)

This Messerschmitt Bf 109E-1 of III/JG 54 crashed at Hengrove near Margate, Kent, at 6.00 pm on 12 August 1940. The RAF personnel seen here during its recovery are almost certainly from No. 49 Maintenance Unit. (Courtesy of the Andy Saunders Collection)

Chapter 2

BOY OF THE BATTLE

I WAS four years old and walking with my Uncle Vic when I saw the Luftwaffe shoot up our local high street. The sirens had just sounded and within seconds a Dornier Do 17 loomed low and growled its menace across the town. Suddenly my Uncle Vic grabbed me and we dived into a shop doorway to avoid the bullets which thudded along the road so fast, there was no time to be afraid. Each bullet spat the ground frantically close to us, leaving small clouds of dust behind it. The aircraft in all its darkness was so close, we could see the pilot's sneering face from the cockpit window. It was a look of pure contempt. Then, as suddenly as the Dornier had loomed up on us, it disappeared towards Biggin Hill airfield. My Uncle Vic just said: 'Oh, I think we'll be getting on home now.'

That day, as we stepped out again in the bright summer sun, still shaken by our near-death experience, my future destiny as a pioneer of Battle of Britain aircraft recovery had been set. A wreck hunter was born and, ironically, if the RAF shot that Luftwaffe bomber out of the sky that day, there's every chance I may well have dug its rusting carcass from a field in Kent – two, three, four even five decades later.

Growing up during the war, I realised every day was potentially full of danger, and that extraordinary experience in 1940 was one of many equally alarming events I shared with my school friends who also lived next to the most important RAF station of the Second World War. Indeed, as the Battle of Britain raged in the skies above, the excited children of Tatsfield Primary School were becoming used to – even addicted to – the sounds of war. Many of them found it irresistible and as seductive as any drug which fuelled thrills and adventure.

I can never forget the steady roar of twelve Merlin engines powering Spitfires or Hurricanes to take off, the drone of the Luftwaffe bombers appearing as fast as Valkyries overhead, the black crosses on their wings an intimidating sight for eyes young and old, the whine of the air raid sirens, and the crash and blast of the Home Defence guns.

I'd smile in a strange sort of comfort. It was my life, and better than any storybook fantasy read to us by schoolteachers in voices made timid by adult thoughts of impending invasion.

More often than not, us kids watched the dogfights in the skies and marvelled at the balletic events unfolding before us. We were bewitched and enthralled. The sound of the guns fired by air crew so high above Biggin Hill resembled cloth being torn in two... a ripping, muffled cracking noise which penetrated the consciousness of all those who heard it.

Spitfires swooping, Me 109s gunning straight for them, the descent of the defending Hurricanes coming down out of the clouds; it is little wonder that such adventure influenced the hearts and minds of any child who saw it.

My memories are sharp and clear and tell of a time when Biggin Hill fostered a vibrant generation of young men and women who lived for the day, not knowing if they'd see tomorrow.

For kids like me, oblivious of the serious threat to our liberty, the aftermath of a dogfight filled us with glee. I was out avidly collecting shrapnel and small pieces of aircraft which had fallen to the ground and scattered, bent, broken and burnt, across local fields, gardens and roads.

I made a note of the places an Me 109, a Dornier, a Spitfire, a Hurricane or a Heinkel had been seen to explode or crash land. Then once the police had finished inspecting the site, me and a few friends would be there to clamber over a burned-out cockpit or comb the area for artefacts.

Such search missions across the North Downs of Biggin Hill and its countryside were an everyday event in the lives of us aircraft-mad little collectors, who scavenged the scattered debris of battle as ardently as if it were gold. Many of us made a business out of it. I joined in the fun of being a member of the shrapnel mafia and we traded this and that, and any piece of a Luftwaffe aircraft in particular was a prized possession indeed!

My grandmother, Esther Parsons, had a lot of other artefacts my uncles had stored in the cupboards of our home. I recall she had a little dish of mercury. I don't know where it came from. I was fascinated how that liquid metal moved around when you lifted the dish. There were all sorts of stuff there, including bullets. My uncles came home one day with an RAF white silk scarf and then one long leather gauntlet! They were always coming home with something from a crash site. The first thing my uncles did when an aircraft went down was to run over and see what they could get. It was normal to get a souvenir but at the time I didn't know this was illegal. They did get shooed off some sites. Especially if there was a Luftwaffe instrument of interest to the RAF found in the cockpit.

My grandfather, Bert Parsons, worked at Biggin Hill throughout the war and was among the construction teams who helped turn it into the top Fighter Command base. He told us stories of some of the aircrews he met and knew by sight and reputation. Grandfather was also at the airfield when a big raid occurred on 30 August and many people were killed. He was cut up about that. On that day Spitfire pilots from Nos. 79 and 610 squadrons were airborne immediately and managed to split the Luftwaffe formation but when the raiders returned at 6.00 pm they let Biggin Hill have it! Nine Junkers 88s followed the Ashford-Reigate railway line at low level before taking us by surprise. My grandfather told me how he used to run for cover and made for wherever he could to avoid the bombs and the bullets. Most of the time all the ground crews and staff could do was fall to the ground as there wasn't a lot of warning. There was only the Observer Corps to let them know what was coming.

The Luftwaffe came in low over Westerham and then you got the hill up to Biggin and they could be seen as easily as that! People could check out the faces of the aircrew, as they flew that low. They were only up about 200 feet. Pilots fly in over Westerham and if they keep straight and level, they are only a few feet above Biggin Hill itself.

When the Luftwaffe struck, there was a feeling of carnage all around but there weren't ambulances screaming about the place. It was always exciting to see all those aeroplanes flying about. I could hear the rattle of machine guns but the most frightening thing of the war for me – and it's laughable now – was the time I was out playing one afternoon and I heard this hissing sound. There was this row of beech trees on a bank at the back of the house and all of a sudden, this barrage balloon came up but we didn't know what it was. We'd never seen one before. It was half inflated really and the 'ear' bits were flopped down. To see this thing looming up over the tree was terrifying. I ran indoors and grabbed my grandparents as they'd never seen anything like it either. There were a quite a few balloons around Biggin Hill and they were made of a light fabric with heavy cables. They were put up in the hope the Luftwaffe would fly into them. Any pilot doing 200-300 mph would not notice a barrage balloon cable, especially if they had a Spitfire on their tail.

Remember, the visibility up there is not great. Even on a sunny day, you think 'good visibility' but it's not like that. The balloons had some success in downing aircraft but the Me 109 pilots used to shoot them up like a clay pigeon shoot. I saw two balloons on fire.

When there was a raid on the anti-aircraft guns, it shook the whole house. I was glad not to have been evacuated though. My grandparents didn't want me to go, so I stayed.

James Eastwood, a relative, recalled how once during an air raid he jumped into a bomb crater with a friend in order to take shelter. When the all-clear sounded, a Spitfire came in to land but unfortunately it overshot the runway and flipped into James' crater. The next thing they knew, the pilot was hanging upside down looking straight at them!

We lived about a mile from the runway and I often saw aircraft taking off. When they left the ground and were very suddenly over our house, you can't get much closer than that, can you?

The only time I did get a big warning from my grandmother was all about 'leaving the Butterfly Bombs alone'. I've got two now in my own personal collection – deactivated, of course. One of them I acquired from a building site in East London in the 1970s. These bombs were weighted so when they hit a building or hard surface they would ignite and explode. I remember they used to hang in trees but most of us kids knew not to touch them.

A favourite commanding officer at Biggin Hill and mentioned by my grandfather was Group Captain Dick 'Grubby' Grice, DFC, who was a veteran of the First World War, and later at Biggin Hill, from 1938, a popular leader among his much-loved No. 32 Squadron. Group Captain Grice, who as a young pilot had flown against the famous 'Red Baron' (Manfred von Richthofen), was noted for his tremendous bravery. Although a decision to blow up a bomb-wrecked hangar at the station got him in trouble and he faced a court martial for his action, having explained that the sight of the half-demolished hangar would invite more attacks from the Luftwaffe, he was exonerated.

I recall the time at our home in the nearby hamlet of Tatsfield when my grandfather told us over supper how on 2 September 1939, the day before the war started, Winston Churchill arrived at the station and called by the Officers' Mess. He told the assembled crowd of young faces: 'I have no doubt you will be as brave and eager to defend your country as your forefathers.' According to some who were there that day, Churchill also asked the aircrews to keep the Luftwaffe away from his house in nearby Westerham! Within a few months, in May 1940, he became Prime Minister. Finally, his warnings in previous years about the growing Nazi war machine were taken seriously by the British parliament.

During the latter half of the Battle of Britain, including 15 September, the Commanding Officer of No. 92 Squadron was Group Captain Brian Kingcome, DSO, DFC*. He was known to be a fair and reasonable individual who along with No. 92 Squadron had recently been transferred to Biggin Hill from RAF Tangmere. He arrived at Biggin Hill a week after the station was almost obliterated by the Luftwaffe, who attacked with might and determination on 30 August 1940. That day 39 people died in a shelter which fell foul to the menace of nine Junkers 88s. The cookhouse, NAAFI and workshops were destroyed and the WAAFery wrecked. Biggin Hill lost a hangar, two aircraft were destroyed and nearly every mode of transport was on fire.

When the shelter full of airmen and women was turned into a pile of rubble, there was no hope for those inside. In the WAAF's safety trench an explosion smashed the entrance, and nearby the concrete walls of another shelter caved in on those cowering inside. Most of the sheltering WAAFs were showered with rubble and waited patiently in the darkness and destruction for help. Finally, these women, previously entombed before their time, were dug free by rescuers using their hands.

I remember hearing stories how the local milkmen, postmen, tradesmen and anyone around who had survived the bombing raid that day descended upon the station to help those in need. In those days, there was no question about such emergency assistance. Most of the WAAF, led then by Assistant Section Officer Felicity Hanbury, survived their ordeal with cuts and bruises, although a few were seriously injured and one, nurse Corporal Lena Button, died from her injuries.

Many of those who perished after the raid of 30 August were dug out of the rubble by miners because the devastation, holes and mountains of rubble were so deep. The medical officer and his nursing staff were working around the clock to deal with the injured, and at one point on 30 August more than twenty casualties were treated in just 45 minutes. By 2.00 am on 31 August most of the bodies of the 39 dead had been recovered.

Much of the motivation of No. 92 Squadron came from Flight Lieutenant Kingcome and Geoffrey Wellum as his wingman. Flight Lieutenant Kingcome became the first to fly from Biggin Hill, as the RAF's battles against the weight of the Luftwaffe turned 15 September 1940 into long, deadly hours scarred by high casualties and destruction. Both the RAF and the Luftwaffe took a beating, but as a 4-year-old, all I could do was watch mesmerized, as the dramatic sights and sounds filled my heart and my mind.

In just twelve months from 1940 to 1941, Biggin Hill was hit twelve times by the Luftwaffe. The airfield had become a prized target for the aircrews of Luftwaffe chief Hermann Goering. And for the commanders of RAF No. 11 Group tasked with defending the South East, there was nothing to do but turn fear into decisive action, which resulted in permanent readiness, combat and successful defence of Britain at whatever cost.

Was I afraid? It never dawned on me to be scared. Excited? Yes! And I knew when an air raid was serious because at home, where I lived with my grandparents and my uncles, we all had to squeeze under the Morrison shelter in the kitchen. I often wondered if the Luftwaffe deliberately decided to attack Biggin Hill around 6.00 pm because they knew we'd all be eating our dinners. I remember many times when I'd grab my plate and finish my meal under that Morrison shelter with my grandmother's elbows nudging me to help myself from the bowl of potatoes she'd placed near our feet! Sometimes we were under that Morrison shelter for three to four hours. The house never got hit, mainly because we were hidden deep in a valley, but we did have a broken window caused by a piece of shrapnel.

For the fighter pilots on high alert, of course the benign procedures of mealtimes and general family life were a far-off memory – surreal even. They'd been thrown into a world full of fear, brutality and dramatic intensity – a game of luck, skill and deep camaraderie.

Flight Lieutenant (later Group Captain) Kingcome, writing about his experiences while stationed at Biggin Hill during the Battle of Britain, recalled: 'Of all the places from which to operate, as I did from August 1940 to June 1942, Biggin Hill was way out in front. It was superbly placed, both operationally and socially.

'Operationally we were just far enough inland from the main German approach lanes to give us time to climb flat out due north to the enemy's altitude before turning south to hit him head on, by far the most effective and damaging form of attack, usually somewhere over mid-Kent.

'Socially it exhausts me just thinking about it. When we were stood down half an hour after dusk there was the choice of either scooting up to London where 10 shillings (the bulk of our day's pay of 14 shillings) would cover an evening at Shepherds and the Bag of Nails (the Four Hundred if we could raise a quid), or The White Hart at Brasted, where 5 shillings kept us in beer until the local bobby moved us on at closing time. Then, with a few girlfriends, on to our billets, a comfortable local country house where we were dispersed at night against the possibility of an air attack on the airfield (all that money that had gone into our training couldn't be put at risk) where one of our pilots, a pianist who could hold his own against any night club musician and frequently did, would play into the small hours, and we would finally snatch an hour or two's sleep in armchairs, fully dressed to save time and effort getting up for dawn readiness.

'Then the dispersal hut with the unforgettable sound of Merlin engines warming up in the grey half-light, the squadron doctor dispensing his miracle hangover cure from a tin bucket, occasionally a pilot, suffering more than usual, climbing into his cockpit for a quick rejuvenating whiff of neat oxygen. And then the inevitable, stomach-churning ring of the telephone and the voice from Ops: "92nd Squadron, scramble. One hundred plus bandits approaching Dungeness at Angels Fifteen."

'The surge of adrenalin, the half dozen or so pilots, that were all that we could normally muster, sprinting to their aircraft, the tiredness and the hangovers disappearing as though they had never been and the flat out climb to 20,000 feet.

'The mud on our flying boots would freeze hard to our rudder bars in our unheated and unpressurised cockpits, but as we saw the sun lift over the horizon at 20,000 feet, it was a hard turn south east to meet the enemy, the swarm of bees against the lightening sky swiftly transforming into a phalanx of bombers as the gap between us magically closes, tier upon tier with their escorting fighters weaving above, forcing one's voice on the R/T to remain calm and relaxed.

' "Gannet Squadron, spread out and pick your targets." The bomber pilots would already be getting jittery at this attack on their most exposed and vulnerable quarter with nothing between them and our guns except a thin sheet of Perspex, the tracer curling out at us, the sound of our own guns, bombers dropping smoking out of formation, three or four seconds of ammunition of our precious fifteen already gone, then into the clear air behind suddenly filled with more aircraft as the enemy fighters hit us from above, the whirling dogfight with friend and foe almost indistinguishable, the last of one's ammunition gone and the sky suddenly empty.

'For those of us safely back on the still darkened earth, the sun would rise again. The day was only just beginning and already behind us a lifetime of action packed into an hour, the memory of two sunrises in one morning and thoughts quickly suppressed of friends not yet accounted for. And ahead of us, life, at least until the next telephone call. Electrifying, adrenaline-filled life. One long, sustained high.'

As a place of action, Biggin Hill has a notable history. Firstly, it had established itself as a world leader in aviation technology in 1917 as a

Wireless Testing Station, and its positioning just 17 miles from London provided a natural area from which to defend Britain against sky-bound invaders.

RAF Biggin Hill's motto was 'The Strongest Link' and in the last year of the First World War it was operating Bristol fighters ready to defend the South East against the German Gotha bombers.

The first ever communication between the ground and aircraft in flight was created at Biggin Hill by the pioneers who developed the art of night flying. The aircrews of No. 141 Squadron made themselves known in and around the station and I recall tales of the hijinks of these young aviators in and around the village – including the tradition of removing a giant teapot from a local cafe at midnight and then replacing it the same time the following night!

However, technical prowess at the station after the First World War needed to be expanded and improved upon, especially if we take note of Winston Churchill's comments of 1933. By then he was already a powerful commentator on world affairs and expressed his concerns about Britain's 'weakness in the air' saying: 'Only a strong British Air Force can protect Britain from invasion and defeat.' His experiences in political office and on the Western Front during the First World War alerted him to the great need for military supplies and training, if Britain was to keep up with the aeronautical progress exhibited by Germany.

By the 1930s three squadrons had been billeted to RAF Biggin Hill and by the start of the war its main purpose was to protect London and the South East from the Nazi invaders. No. 92 Squadron was billeted on 'the Bump', as Biggin Hill became known, and the Women's Auxiliary Air Force, led by Assistant Section Officer Felicity Hanbury (later Dame Felicity), had arrived in force by 1939 to ensure the station ran efficiently and with purpose.

By the end of the war among those who had served with great distinction and honour at RAF Biggin Hill were three WAAFs – Sergeant Elizabeth Mortimer, Corporal Elspeth Henderson and Sergeant Helen Turner, who all received the Military Medal for bravery and had local roads named after them.

The courage and actions of all those who served at RAF Biggin Hill during the Second World War have been well documented over the years. Its squadrons are recorded as having destroyed 1,400 enemy aircraft at a loss of 453 aircrew who flew out of its famous base between 1939 – 1945.

As a child, while such history was taking place at the airfield, I was at Tatsfield Primary School listening out for the sounds of war at the same time as paying attention to my books, and Mrs Snow's sweetshop in Tatsfield was selling liquorice wood. Us kids didn't need any ration coupons to buy that for half a penny and it would last all morning. By the afternoon though, a trip to the school lavatories was a must. I seem to recall a lot of the teachers at school were good, kind people who were always happy to help us kids out with our problems. Any bad behaviour though, would result in a whack with a wooden ruler in front of our classmates and we never played up again.

But despite the regime of school life, there was nothing better than to get outside and watch the war in the skies, or at least listen and learn, and take every opportunity to visit the site of a crashed aircraft and look for souvenirs.

During the raids over the school, we had to run for some rickety shelters which wouldn't have been much good if they had been hit! Did I ever see any Luftwaffe aircrew parachute out of their aircraft and get marched through the village? No. I saw them bale out, but they were often too far away to go out to the place they landed. I don't think my grandmother would have let me. It was all very exciting though, as we thought about what we could find at a crash site. In Biggin Hill it's heavy clay and massive flints. To me it was all treasure – the shrapnel and bullet shells, and the Perspex. My uncles used to shape Perspex into RAF wings, and to make the shape of the wings themselves like feathers, they used a hot needle. I used to take them to school and swap for a bullet or a shell.

One lad, who was about eight years older than me, was Charlie Buck, and his parents ran the fish and chip shop just at the end of Tatsfield Road. One day as there was a bit of a dogfight going overhead, he suddenly heard this whistling noise. He just fell to the ground, as that's the thing to do if there's a bomb coming down. Anyway, this shrill noise stopped and Charlie thought, 'Oh, phew, it didn't go off.' so he got up and a few yards away from him was a German oxygen mask and a helmet! That's what the noise had been, the sound of it spiralling down. It was one of those funny stories that became folklore among us kids hooked on the adventure of it all.

I mentioned earlier my memory of a Spitfire going down in Westerham and described how the pilot managed to get out and walk away as calm as you like. I've little doubt he knew a local contractor would be called to come out and collect his aircraft and it was even likely the RAF would arrive with a Queen Mary trailer to carry off the battered airframe.

There was one time during the Battle of Britain when an Me 109 was roaring over Sevenoaks and shooting up the town and firing at the locals going about their business. Anyway, it got shot down; itself and the whole lot, pilot too, came crashing down near a pigsty. Well, as you can imagine, the people of Sevenoaks were more than happy about that and the pigs in the sty didn't need feeding that day. That's a true story and has stuck in my memory all these years. Retribution was never far from the hearts and minds of those keen to see the end of the enemy.

The village of Biggin Hill during the war wasn't as large as it is today. It had a church which was a corrugated iron building painted green and it sat next to the Post Office on the top of Stock Hill. In the 1950s the make-shift place of worship was replaced by a real brick building mostly constructed from the debris of a church which had been hit by Luftwaffe bombs in Peckham, London.

Former Biggin Hill schoolboy Peter Haliday recalls, like me, how the most important people in the village were notably the vicar, or 'old rubber neck' as he was called owing to his strange habit of moving his head side to side during religious education classes; the village police constable, whose name was Cannon – or PC Cannon for us kids; and the butcher.

Peter is recorded as saying: 'Using the back roads to school one morning, after a particularly noisy night, we were surprised to see a number of houses near the school had a heap of partly burnt incendiary bombs in the garden. Some had perhaps as many as eight or nine tails, together with other bits and pieces.

'As we were standing looking at the collection, an ARP warden came out of one of the houses and crossed over the road to us. He yelled, "Don't touch anything you boys! The Jerries dropped a bread basket of incendiary bombs all around here so if you see anything, don't touch it." He gave us a look as if he had heard of our reputation as souvenir hunters and did not trust us!'

The 'bread basket' was a name we all had then for the Luftwaffe container which held these particular bombs together. I recall it was about a diameter of a dustbin and three times as long, with a bomb tail on one end. Inside of it were several trays in which the incendiaries were loaded. The whole thing could house around 150 bombs. Once the container had been dropped from an aircraft, it threw the bombs out far and wide, especially if it had been dropped from a great height.

One day there was mass confusion among the grubby-kneed young excavators of Biggin Hill as they saw the area around them littered with what looked like pieces of tin foil. I later discovered it was what the

RAF called 'window', which was dropped by aircraft to confuse radar signals. The scattered glitter all over our village had been dropped by the Luftwaffe and I recall my grandmother telling me not to touch it, as she wondered if it was poisonous.

More often than not, our teachers warned us to keep away from anywhere which might have unexploded bombs. We obeyed, especially when we saw Mr Hicks striding along, waving his stick around the school field and playgrounds, where likely explosives sat waiting for victims. Us kids never really forgave the Luftwaffe for failing to hit the school after we'd left for the day!

The war gave the people of Tatsfield an edge. More often than not their attempts to survive appeared in the local newspaper. I have a copy of a wartime *Kentish Times* and it contains a report about our local priest, a person I remember very well as he wore a very large, round traditional cleric's hat, who was fined fifteen shillings for not taking heed of the blackout warning. It seems even men of God weren't immune to penalty charges!

When I was just of school age there was a tragic tale in the neighbourhood about two Hurricane pilots of No. 32 Squadron who had taken off from Biggin Hill on 11 August 1939 to test the blackout. The first to meet his death in a mysterious crash that day was Flying Officer Arthur Buchanan-Wollaston. For some unknown reason, he was killed as his aircraft went down at The Scout Hut, near my home in Tatsfield. On the same day, Pilot Officer Harold Olding took off and then he died, too as his Hurricane inexplicably nose-dived into the road behind Lusted Hall Farm Tatsfield.

In the Royal Air Force official announcements report carried in *Flight* on 17 August 1939, it confirms both pilots had died in 'flying accidents' on the same day while carrying out the same attempt to 'test the blackout'. It seems a total of ten RAF aircrew lost their lives across Britain's airfields that day.

Tragedies like this proved to be among the many to hit us during the Second World War. Like many other communities all over Britain, the essence of struggle and survival opened hearts and minds to all sorts of behaviour, mostly extreme. But when it came to the act of human kindness, I found it was never far away in Biggin Hill. It was out of our quiet sense of never knowing if we would have a tomorrow, that a great bonding flourished between us. Even after the war, the old values of hope, by then deeply engrained in the lives of our friends and neighbours, taught us that however tough life got in so-called peacetime, there was always a spirit of unity to obliterate our fears.

Ruined homes blasted by the Luftwaffe during a raid on Biggin Hill in 1940.

A photograph of Biggin Hill airfield in action in 1944.

WAAF heroines of Biggin Hill who carried out their duties with courage and honour during a bombing raid on the station in 1940. From left to right they are: Sergeant Elizabeth Mortimer, Corporal Elspeth Henderson and Sergeant Helen Turner.

Dornier Do 17s heading towards Biggin Hill. It was the Luftwaffe aircrew of a Do 17 that shot up Biggin Hill High Street in 1940 and caused 4-year-old Terry to dive for cover in the doorway of a nearby shop.

Above left: One of Terry's heroes of No. 32 Squadron at Biggin Hill – Flying Officer Douglas 'Grubby' Grice.

Above right: Terry Parsons aged 4 in 1940.

Terry's childhood home in Tatsfield, near Biggin Hill.

Left: One of the key figures from the wartime history of RAF Biggin Hill – Wing Commander Brian Kingcome, DSO, DFC* of No. 92 Squadron.

Below: Wing Commander Brian Kingcome, left, with Squadron Leader Geoffrey Wellum, DFC.

Chapter 3

MY FIRST DIG

SURROUNDED by walls of dark, damp earth, I dig gently around the blackened metal carcass before me. To the casual observer it doesn't look much. A lump of mangled iron perhaps? Or a redundant old container? But to me it's the ultimate prize, as it's a rare Merlin engine from a Hurricane or a Spitfire, and despite its mud-caked appearance, I know I have unearthed a genuine representative of the greatest aerial conflict of time – the Battle of Britain.

Oh-so-gently, I pick up various fragments of the defeated warbird which now protrude from the clumps of sticky soil around my feet. I breathe in the musk of rich earth which now surrenders its treasures. There's part of an altimeter, a slice of cowling, and what looks like the top of a wheel is daring to poke out of the ground. The instrument panel is gnarled and misshapen, and the glass which had once protected the fuel and speed gauges lies in splinters which catch the sunlight and twinkle in a macabre broken beauty in the freshly dug earth.

These pieces of history, these scraps of archaeological significance had decades earlier been part of the battle which saw the RAF chase the Luftwaffe from our skies. Now these artefacts, once touched by warriors of 1940, were in the daylight again as I gently unearthed and prised them from their mysterious, dark burial ground.

I'd happily argue that the earth-shielding history has a certain smell – a rich, dark, lavender musk of protection.

On every dig, I remembered again and again how I'd watched with child's eyes in 1940 a type of warfare comparable in importance to Waterloo take place in the skies over my home near Biggin Hill. The sight of those dogfights swam again before me, as I scrape away the mud from the engine at my feet. Two eras now melt into the moments of one.

I wonder if I saw this Hurricane, this Spitfire, a once-beautiful fighter aircraft, go down in 1940? Did I watch it scream in flames to its death at 500 mph? Or did it tumble serenely down and slice through trees in its haste to hit the ground before breaking into a thousand pieces? I feel ashamed as I recall my reactions to such sights as a 4-year-old. The death of the Hurricane, Spitfire, Me 109 or Dornier Do 17 and the fates of their pilots were all part of a day to me then which I embraced as nothing but an exciting adventure. I was a boy of the 'battle' and sentiment never came into it the black and white world of my early youth.

My first dig took place in the summer of 1963. I was 22 years old and found myself chatting with kindly Mrs Gell, who ran a restaurant on the outskirts of Biggin Hill. I'd known her for a few years and during my rounds as a lorry driver stopped off for a cup of tea and a catch-up. Then by chance I happened to tell her I was interested in the Battle of Britain and I asked her if she had seen any aircraft go down in the area. Suddenly she pointed over the road and told me if I crossed the two fields ahead of us, I'd find an aircraft.

'I remember it as plain as day,' said Mrs Gell. 'It went down in 1940 – just in that spot. I will never forget it. That was the closest to us. The others of course are also within walking distance!'

So I took note of her observations and as soon as I could, I visited the site she'd pointed out. After a few scrapes around the field with the shovel and keeping my ears strained to the sound of the little metal detector I was waving about near my feet, it wasn't too long before I was digging away with my spade and soon staring down a hole in Botley Hill, Tatsfield, Biggin Hill.

And there it all was. The pieces, the wreckage of battle. After I'd surveyed the debris, I wondered who had flown this warbird and how they had escaped. It wasn't long before I discovered from RAF archives and Mrs Gell that the pilot of Hurricane P3943, which was now the charred and blackened collection of twisted metal and scraps of canvas and Perspex I'd unearthed, had been flown by Sergeant Harry Snow Newton, AFC, (1920 – 1996) of No. 111 Squadron. Sergeant Newton baled out on 18 August 1940.

Now, twenty-three years later and I was to spend days unearthing the wreckage of his aircraft. I was excited by my discovery and heard from Mrs Gell that an individual calling himself Sergeant Newton returned every year to the area to look for his aircraft! 'He's been in the restaurant so many times asking for information. To be honest, he seemed a lost soul to keep returning to see us like that every year.' she said.

As soon as I heard this story, I looked into the history of the crash as much as I could. All I had in those days was a map of the area and eyewitness accounts. (Frank Mason's book *Battle over Britain*, which was like a Bible to me, as it was a superb and informative record of RAF and Luftwaffe aircraft which had been shot down during the conflict, wasn't published until 1969. It was very ahead of its time and was an important reference source which also included diagrams of every aircraft of the time.)

I began excavating aircraft crash sites mainly as a recovery specialist with an awareness of what any found items represented. When I was able to check in Frank Mason's book who the pilot and aircrew had been on the day the aircraft went down, it added another important dimension to my passion. Also, there were still many, many eyewitnesses around like Mrs Gell at the restaurant who I could talk to about the Battle of Britain. Of course, people's memories can become hazy or muddled and there were times I was sent off on a wild-goose chase. It was hard work at times acquiring the exact location of an aircraft when Mr Y said he had seen a Spitfire go down in a field about a mile to my left, and Mr Z argues it was a mile to my right! It was always a lucky break though, if I got to speak to a farmer who was usually pretty certain about the whereabouts of any buried RAF or Luftwaffe aeroplanes on his land.

In the 1960s it was all so very different to the excavations carried out today by highly qualified archaeologists, technicians, Ministry of Defence inspectors and forensics, and the media. They will spend weeks at a site now, whereas fifty years ago I would do up to three or four digs a week with a group of friends.

What I always endeavoured to do though, once I'd researched the site, was only dig aircraft from which the pilot and aircrew had baled out. A policeman told me then, that while you may know you've suddenly found human remains, it is best to be sure, to find out if the body is not part of an ongoing criminal investigation. The police like to be one hundred per cent certain it wasn't someone killed there and buried on the site.

Of course, the discovery of any human remains during a dig must be reported immediately. I discovered that there were occasions in 1940 where remains had been removed from an aircraft and officially been given a decent burial. Believing this information to be correct, I went on one or two digs only to discover not all the remains had been removed and the eight pounds rule had just been a token representation to officialdom by busy salvage men during wartime.

If a small bone was ever discovered during any of my digs, then everything stopped and the police, coroner's officer and RAF medics had to be called. Bones, teeth and skin can last a long time especially if they have been in the clay of east Kent. Clay can seal off a cockpit so it's completely airtight and nothing can deteriorate. Any of us who had been digging at the site would leave immediately and return once the police gave us permission.

If I had contact with the family of aircrew, I would write and ask if they would like any personal items found at the site returned to them. I always played the honesty card, as it is important to tread carefully and sensitively with families whose loved ones were killed in action. Some relatives welcomed the fact I'd taken the time to contact them, and I cannot stress enough how I made every effort to ensure any aircraft I dug was free of human remains.

When it came to finding out more about the pilot of my first-ever-dig, I discovered Sergeant Harry Newton had been scrambled from RAF Kenley (Croydon) and his aircraft had been hit by heavy-duty bullets from the marauding Luftwaffe. He couldn't get out of his Hurricane too easily, so he flipped it over and when clear, managed to parachute out. The Hurricane went down in flames having suffered the fiery wrath of return fire from a Dornier 17.

The Dornier crashed at Hurst Green. Sergeant Newton went to The Oxted and Limpsfield Cottage Hospital and was treated for burns. Sadly, I never got to meet him during the dig in 1963 but we did get a chance to write to each other, and I treasure those letters from this hero of the Battle.

So, who was Sergeant Pilot Harry Snow Newton? Well, he was born on 13 July 1920 in Nottinghamshire, and in early 1939 he joined the war. He joined No. 504 Auxiliary Air Force Squadron as an AC2 photographer. By the spring of that year, he joined the Royal Air Force Volunteer Reserve as an airman – pilot-under-training – at Tollerton. When the war broke out he was posted to 8 FTS Montrose, where he stayed to learn the intricacies of the cockpit until 10 May 1940. A few days later he passed as fully competent at the controls of an aircraft and he was transferred to 6 OTU at Sutton Bridge, and by 18 May 1940 he was posted to No. 111 Squadron at Kenley to fly Hurricanes.

Sergeant Newton had a successful June and July, but on 11 August during the Battle of Britain he had no choice but to make a crash landing on marshes near Boyton, Martlesham Heath, Suffolk, in Hurricane P3548. According to the combat report, he appears to have run out of fuel following intense battle over Thanet, Kent. On

16 and 18 August Sergeant Newton continued to prove to be a pilot of great courage, and destroyed several Dornier Do 17s. However, after another victory on the 18 August, his Hurricane P3943 was struck by fire from a vigilant Luftwaffe airman and he was forced to bale out over Botley Hill.

Although badly burned, Sergeant Newton was able to return to his squadron on 10 October 1940 and by February 1941 he was posted to Air Navigation School at Staverton as a staff pilot. By August 1942 he was commissioned from flight sergeant and served as staff pilot with an air gunnery unit in Andreas on the Isle of Man.

By September 1944 Harry Snow Newton had been awarded the Air Force Cross (AFC) and released from the Royal Air Force with the rank of flight lieutenant in 1946. That same year he joined the RAF again and remained until his retirement in 1975 as a squadron leader. During his long career as an aviator he logged more than 10,000 hours.

This is one of Harry's heartfelt missives to me describing in great detail what happened to him on 18 August 1940:

'Dear Terry,

On Sunday, 18 August 1940, I was aged 20 years and 1 month. It was a fine, sunny day. I had just eaten a huge lunch with double helpings of sweet with masses of custard and was sitting out in the sun, complete with "Mae West" at the ready. The "Scramble Bell" rang out from the "Ops Room". Ten pilots rushed to their aircraft some 50/100 yards away on the grass airfield at Croydon. By the time I reached mine, grabbing the parachute which hung ready over the tailplane, strapping it on and climbing up onto the left wing, the engine was running, started by the two ground crew – one permanently sitting in the cockpit, the other stationed by the starter trolley. As I jumped into the cockpit, the airman was already passing my shoulder straps before he leaped off the wing with a quick "good luck". All this had taken only 45 seconds. I moved the aircraft into take-off position and we climbed into the blue sky taking up a broadcast heading from the ground controller. The vectors began to change rapidly as we gained height and I began to wonder just how many he had found for us this time. There was no time to ponder – I suddenly found myself in the midst of a dogfight. It was every man for himself. I could see the yellow-nosed Me 109s all around, with occasional Hurricanes flying in all directions. It was very difficult to sort one out and have a go – there was so many – the best policy I had adopted previously, was to try to stay in the middle of the fight – there I was safe – I just had to keep changing heading and height, make difficult turns and remember what the CO had said – "Don't fly a straight course for more than one second."

If I had tried to keep on the outside of the fight, I would have been picked off in no time at all. This way I could be the greatest ace in Britain – no one would see me sweat. Within minutes, vital height was lost zooming about and trying to lock on to an Me 109 – I was near the ground. The dogfight had dispersed as quickly as it had begun. I look around – still in one piece – and saw a lone Dornier 17 (or was it a 215?). It was breaking away to the south – flying low over houses just south of Croydon. I remember thinking that this one will not get back. It obviously saw me coming from above and behind. I then saw a row of houses blown up by bombs and assumed the Dornier had jettisoned its load. A whole street of beautiful English houses disintegrated. I don't remember ever feeling so mad. I opened the cockpit hood (you were supposed to fight with it opened in case it jammed in action – not like the Battle of Britain film!) my maps flew out of the cockpit as speed increased in the dive. I rapidly closed the range and began to fire all guns. The tracer was passing just above and to the right of the Dornier, when I saw the rear gunner pop his head out and swing his gun in my direction, and fire. It was my eight guns to his one. I could see every detail of the aircraft and the gunner, and knew he could not miss. I fired another burst after a slight correction, when my cockpit burst into flames. Fire was coming from the right-hand side from where the K-Gas fuel pump was sited. The slipstream carried the flames up and over my head. I was now more annoyed at the thought of losing my target.

I let go of the stick on feeling the heat and closed my eyes. Then I realised that my aircraft could either blow up or fly into the ground when the flames reached the main fuel tank of 65 gallons just behind my instrument panel. More furious than ever at being cheated, I deliberately put my hands back into the flames to grab the stick, fired my guns continuously, kicked the rudder about to squirt bullets everywhere, eyes now cemented shut by the burning oxygen mask on my face.

I then felt the fire burning through three pairs of gloves on my right hand. I pulled back the stick to gain height, as I estimated that I must have passed over the Dornier. It was not recommended to expose your underside to the enemy but I had no choice.

As I felt the aircraft climb away, I let go of the stick, trimmed with my left hand, released my harness and began to climb out of the machine by standing on the seat to avoid the flames. I remember feeling the cool air on my face and felt the heat now on my body. I now had to force myself to wait, either the aircraft blew up in which case I was not interest, or I could gain enough height to bale out. My last sight was of tree-tops and houses; I had to stay.

After what seemed to be a very long time, the engine suddenly coughed and stopped and made up my mind for me. I was ready with my right foot to kick the control column down to the right as I flung myself off to the left. As I had no idea of height I just had to pull the ripcord at the same time, risking it catching in the tail on opening. I fell out and remember pulling so hard that I thought I had broken the ripcord, as there was no resistance. The next second there was a jerk. I forced my eyes to open and looked down to find myself hung over a nice, friendly green field with a circle of soldiers all pointing rifles up in my direction. I yelled something in British English and landed in their midst. I even remembered to flex my knees together, pull down the parachute cords as I hit the ground in a perfect landing. The parachute disconnected and floated off into a hedge. I was greeted and rushed into a concrete bunker for a cup of tea. There a chap and his girlfriend were sheltering from the raid. She took one look at me and fainted. I suppose I must have looked a mess. In no time at all a very excited lady with a Red Cross apron herded me into her small ambulance and drove me to Oxted Cottage Hospital.

My parachute was returned by the army with 36 bullet holes all over it. Either a lucky shot had entered the pack before I had used it or someone had shot at me on the way down. I can't say. The army said they saw the Dornier dive into a field to the south-west. I relaxed in the ambulance and enjoyed the peace of the countryside in the warm air, wondering just how to report my crash in official terms. The hospital put me in the casualty ward and sent for a doctor, being Sunday afternoon. A nurse appeared with a bottle in traditional style! I refused and asked for a doctor as I was now feeling pain and worried about losing my right hand, which was covered in oil dirt and I could see all the moving parts. My leg was burned to the bone in one place, but did not hurt. My face was beginning to dry up and become stiff. My eyes ached. The doctor arrived and quite cheerfully said that all would be well after an immediate operation and I would be seeing my Sunday lunch again later! I did.

Nurse Joyce Banks gave me a lot of attention over the next four weeks. When I left in bandages and returned to my squadron, none the worse for the action, I was told I had shot the Dornier down and received a piece of the aircraft from an army sergeant stationed in the area. I had the greatest respect for the staff and local people who came to see me with all sorts of goodies. I returned to the field after the war and met a local farmer who said he saw the whole thing on his way home from the pub.

Yours sincerely, Harry'

When I read this particular letter from one of my heroes, it made me realise just how important it was to recover the aircraft and salute the aircrews who had taken part in a desperate and historic conflict which shook the foundations of Britain and indeed, the world. Such days would never be seen again. Their impact was great, the actions of those involved should never be forgotten and it was always in honour of men and women as courageous as Harry that I was motivated to unearth aircraft of the battle. Someone had to.

When I first wrote to Sergeant Newton to let him know I had found his Hurricane, he was delighted I had taken so much care to track down the aircraft. He told me he couldn't get the events of 18 August 1940 out of his mind and that was why he visited the area of the crash site each year.

However, I did let him know he probably would never have found it without the use of a metal detector, as it was good and buried down deep. It would have been difficult to find an exact location after more than twenty years since it hit the ground.

I kept him up to speed with the progress I had made though, and I'd like to think it gave him some peace of mind to know there was now a poignant collection of artefacts to mark that dark and dangerous day in his life on display in the (now former) Halstead Air Museum. I did send him a few artefacts from his Hurricane, so at least he had these as a certain reminder of his gallantry in the Battle of Britain. Sergeant Newton as one of 'The Few' who served with honour in the Battle of Britain, died in Trowbridge, Wiltshire in 1996.

In the early 1960s, when I dug his Hurricane – my first aircraft –, such activity was mostly unheard of. I didn't know I was a pioneer of aviation archaeology, as to me it was a hobby but rapidly became a passion and a serious one at that. In those days for me it was all about finding the wreckage and paying tribute to the heroes and heroines of the Second World War. If I was lucky, I could discover the serial number of the aircraft, albeit RAF or Luftwaffe, and if there was information around about the pilot or aircrew then that was a bonus, especially if they survived the war.

I had been a keen collector of wartime aircraft memorabilia since childhood and for many years my boxes of shrapnel and various items of significance stood piled high in a cabinet in my grandmother Esther's perfectly dusted and clean dining room. The fact she stored these items for me for so long says a lot about the way she encouraged my interest in preserving the memory of those men and women who took part in the Battle of Britain and the rest of the war. My grandmother brought me up at a time when my own mother, her daughter, and my father were unable to be responsible for me.

I remember my grandmother as a warm and caring woman who taught me right from wrong and gave me a sense of purpose in life. We'd also got through the war together and I suppose once you've sat under a Morrison shelter eating your dinner with someone as bombs explode all around, there's a certain bond that never leaves a soul. Our house was in the dip of the valley and we were lucky never to have been directly hit by the Luftwaffe. The property was quite hidden until the aircraft came over the hill and by the time it was spotted by the Luftwaffe, it would have been too late to use it as a target. Our neighbours and friends suffered though, and more often than not, my grandmother would be dishing out tea and sympathy to those who had suffered during a raid – had holes in their roofs or their bedrooms had suddenly disappeared and crumbled into a heap of smouldering rubble.

It was in the 1960s and around the time I dug Sergeant Newton's Hurricane that I met with the founder of the Halstead War Museum, Ken Anscombe.

I had bought a metal detector which was a little plastic object that made a buzzing noise. It was a very basic bit of kit. I telephoned Ken who I knew shared an interest in finding aircraft from the Battle of Britain and he came over to see the site at Botley Hill and he told me, 'You've done well here boy.' Then suddenly Ken spotted someone in the distance digging for a pipeline so he went over to this individual and asked if he would bring the digger over to the Hurricane crash site which I had been sweating over with just a shovel.

Anyway, with a mechanical digger removing the earth, it made all the difference and we managed to get the propeller hub up out of the sticky mud and I gathered up two bags full of pieces. I couldn't believe what I had in my hands that day. Ken organised for the discoveries to be removed via a large truck and along with the prop hub and the smaller artefacts, he transported my finds back to what was known as his Halstead War Museum.

The pieces of the Hurricane once flown by Sergeant Newton were then cleaned up and labels were prepared and the evidence of my first-ever dig and discovery were put on display. It was then I realised how important it was that the remains of these aircraft were found and treasured and shown as memories of a brutal and bloody war.

The Hurricane had gone into the ground to a depth of about a hundred feet. It had nose-dived down and that's why the prop hub was located first. The main fuselage and the engine, which may well have been sticking out of the ground, had probably been taken away in 1940 by the haulage and scrap merchants employed at the time to remove aircraft remains. Don't forget, the aircraft had been on fire when it ploughed into the field, so it was a sorry sight by the time its sad carcass went off to the scrap heap.

In the 1960s though, no one really wanted to remember the war and all its strife and sadness. My hobby, as it was perceived then, was rare – strange even – and perceived by many as a waste of time. Who wants pieces of old metal clogging up the living room, the garage, the shed? The war was deemed by some then as all too recent and not remotely of any archaeological interest at all. Why bring back bad memories of death and destruction? People knew war and grew up with it. I suppose then in the 1960s the new world order was very much in place and life in Britain was all about pleasure and entertainment, and the new generation wanted to forget, and forget hard. But I knew, and still feel the same, that there would always be a debt to pay to those men and women who had risked and lost their lives in the cause of our freedom. Looking back, I see my youthful belief and ensuing actions qualified as more than a whim and a 'hobby'.

My childhood memories of 1940 flood back to me often. They will never leave me, as the Battle of Britain is well and truly in my blood. If, during my life, the spirits of those aircrews have in a mystical way choreographed my long path to find and unearth the charges upon which they flew into battle, then so be it. The thought of such a hidden, mysterious power untouched by the cynicism of today's reality comforts me as if I had been chosen by these warriors to help keep their memory alive.

Not long after I began digging aircraft, I met Tony Graves who was and is as keen as I am to keep the memory of 'The Few' alive. Tony set up the popular London Air Museum (which sadly closed some years ago) and he still plays a significant role in the world of aviation archaeology. In recent years Tony has recovered many aircraft and worked with families keen to know what happened to their loved ones who were 'missing in action' over France during the war. Finding the prop hub from Sergeant Harry Newton's Hurricane started it all off for me in 1963.

One memory which will always remain clear and sound is the day a group of us were joined by a Battle of Britain pilot who was keen to join a dig for a mystery Spitfire. That pilot was the late, great Group Captain

Tom Gleave, CBE (1908 – 1993) who himself had been shot down in 1940 and was sent to recover from his burns at the famous Sir Archibald McIndoe Hospital in East Grinstead. Gleave's Hurricane had been shot down between Cudham and Downe, Kent. In recent years a farmer ploughing a nearby field discovered the pilot's battered cigarette case. This he presented to Group Captain Gleave's daughter, Angela Lodge.

Group Captain Gleave, who became known as the first and only 'Chief Guinea Pig' at the burns unit, was thrilled to join us forty years on as we dug the earth around Chiddingstone Hoath, near Edenbridge, Kent, searching for artefacts and even the engine from that Spitfire. That day we didn't find much, and the identity of the aircraft or the pilot who had been at the controls remains a mystery to this day.

During the war he commanded No. 253 Squadron, and his tally of victories against the Luftwaffe included an impressive five Me 109s (over the course of just 24 hours!), and a Ju 88. Having recovered from his facial injuries after being shot down during the Battle of Britain, he was given command of RAF Manston. It was from this famous base on the Kent coast he ordered six Fairey Swordfish of No. 825 Squadron into action with specific instructions to sink the *Gneisenau, Scharnhorst* and *Prinz Eugen*.

During the dig for the Spitfire remains, he told us about his time serving as General Eisenhower's Head of Air Plans at SHAEF (Supreme Headquarters Allied Expeditionary Force) from 1 October 1944 to 15 July 1945. Tom was later elected a Fellow of the Royal Historical Society and became a successful aviation historian and deputy chairman to the Battle of Britain Fighter Association.

I recall him as an enthusiastic person with a great thirst for information. He took part in the dig with great aplomb, asking questions about the other aircraft we'd dug. He said he was tremendously impressed with our efforts and felt proud there were 'a few authentic souls' doing their best to pay tribute to the fallen and all his RAF colleagues who risked and lost their lives during the Second World War.

In his own Battle of Britain memoir, *I had a Row with a German*, which was published in 1941 under the pseudonym 'An RAF Casualty' as the censor of the time insisted, he wrote an awesome description of the day he baled out of his burning Hurricane. It is one of the most remarkable and genuinely authentic insights revealed by a true man of the Battle of Britain. Shortly before he penned the book, he was still angry that many of his friends had been shot down and killed, including No. 253 Squadron Leader Harold Starr, who on 31 August 1940 baled out of his aircraft only to be shot at and fall dead at Hamill Brickworks, near Eastry, Kent. His Hurricane L1830 came down near Grove Ferry.

Squadron Leader Gleave wrote: 'On 31 August 1940 I had to break the news about Starr's death to the squadron. Nothing can describe their feelings; they were expressed by all, crews and pilots alike, in no uncertain terms. Tempers were raised to white heat; nothing that they had heard or read could have brought home to them more forcibly the ruthless type we were fighting against. Their determination to smash the Hun now knew no bounds. Although they had missed the first mass raids of the blitz, their subsequent efforts bear testimony to the fact that this act profited the Hun nothing.

'That day just before 1.00 pm we heard about a large raid of Luftwaffe coming in from the south, and the lull of the past two hours or so changed to frenzied activity. I grabbed my helmet and parachute and ran to the aircraft which I was to use in place of "X", which I had lent to another pilot during a previous raid when it had been damaged. The crew had already started up – they never needed asking – and I jumped in.

'We received orders to join up with another squadron at 2,000 feet over the aerodrome, and in a few seconds, were climbing up as hard as we could go. The sections formed up as we climbed, and I turned slightly at 1,000 feet to make a wide circuit and to look out for the other squadron, which, a few seconds later, I saw coming south flying in an inverted "J" formation; one flight was in "vic" with the other in line astern behind the left-hand man of the leading flight. We followed suit, but joining up on the right, thus making a total formation in the shape of an inverted "U".

'After a few minutes we turned north, and I glanced up to see what we were chasing. Right above us were rows of Hun bombers – Ju 88s in line astern – and my aircraft were directly below one line of them and closing distance rapidly. We were soon within about 1,000 feet of them, well within cannon range and approaching machine-gun range, but the formation was still going ahead. I did some rapid thinking: if we maintained our position, we would, in a few seconds, be sitting shots for both front and rear Hun gunners. I therefore decided to attack before they had a chance to open fire, and certainly before we came within danger of collision. I rocked my wings and then eased the nose up, taking a bead on No. 5 of the line of Huns and giving him a raking burst. I turned on to my side as I finished firing, kicked hard on bottom rudder to fake a stalled turn, and dived down, straightening out as I gathered speed. I repeated the process on No. 3 and, glancing over my shoulder as I skidded sideways over the top, saw clouds of greyish-white smoke issuing from his port engine. I could not see the effect of my fire on No. 5; he was too far behind. I was about to pull up to attack No. 1, who incidentally was now losing height preparatory to a dive-bomb attack, when I heard a metallic click above the roar of my engine. It seemed to come from the starboard wing and I glanced in that direction, but a sudden burst of heat struck my face, and I looked down into the cockpit. A long spout of flame was issuing from the hollow starboard wing-root curling up along the port side of the cockpit and then across towards my right shoulder. I had seen neither tracers nor cannon tracks near my aircraft; the fire could not have been caused by structural or other failure, and I therefore presumed I had picked up a stray incendiary. I had some crazy notion that if I rocked the aircraft and skidded, losing speed, the fire might go out. Not a bit of it; the flames increased until the cockpit was like the centre of a blow-lamp nozzle. There was nothing left to do but to bale out; a forced landing was out of the question as I was still 7,000 to 8,000 feet up. I reached down to pull the radio telephone lead out of its socket, but the heat was too great. The skin was already rising off my right wrist and hand, and my left hand was starting to blister, the glove being already partially burnt off. My shoes and slacks must have been burning all this time, but I cannot remember any great pain.

'I undid my harness and tried to raise myself, but I found I had not the strength. I was comforted by the thought that I had my gun ready loaded if things came to the worst. I decided to pull off my helmet, open the cockpit cover and roll on my back so that I could drop out.

'My helmet came off after a determined tug: I opened the cockpit cover and that was the last effort I had to make. There was a blinding flash, I seemed to be travelling through yards of flame; then I found myself turning over and over in the air, but with no sense of falling. Gradually I ceased to travel forwards and fell downwards, still turning head over heels. My hand instinctively passed over the harness release and on to the ripcord handle. I pulled hard and felt the cord being drawn through the strongly woven fabric tubing; then came a gentle jerk as I was pulled into vertical position, swinging comfortably, secure in my harness. An interminable space of time seemed to have elapsed whilst I was endeavouring to escape from that inferno, but actually it was less than a minute.

'Now only the earth below had any interest for me; I was feeling distinctly browned off. As I approached the ground I seemed to gather speed; the swinging appeared to be accentuated, and the sight of a barbed wire fence below gave me a start. I was then about 50 feet up, and as I went through the last swinging motion, the fence disappeared from view, the ground came up in an unfriendly way, and I closed my eyes. I felt my left hip and head strike the ground simultaneously and then all was still.

'I sat up and looked around, and was surprised I had not received any injury from my impact with the ground. With an effort, I stood up and surveyed the damage. My shoes still looked like shoes and I found I could walk; why I don't know, as my ankle and each side of my right foot were burnt and my left foot was scorched and had small burns. My slacks had disappeared except for portions that had been covered by the parachute harness. The skin on my right leg, from the top of the thigh to just above the ankle had lifted and draped my leg like outsize plus fours. My left leg was in similar condition except that the left thigh was only scorched. My right arm, elbow and face were burnt and so was my neck. I could see all right, although it felt like looking through slits in a mass of swollen skin. I realised the services of a doctor were necessary!

'There seemed to be nobody about, so I decided to walk to the end of the field where I could see a gate. I remember calling out in the hope that someone would come along as I made my way across the grass. I reached the gate, managed to open it, and found myself in a country lane. Lower down, on the opposite side of the lane, was a cowshed, and I walked towards it. A man came out; he had apparently heard me calling and when he saw me he stopped and stared. I guessed I must be looking a little strange, and promptly blurted out, "RAF pilot. I want a doctor..."'

I remember, too, the day in the 1970s when Squadron Leader Kenneth Carver, DFC, joined us during the excavation for his Hurricane N2466 which had crashed at Spelmonden, Goudhurst Road, Horsmonden, Kent.

We learned how Squadron Leader Carver (Pilot Officer in 1940) had been with No. 229 Squadron when during combat with He 111s high above Maidstone on 11 September his Hurricane caught fire and he baled out, landing near to Flimwell. His injuries meant a month's stay at Rumwood Court Hospital near Maidstone and then he was taken to the RAF Hospital at Wendover to recuperate.

The search for his Hurricane was tough, as the main part of it sat under the A21 near Goudhurst and still does! It was impossible to get to but we know the engine is there as well as the cockpit. We did find the stick from the aircraft, and Squadron Leader Carver, DFC, went home with some instrument facings and part of the instrument panel. He was a lovely man and seemed genuinely pleased to join us on the hunt for the aircraft which had helped him fight the enemy so gallantly.

Whenever we could, we always tried to contact surviving pilots and aircrew about digs for their aircraft. Having them with us made a huge difference of course, as we heard their stories as we ploughed through the deep earth to reawaken history. They were special days I will never forget.

Squadron Leader Carver, who came from Surrey, was 78 when he died in 1996.

Imagine how honoured I was in 2015, when on the 75th anniversary of the Battle of Britain I got to meet the amazing Squadron Leader Tony 'Pick' Pickering of No. 501 Squadron at the Battle of Britain Memorial at Capel-le-Ferne, Kent. I had a chance to let him know I had located and excavated the site of his Hurricane P5200 which had been shot down on 1 September 1940 over Caterham during combat with Me 109s.

Then aged 20, he had managed to bale out, unhurt, and drop in on the Guards Depot where at first it was believed he was a German! His aircraft had smashed into the ground at Happy Valley Old Coulsdon, where some of us diggers spent a day in the 1970s unearthing artefacts.

During our chat at the Memorial event in 2015, Squadron Leader Pickering told me that when he was a young sergeant pilot in 1940, he was full of determination to 'do his bit'. He said the idea of Hitler ruling Britain was unimaginable and everyone he knew was united in the cause to defend the skies and the land with all their heart. I will never forget meeting this friendly, unassuming man and it is fortunate he was invited to appear on various television programmes over the years. His memories of the Second World War are now on record for generations to come. Squadron Leader Pickering died in 2016 having left the RAF in 1945 and then having led a full life travelling the world with his work for GEC.

The second-ever dig I carried out in the 1960s was on an Me 109 which had come down at Norheads Farm, Owl's Wood (also known as Mullards Wood) Tatsfield, Biggin Hill. It had been shot down just after noon by Pilot Officer John MacPhail of No. 603 Squadron on 15 September 1940 – a date which marked the brutal climax of the Battle of Britain with record losses of both RAF and Luftwaffe aircrew and aircraft in just 24 hours.

The Luftwaffe pilot, Oberleutnant Julius Haase of 3/JG53 (Staffel Kapitan), had been based at Etaples, France when he had taken off that day. Oberleutnant Haase baled out of his stricken Me 109 but when locals found him, he was slumped dead at the back door of a house in Lusted Hall Lane – the shroud lines of his parachute had been tied together. He had no chance of survival if he'd attempted to employ the device.

When I began researching Oberleutnant Haase's Me 109, I was told by a farmhand it was in the local woods with its tail sticking out of the ground. So I followed his instructions and there in the trees I saw this steel hawser (rope) and I thought, 'Oh blow, someone's already dug it.' They had already got the engine out and Ken Anscombe (who used to be in the RAF as a fitter) told me he had caught someone digging it out and told them he was from the Royal Air Force Association and they promptly gave him the engine.

Anyway, that day, even though I knew the site had already been dug, I thought I would carry on looking and suddenly I picked up this disc poking out from the ground. When I turned it over, there it was... The Mercedes Benz engine badge! What a prize. When I showed Ken, he said, 'Never seen one of them, I'd like that.' and so as good-natured as ever, I gave it to him. Ken then invited me to join his club. Artefacts discovered at this site included the complete Daimler-Benz DB601 engine, which was buried in clay fifteen feet beneath the surface. I know the engine went on display at Ken's Halstead War Museum – which is now sadly no more.

Over the years I added lot of artefacts to Ken's collection. Once we dug a Dornier 17 which had gone down on Gincocks Farm, Warren Lane, Hurst Green, near Oxted, Surrey on 18 August 1940. It had been shot down by a Hurricane of No. 32 Squadron flown by Pilot Officer Alan Eckford during an attack on RAF Kenley. The Do 17 crew included its 27 year old pilot, Hauptmann Walter Stoldt (Killed in Action), Feldwebel Johann Beck, observer (POW), Unteroffizier Paul Gengel, radio officer (KIA); Oberfeldwebel Wilhelm Lautersack, flight engineer (POW) and Oberleutnant Walter Surk, a war correspondent (KIA). The three deceased were buried in a collective grave at Cannock Chase Cemetery.

The dig for this Do 17 was unusual, as it was one of two Luftwaffe aircraft I'd found which had a so-called 'mystery body' among the wreckage. It is rare, too, for a Do 17 to carry more than four crew. There was also a German helmet among the artefacts I found at Hurst Green which wasn't the type worn by the Luftwaffe. In recent years the excellent Kracker Archive listing Luftwaffe aircrew indicates the mystery fifth man was probably Oberleutnant Surk – the journalist on board. The sight of the three dead crew was reported to me by Mr Addison, who lived at the nearby farmstead and was witness to the crash.

The questions over the identity of this fifth person have been discussed for years. I discovered that Luftwaffe chief Hermann Goering became so tired of being blamed by the Fuehrer for not winning the air battle over Britain, that he sent Gestapo officers up with bomber crews to make sure they weren't dropping bombs just anywhere and turning tail back to Germany the minute they saw the RAF approaching. To be spied on while doing their duty must have irked many young Luftwaffe crews if this was the case. It seemed Goering would do anything to save his own reputation with Hitler and thus encouraged his aircrews to believe it was an honour to die for the Fatherland!

At that dig we found oxygen bottles, tools, and a tail wheel. I found out later that a Mr Dixon, a farmer who lived nearby, was selling his land and someone told me he had some pieces from the Dornier which he'd found not long after the crash in 1940. I approached him about this and he gave me the propellers which were in beautiful condition and still dark green in colour. They were extraordinary and powerful artefacts from the Battle of Britain. Once again, these went to Ken's museum.

I recall how I was digging two or three aircraft a week in the 1960s. This number grew in the 1970s. Some of us dug aircraft all year around. I've been out in the deep, dark winter and I have had to dig the ice out before you could bale the haul out. I did that when I visited the crash site of an Me 110C-4 at Worcester Park in Cheam, Surrey. I was digging that site with Tony Graves. The aircraft went down in 1940 in the middle of a cricket pitch. We started the dig on the Saturday and it rained hard overnight and froze. Anyway, when I got there that morning, the ice was about six inches thick. I grabbed a pickaxe from my truck and broke the ice as best as I could. I got down about three feet and suddenly all this wreckage loomed out of the hole! I dug around a bit more, then just levered it up and snapped the ice again. I grabbed hold of the wreckage I could see and pulled it up with all my strength and I saw a swastika on it... I had pulled out a tail fin! What a find!

This incredible artefact soon went on show in the London Air Museum founded by Tony. The artefacts from this Me 110 were later passed onto Tangmere Aviation Museum in West Sussex. Sadly, I've no idea where they went from there. It wasn't long before I had enough items of the Battle to establish my own collection and create displays, but I soon realised I couldn't let it take over my whole life. That's what running a museum can be like, and I've seen evidence of the responsibility taking its toll to the detriment of many people over the years. I have seen the extent to which some people can go to in order to claim certain pieces of history and it's not pleasant to witness.

But of all the mysteries I have pondered over the years, there's one that's sparked debate among historians for years. These fascinating questions and theories revolve around that dig I mentioned earlier for the Me 110C-4 (Werk 3298), which on 9 September 1940 was among a group of 300 German bombers and fighter escorts on their way to attack the Hawker Hurricane fighter aircraft assembly plant at Brooklands, Surrey, and the London Docklands.

It has been established that the Me 110 I dug from the ice had been flown by Unteroffizier Alois Pfaffelhuber and Unteroffizier Otto Kramp. They had encountered the wrath of RAF fighters over Croydon, Purley and Kenley but still they pressed on in a bid to reach their targets. But within minutes, they were hit. By then, many of their German colleagues had ditched their bombs in haste to avoid destruction and made attempts to turn back towards the Channel. On this day, the RAF proved too effective as Hurricanes and Spitfires hit target after target. Among the RAF fighters in the sky that day was No. 242 Canadian Squadron led by Squadron Leader Douglas Bader.

For Unteroffizier Pfaffelhuber and Unteroffizier Kramp, time ran out, as it was the guns of Pilot Officer Hugh Tamblyn's aircraft which tore into the Me 110.

Pilot Officer Tamblyn's combat report reads: 'I saw a 110 making across me a steep turn. I gave it a short burst and went into dead astern where after a burst of about seven seconds the port engine caught fire. The machine went into a fairly steep dive and I followed him down and watched him crash in front of a cricket clubhouse.'

This pavilion was what was then the New Zealand Shipping Company's Maori Sports Club headquarters. The area became part of the P&O Shipping Company sports ground and part of Worcester Park. Nearby is the A3 landmark, Tolworth Tower.

At the age of 23 years old, Pilot Officer Hugh Tamblyn, DFC, had an incredible survival rate and record of successful combat action until his death on 3 April 1941. He is known today as one of only two airmen to have survived the 'slaughter of the innocents' after nine of twelve Defiants flown by No. 242 Squadron were shot down over the Channel by the Luftwaffe on 12 July 1940.

When Pilot Officer Tamblyn met his own death, he had been on convoy duty east of Felixstowe when what was believed to be return fire from a Do 17 caught his Hurricane and he went down into the sea. When his body was found, it was revealed he had died from exposure and cold.

When he met the Me 110 on 9 September 1940, however, he logged the time of his attack on it as 6.00 pm and Unteroffizier Pfaffelhuber and Unteroffizier Kramp joined the growing list of casualties from the Battle of Britain.

This is where the mystery begins. Records made at the time by Surbiton Mortuary staff reveal a third man died with the two Luftwaffe crew. The man was allegedly a civilian, and to this day, British and German historians still ask who he was and why he was in the Me 110. RAF Intelligence of the crash site at the time does not mention a third man. The situation had begun to resemble the story-line from the famous Graham Greene novel, *The Third Man*.

Meanwhile, the Surbiton Mortuary archive contains a death certificate bearing the name of a D.R.K. Gelferin, aged about 23, and the address of 30 Wielandstrasse, Frankfurt. But there isn't a record of the remains of this alleged third crew member being buried.

According to historians specialising in the Luftwaffe, it wasn't exactly usual for an Me 110 to carry more than two crew members but it wasn't unheard of, either, for an aircraft of this size to have three on board.

There are three possible scenarios – number one suggests there was no third crew member and no body and the mortuary staff member compiling the list of remains was wrong.

Number two: it has been discovered that staff at the Volksbund Deutsche Kriegsgraberfursorge (German War Graves Commission) claimed that the Surbiton Mortuary had recorded the death not of a person, but a title. The VDK also believed what had been unearthed at the site of the wreckage and the body parts at the time had been a piece of paper with the words 'DRK Helferin' and NOT 'Gelferin'. The initials DRK represent Deutschen Roten Kreuzes (German Red Cross). The word *Helferin* translated to English means 'female helper'.

Historians then began asking if it was possible that a medical worker had been flying with Pfaffelhuber and Kramp that day, and if so, why?

The third potential explanation for the mystery body was that it had all been part of a British Intelligence cover-up. The date the 'body' is shown to have been admitted to the Surbiton Mortuary is four days after the remains of the two Luftwaffe crewmen were brought in, and six days after the crash. The delay poses even more questions.

Writing in *The Surrey Advertiser* in 1996, reporter Tony Thomas, who had received research assistance from historians including Dennis Davenport and various eyewitnesses to the crash, asked: 'Did British intelligence officers delay the identification of the third person in the Me 110 because he or she was on a special mission, details of which were to prove of vital help to our war effort? And who had given the name 'DRK Gelferin' to the mortuary? Was it British intelligence in an act of misinformation to cover up their vital find on the first XI cricket pitch at the Maori sports ground?'

German journalists were also intrigued by the story, with one, a Fred Kickhefel of the *Frankfurter Rundschau*, visiting the address of DRK Gelferin as recorded by the Surbiton Mortuary staff.

He wrote: 'It is a typical German house from the turn of the century, consisting of a ground floor and four storeys. The house survived the war but of course there are listed totally different names in today's (1996) address book. 'One thing that strikes me as an interesting coincidence is how one of the people listed as living there in 1940 is Fritz Jahn, Flugleitung Assistent, which in English is translated as air-controller. As this was a rare profession in 1940, there might be a chance this man joined the Luftwaffe and did some research, like testing the Knickebein system, which led the German bombers to England.' It would be interesting to know if Fritz Jahn was indeed the third man in the Me 110. Maybe the fragment of document found among the wreckage indicated that a DRK Gelferin was next of kin in case of Jahn's death? The scrap of paper might have been blown out of his pocket? Was that relative a Red Cross worker who lived at the same address? The third and final possible answer suggests the mystery man or woman was a war correspondent, or even a photographer covering the Battle of Britain for German newspapers and radio.

Stephen Flower, author of *Raiders Overhead*, came up with a good point. He said the LG1 Luftwaffe squadron, which the Me 110 had been part of, had in fact been testing new tactics in aerial warfare, and any film or photographs taken by someone on board at the time would have been a valuable training aid.

Soldiers camouflage Leutnant Bernhard Malischewski's Messerschmitt Bf 109E-4 of Stab II./JG 54 to prevent its possible destruction by the Luftwaffe. The aircraft was shot down by RAF Flt Lt Bob Stanford Tuck DSO DFC** AFC on 12 October 1940 during a combat over Tenterden in Kent. Malischewski was captured at nearby Chapel Holdings, Small Hythe. Malischewski's Me109 was was one of many Luftwaffe aircraft transported around the country and used a propaganda exhibit by the War Office.

The remains of Alois Pfaffelhuber and Otto Kramp were later buried at the German Military Cemetery at Cannock Chase. The questions over the 'third man' remain to this day.

It was on a freezing winter's day in the 1970s that I joined Tony Graves from the London Air Museum at the crash site on that cricket pitch in Surrey. Tony had gained permission to dig the area and mostly by hand and with shovels, we found what was left of both Daimler Benz DB601 engines along with oxygen bottles, the remains of a rubber dinghy, both undercarriage legs, a first aid kit, a parachute, plus the tail fin and its swastika!

The eyewitnesses to the death of the Me 110 and its crew included Pilot Officer Tamblyn of course, and several boys. One of them was 11-year-old Tony Cornell, who lived in nearby Old Malden Lane in 1940. He recalled:

'At around 5.45 pm, as we stood around in the garden staring up at the even ranks of German bombers high overhead, incendiaries and high explosive bombs whistled down and we dived into our Anderson shelter.

'Then we heard the frightening sound of an Me 110 making its last journey earthwards. Just when those Daimler-Benz engines sounded as if they were about to burst, the noise ceased abruptly and there was just a fraction of a second of eerie silence before the ground shook and the sound of an almighty explosion reached us. About an hour later I went up to the cricket pitch to see the wreckage. I remember being scared stiff by the sudden transformation of familiar surroundings into something like a scene from hell.

'The force of the explosion had totally reduced the aircraft to a thousand small pieces, or so it seemed to me, spread outwards from the smoking crater. Ammunition was still exploding with muffled bangs deep underground.

'I had intended to find a nice interesting piece of German plane to add to my growing hoard of shrapnel, spent machine gun cartridge cases and other souvenirs.

'What I suddenly found was a human ear. Not bloody or torn but sitting forlornly on the greensward of the first XI cricket table. This was the last straw. Courage deserted me and I ran home feeling sick. That was the moment I realised that war was about death and destruction and not at all the glamorous existence that schoolboys imagined a fighter pilot might lead.'

Seconds before the Me 110 hit the ground, teenager Fred Waterfield was cycling along Old Malden Lane near the junction of Barrow Hill when someone from a nearby cottage ran out and told him to take cover in a ditch. He woke up in a dressing station near St Mary's Church having been found unconscious in a bomb crater.

Eddie Colvin, who was 14 at the time, recalled the Me 110 as being a 'mass of smoking, twisted metal' and he thought it would take the roof off the top of his home. The aircraft was blown into tiny pieces which scattered far and wide.

Eddie had cycled to the scene of the crash with a friend to look for Luger pistols. What they found was the aircraft control column and the German cross from the fuselage which had been blown out intact. When the RAF arrived, it was Eddie and his chum who directed them

A Hurricane Mk.I of the type marking Terry's first-ever dig in 1961.

Above left: A portrait of Sergeant Harry Newton.

Above right: Sergeant Harry Newton.

Right: Pilot Officer Kenneth Carver, DFC, who years later accompanied Terry on a dig for his Hurricane that came down at Horsmonden, near Maidstone in 1940.

Below: Oberleutnant Hasse's aircraft was not the only crashed Me 109 to be examined by Terry, who is pictured here (third from left) with his daughter Mandy, Ken Anscombe's daughter Roslyn and fellow diggers. They had unearthed the wreckage of an Me 109 shot down at 10.30 am on 26 October 1940. Its pilot, Unteroffizier Geisswinkler was killed. The wreckage was located at Chalklet Farm, Pembury, Kent.

A gigantic digger at the scene in the late 1960s removes the mud-caked, historic engine of Unteroffizier Geisswinkler's Me 109 from its grave. The picture shows Ken Anscombe and two of the digging team to the right. On the far left of the picture, taking great interest in the making of history, are Terry's wife, Rose Parsons, and Ken's wife, Win Anscombe. The aircraft had been shot down by Sergeant Ronald Fokes, DFM of No. 92 Squadron. Sadly, Sergeant Fokes was killed in 1944 after his aircraft was hit by flak during his attempt to strafe enemy vehicles near Caen, northern France. (Picture: Courtesy of Gordon Anckorn)

Battle of Britain veteran Group Captain Tom Gleave, CBE, pictured on the far right of the picture, joined Terry (second left) and his team during the dig for a mystery Spitfire. This dig was organised by Ken Anscombe (far left).

One of the most exciting discoveries Terry made was this piece of tail fin from an Me 110-C which he dug out of ice six inches thick at Worcester Park, Cheam, Surrey. The aircraft had come down in 1940 in the middle of a cricket pitch. The story around the crew and a 'mystery corpse' proves fascinating, as Terry was soon to find out.

Terry's excavation team at Happy Valley, Old Coulsdon, Surrey, digging the site of a Hurricane flown by Sergeant Pilot Tony Pickering of No. 501 Squadron. The team was delighted the former pilot could join them on the hunt for artefacts from his aircraft which was shot down on 1 September 1940. Terry met Sergeant Pickering again in 2015 during the 75th Anniversary events marking the Battle of Britain.

to the scene and watched them collect pieces of flesh and bones and place them in sacks for burial.

He recalled: 'I wanted to hang the piece of fuselage with the German cross in my bedroom, but my mother said "no". For years it sat in a cupboard under the stairs with other wartime relics. When the house was sold, it all went out to the dustmen.'

Chapter 4

THE WORLD'S
FIRST TELEVISED DIG

IN March 1970, the producers of Thames Television's programme *Magpie* made history when they decided to film what was to become the world's first-ever televised dig of a Battle of Britain aircraft. (First screened in 1968, *Magpie* was offered to younger viewers as an alternative to the BBC's *Blue Peter*.)

The programme's creators, Lewis Rudd and Sue Turner, obviously mindful of the valuable archaeological lessons to be learned, sent a camera crew along to Ightham Place, Kent where I was part of the group recovering the wreckage of Hurricane N2652.

This aircraft had been flown by Canadian Pilot Officer Noel Karl Stansfeld, (sometimes spelled 'Stansfield') DFC, Czech medal for bravery, of No. 242 Squadron. He baled out, wounded, after combat with Me 109s over Edenbridge, Kent on 30 August 1940.

I remember the dig for Pilot Officer Stansfeld's Hurricane well, as I knew it was the first time ever the work of us wreck hunters would be seen on national television. I also thought to myself, how at last it would provide us with a chance to make the world remember the courage of 'The Few' who fought in the Battle of Britain.

The sight of an aircraft being removed from the ground piece by piece would provide a serious reminder to millions of people just what warfare was all about and what a vital role the RAF played in the defence of Britain's skies.

The presenter of *Magpie* who visited us that day was Tony Bastable, who was tremendously interested in the excavation. There were huge, old cameras and spotlights trained onto the site and while it was only being filmed for the television screen, it was more like a Hollywood blockbuster when I recall the amount of equipment there.

51

At the time, I was part of Ken Anscombe's digging team. He was in contact with Gordon Anckorn from the local newspaper. Well, this journalist often got to learn about aircraft crash sites, as readers of his column used to write in and tell him what they'd seen go down in 1940. He would then tell Ken, and off we'd go to check out the information.

Remember, eyewitness accounts were still very much relied on, and if they came good then it was a great feeling when a piece of wreckage set the metal detector buzzing. That day at Ightham Place was messy, muddy and wet with a great deal of slurry. There was a digger on site, which made a huge difference to the excavation and without it we wouldn't have uncovered as much as we did. The local newspaper, *The Sevenoaks Chronicle* reported that week '*Magpie* cameras see Hurricane unearthed from a watery grave'.

The site was in the corner of a wood and we found a vast amount of aircraft pieces – a complete aircraft, really. I planned to go back and retrieve it all after the television crew had left. However, when I returned to the site with my friend Ed Francis to collect the various artefacts from the wreckage, someone had beaten us to it and already removed a lot of the larger pieces. But not to be deterred, we had another scratch about and suddenly Ed called out, 'Look what I've found.' In his hand Ed was waving the much sought-after control stick which had last been touched by the hand of Pilot Officer Noel Stansfeld, DFC!

To any aircraft recovery specialist, the finding of the 'stick' is an important moment. A little like a bloodletting, really. It means you've found a real piece of history which had been used by a warrior of the Battle of Britain to steer his aircraft into combat. Well, Ed and I were triumphant about finding that stick. I went over to the place Ed was looking around and found for myself nine instrument casings. Being the good, honest person that he is, Ed handed in the prized find to the Halstead War Museum and was reprimanded for going back to a dig without permission!

So, after that we both felt a little put out and decided to call it a day and stop working with groups.

Then some years after I joined Ken for the televised dig for Noel's Hurricane, I was delighted to find a rare copy of an article which appeared in a magazine of 1970. The writer had created a wonderful description of the day of the dig under the headline 'The Search for a Fighter Pilot':

'Thirty years ago the skies of Kent were full of German and British fighter planes, fighting it out to the death in the Battle of Britain.

Many of those fighters, of course, were brought down, and that, as far as history is concerned, was the end of the story; the fates of individual fighter pilots were not recorded.

But it was only the beginning of the story for Ken Anscombe and Gordon Anckorn and the team from the Halstead Museum of War Relics, which contains all the aircraft they have dug up. And, as it turned out, it was only the beginning of a real-life detective story for Tony Bastable (presenter) and *Magpie* researcher Helen Best, who joined Ken and his team (including Terry Parsons and Ed Francis) on a search for a Hurricane Fighter which, according to eyewitnesses, had crashed on 30 September 1940 between the hours of nine and ten in the morning.

The site where the plane had crashed was a very wet and soggy wood. It was obviously impossible to dig by hand so a mechanical excavator was brought in to help. As the hole got deeper and deeper, tension rose. Were they in the right spot or was it all a fool's errand?

Then suddenly, at about ten feet down, Tony saw something that made him yell, "Hey! What's that! There's something in the scoop!" Ken rushed over and examined the find. "That", he said, grinning, "is part of the plane's gearing mechanism. And it's in extraordinarily good condition."

With renewed energy, Tony, Ken, Terry, Ed and Gordon Anckorn of the team continued the dig, and soon, to Tony's astonishment, they had discovered many different parts of the Hurricane the cockpit cover, still waterproof; the control column with the firing button in firing position, showing that the pilot had been ready to fire as his plane came down; and best of all, the plane's engine number, which proved beyond doubt which particular Hurricane this was.

With the information gathered from these excavations and from accounts of eyewitnesses, Ken was able to say with some certainty that the plane had been engaged in battle six miles up in the sky, and that when it was hit it fell in a dead-drop straight into the ground.

After finding out so much about this Hurricane, Tony became extremely curious about its actual pilot and decided to find out whether by some chance he had survived that September morning. If he had, and was still alive all these years later, Tony determined to reunite him with the plane that had been buried so long.

Tony and Helen's first step was to contact the Ministry of Defence with the information they already had and to see if they could be given the name of the Hurricane's pilot. But the records showed that he might be one of two men; one came from Wales, the other from Canada. They decided to start with the pilot nearest home, and after what seemed at times like a wild goose chase, they managed to locate the man from Wales. But disappointment was in store, because the pilot told Tony and Helen that he had managed to crash-land, and his plane had been recovered at the time.

That left the Canadian, Flying Officer Noel Stansfeld, DFC. Tony was afraid that, after all, the investigation was to come to nothing, but Helen rang Canada House in London. Officials there searched through their files and came back with the answer, "Yes, Noel Stansfeld did survive that September morning but we don't know what happened to him afterwards. The best we can do is give you his wartime address, in Vancouver."

The chance of the pilot still living at that old address seemed very slight, but Helen wrote all the same. And to her and Tony's astonishment, they received a reply by return of post – from Noel Stansfeld himself. He said he was astounded to hear about the Hurricane which he reckoned must be his, and would come to England as soon as possible to meet everyone on the programme and see his Hurricane again.

So it was, that Noel Stansfeld appeared on *Magpie*. He told Tony how he had begun his RAF service in Group Captain Douglas Bader's 242nd Squadron. Bader wrote of Stansfeld: "As a fighter pilot in Hurricanes, this pilot is exceptional; a most reliable and intelligent section leader and a good fighter." And for his fine record of shearing down enemy aircraft, he was awarded the Distinguished Flying Cross.

Then on 29 September 1940, Noel Stansfeld was posted to No. 299 Squadron. Tony asked him what happened the very next day.

"I got up at about 6.30 am on that particular day and went down to the flight office. I hadn't time to get a parachute, nor a Mae West, but I borrowed a parachute from another pilot who wasn't flying that day, and we took off, as I recall, at about 9.00 am. We flew to about 17,000 feet, and I had seen water beneath me. Then at this particular time, I spotted above us some Me 109s. I called up on my radio to tell the CO they were there, and I realised as soon as I tried transmitting that the radio was not functioning. It was not too good.

"However, within a few seconds I spotted cannon shells going over the wing on my left and cannon shells going over the aircraft on my right. And at that moment I was hit myself. I was above cloud but I realised as soon as my parachute opened that, as I said, there was water beneath me, and I had no Mae West. But, fortunately, as I went through the cloud there was lovely England beneath me. I landed beside a searchlight battery and the chaps there took care of me."

After a while in hospital, Noel Stansfeld became a flying instructor in Canada where he is now (1970) a law court reporter.

So for Ken and Tony and the excavation team, and the fighter pilot himself, the story had a happy ending. And on the programme Tony gave Noel the actual gunsight through which had he looked a few moments earlier, he would have seen the Luftwaffe pilot who hit him.'

Another important historical fact revealed by this dig was the potential for confusion when it came to the identification of a particular aircraft. In the case of Hurricane 2652 (Noel's Hurricane), the same serial number was found on the parts of an airframe recovered during a surface dig at Elmley, Isle of Sheppey by a group from another museum in 1971. This dig was abandoned because of the marshy conditions. Both Hurricanes were on record as being under repair at Number 4 Maintenance Unit Rolls Royce during the first days of July 1940, and according to the noted aviation archaeologist and author Winston Ramsey, 'It indicated just how much cannibalisation of aircraft was prevalent at that time.'

The crash site at Elmley, Isle of Sheppey was where the remains of 24-year-old Flight Lieutenant Hugh Beresford of No. 257 Squadron and his Hurricane (registered as P3049) were discovered during a full excavation eight years later. Flight Lieutenant Beresford was killed on 7 September 1940. I appeared on television again when the BBC's *Inside Story* producers decided to film this dig in September 1979, and a tail wheel, aircraft identity plate, steering control column and a parachute pack were discovered. A funeral then took place for Flight Lieutenant Beresford at Brookwood Military Cemetery in Surrey on 16 November 1979 and quite rightly, this pilot hero was buried with full military honours. His sister Pamela and friends from his home in Hoby, Leicestershire were in attendance – 39 years after Flight Lieutenant Beresford's death.

Sadly, as so often happens within museum groups, personalities can clash and petty politics poison the sense of collective purpose. For me and many good friends it was about honouring the memory of 'The Few', and over the decades I have given whole truckloads of unearthed artefacts to various museums which claimed to put them on show all over the UK. More often than not, the identity of the archaeologist who unearthed them is seldom mentioned on anything resembling a label or reference.

What was splendid at some digs though, was how I did manage to give the actual pilots one or two pieces from our excavations, and this we did after the television programme researchers had managed to track down Noel Stansfeld, DFC. He was flown from his home in Canada to London so he could appear in the *Magpie* studio and talk to viewers about his experiences in the RAF during wartime.

He told everyone how he was born in Edmonton, Alberta in Canada in 1915 and was educated in Vancouver. He decided to join the RAF on a short service commission in April 1939.

As a trainee pilot, Stansfeld did his initial courses at 3 E&RFTS in Brough, Yorkshire before advancing his skills at RAF Montrose in Scotland. By the end of the year he had converted to Hurricanes and was posted to No. 242 Squadron at Church Fenton, North Yorkshire on 20 January 1940. By May, the squadron was resident at Biggin Hill under the command of Squadron Leader Douglas Bader.

For three months, Noel took part in mission after mission to drive back the Luftwaffe approaching British shores. But morale at No. 242 Squadron was low after heavy losses, battle fatigue and lack of equipment during the Battle of France earlier that year. It was because of these factors the young Canadians got off to a rocky start with their new all-achieving commanding officer until they realised Bader would be an effective and energetic leader after all, and he also seemed to have some understanding of their concerns.

During the early summer in this crucial year for the defence of Britain, Noel shared the destruction of a German observation aircraft, a Henschel 126. Weeks later he proved to be a supreme fighter over Dunkirk on 31 May by destroying an Me 110 and a Ju 87 on 1 June. The young Canadian was proving a fearless young pilot and a key member of a busy, courageous squadron. No. 242 Squadron soon became part of No. 12 Group and was posted to RAF Duxford from where it took part in the Battle of Britain.

Records show that on 8 June Noel was sent to France and on 14 June he had to make a forced landing after his Hurricane was hit by Me 110s near to the town of Nantes in Brittany. He was lucky, as he was unhurt but the aircraft was written off.

Noel's days as a pilot continued to test his courage and skill. On 18 June he destroyed an He 111 and a few days later he learned he had been selected for a navigation course at St Athan in Wales. Noel remained at this training base for most of August 1940 before he was returned to the fold of No. 242 Squadron.

Once back in the air, there was no stopping the young aviator who on 30 August shared in the destruction of an He 111. (On 30 August, in the space of one hour, 12 Hurricane fighters of the all-Canadian squadron shot down 13 German bombers and fighters in a great air battle, in which the Canadians were outnumbered six planes to one. While in France, the squadron was officially credited with 72 enemy planes and by the time the Germans gave up their mass daylight attacks on Britain, it had added well over a hundred more.)

On 7 September, the squadron records reveal, he shot down and destroyed a Dornier Do 17 and on what became known as the hardest day/Battle of Britain day on 15 September he excelled by destroying another Do 17 and an He 111. On 27 September the Luftwaffe aircrew of a Ju 88 encountered the young Canadian and came off the worse, as he played a role in the destruction of their aircraft.

Two days later Noel learned he was to be transferred to No. 229 Squadron based at RAF Northolt under the command of Squadron Leader Frederick Rosier (later Air Chief Marshal Sir Frederick Rosier, GCB, CBE, DSO). It was not a lucky move. On 30 September and just one day after joining his new squadron, Noel was shot down in combat with Me 109s over Edenbridge, Kent and baled out. His Hurricane N2652 went into the ground at Ightham Place, as I was to discover when up to my waist in mud, thirty-odd years later!

The Air Raid Warden's diary for 30 September noted that the east Kent area was on Red Alert. 'The warning sounded at 8.55 am as large number of Luftwaffe (enemy) bombers and fighters were spotted flying overhead. Heavy barrage balloons were put up in the distance and engagements with our fighters were heard overhead but no bombs were dropped in the Ashford area.'

At 12.54 pm the air raid sounded again. 'Further large numbers of enemy aircraft were seen and engagements with fighters took place.' Once again, Ashford escaped the Luftwaffe's bombs.

In October 1940 Flight Lieutenant Noel Stansfeld was awarded the DFC and he returned to Canada. Citation: 'This officer has destroyed *seven enemy aircraft during engagements over Dunkirk and England. He has exhibited excellent fighting q ualities, i nitiative a nd m arked p owers o f leadership.'* As hero of the Battle of France and the Battle of Britain, Noel went on to train scores of young RAF pilots. He returned to the UK in 1943, and in 1945 he joined RAF Transport Command to ferry troops in and out of India. Noel was posted to RCAF Station Sea Island in Canada and left the services in 1948 after recovering from tuberculosis. That year he was awarded the Czech medal for bravery. He died in Canada aged 80 in 1995.

There are several reasons why I will never forget the dig for his Hurricane. Obviously, all the show business activity surrounding the *Magpie* programme left a lasting impression, but later came the realisation that Noel could have been a character in the famous *Reach for the Sky* film about the life of Sir Douglas Bader.

In this 1956 biographical BAFTA-award-winning epic, the well-known actor Kenneth More portrays Bader, who takes over command of the 'dispirited Canadians' of No. 242 Squadron. We see Bader arrive to meet his new squadron only to find them slumped in chairs, unshaven and wearing scruffy Irvin jackets, out of regular uniform and truculent towards authority. When Bader realises he's taken on a bunch of disillusioned young men suffering from battle fatigue, who feel forgotten and neglected, he begins to fight for their needs and eventually gains their respect to lead them through the Battle of Britain.

From various reports about Noel, I know he went through a phase of 'burnout'; and who wouldn't, after surviving the horrors of air warfare over France in 1940? He'd seen his friends get killed and had no knowing whether his own life would be spared from the merciless attacks by the Luftwaffe. When I met him on the dig for his Hurricane that day in the early 1970s I wish I had spoken more to him about his experiences of the war, but it's good to know that film director Lewis Gilbert did include the heroism of the Canadians in *Reach for the Sky*. What Noel thought of the film I don't know, but the all-Canadian squadron served with complete honour and valour during every action.

Squadron Leader Bader's assessment of him from 26 September 1940, at which time Noel had flown 422 hours (198 hours in the previous six months), reads: 'Conduct, very satisfactory. Temperate. This officer is the first Canadian in the squadron. He has a good brain, plenty of courage and is most reliable. Has a mature sense of judgement and is an excellent pilot. In combat, he is ferocious and a good shot. Have a very high opinion of this officer and consider he should make a good flight commander with a little more experience. The best junior section leader in the squadron.' On 2 September 1940 during Noel's time at No. 34 SFTS, Group Captain Ellis wrote of him: 'An extremely loyal officer. Is a Canadian serving in the RAF. Splendid spirit and a good example to others.'

The following month on 9 October a reporter from the Canadian Press must have spoken to Noel. The headline on the report reads 'Canadian Says German Flyers Really Scared'. The text goes on:

'Vancouver, Oct. 9, 1940 — (CP) — Pilot Officer Noel K. Stansfeld, Vancouver's latest Distinguished Flying Cross winner, believes German pilots now raiding England "are really scared to death".

Pilot Officer Stansfeld, who was awarded the DFC recently for operations with the Royal Air Force over Dunkerque and England, was describing how he shot down his seventh aeroplane in a letter to his parents here in Vancouver, Mr. and Mrs. J. K. Stansfeld.

After a brief gun duel with the rear gunner of a Heinkel 111, north of London, which ended when a machine gun burst killed the Nazi gunner, Stansfeld said he poured "the rest of my ammo into him".

"I could see three chaps in the front as they circled lower and lower," Stansfeld wrote. "They landed in a field and the three chaps, looking very dejected, crawled out with their hands high above their heads. I saw some local defence volunteers come out and drag them away. It is my firm belief that the Jerry pilots coming over are really scared to death. Except for the gunfire I had from the Heinkel 111, the Luftwaffe tried no evasive tactics at all. All he wanted to do was to land, and land anywhere."

On 22 September 1943, Group Captain E.S. Weston (No. 32 OTU) described Noel as 'a loyal officer; suited to instructional duties.' However, two days later, Squadron Leader N.K. Lloyd (No. 32 OTU) made a statement which makes me wonder if Noel's battle fatigue was working its way to the surface.

Squadron Leader Lloyd wrote: 'A good average training officer – not likely to provide good leadership on operations.' However,

Group Captain E.L. Wurtele assessed him as follows: 'Has done good work in conversion flight; a loyal officer more suited for training duties.'

At No. 20 (P) AFU, however, having flown 1,579 hours (120 hours in the previous six months), Group Captain N.W. Timmerman wrote: 'An above average officer who is a useful flying instructor and has done a good job as assistant to the Wing Commander Training.'

Thirty years later, as I was digging the earth looking for Noel's Hurricane, some research revealed how just a few yards away there was another Battle of Britain crash site. Sadly, the pilot in that Hurricane was killed as the aircraft went down in flames. His name was Flying Officer Malcolm Ravenhill, who was unlucky enough to be shot down by Me 109s during the same raid at the same time, 10.40 am, which saw Noel bale out. Flying Officer Ravenhill had been flying Hurricane P2815 when it came down near Church Road, Ightham on 30 September 1940.

I recall going over to this area not long after we had dug Noel's Hurricane but there was nothing but a dark place in the grass, and I think one or two pieces from the Hurricane were found just beneath the surface. Why Flying Officer Ravenhill did not bale out can only leave me to presume he was killed by gunfire from the marauding Luftwaffe before his aircraft went down in flames.

His RAF career began in 1938 when he was sent to a flying training unit in Egypt and by January 1940 he was with No. 12 Group Pool at Aston Down. When he successfully converted to Hurricanes, he joined No. 229 Squadron at Digby on 9 March that year, and on 1 September he survived being shot down by Me 109s during heavy combat over Biggin Hill. He had been at the controls of Hurricane P3038 before he baled out and was admitted to Shorncliffe Hospital, suffering from shock. The second time he was attacked by the Luftwaffe, twenty-nine days later, he wasn't so lucky. The grave of 27-year-old Flying Officer Malcolm Ravenhill is in his home town of Sheffield at the City Road Cemetery. On the tombstone, there is an inscription 'One of the Gallant Few'.

A portrait of this hero was drawn just weeks before his death by famous artist Cuthbert Orde and it depicts a handsome man who appears so much older than his 27 years. The eyes are wise and dark and he sports the fashionable RAF moustache, to denote an air of authority, above a kind mouth and a strong chin. If there was fear in his heart, his face in this remarkable portrait doesn't show it.

Magpie cameras see Hurricane unearthed from a watery 'tomb'

DIGGERS from the museum (left to right): Terry Parsons and Lusha Francis searching in the slurry; Helen Beal and Tony Bastable of Magpie programme; and Rosalind and her father Ken Anscombe (curator of the museum).

ON September 30, 1940, when the German air offensive was reaching the last stages of the Battle of Britain, the people of Ightham were watching a furious battle in the clouds above their heads.

A crowd of Spitfires, Hurricanes and Messer- ... landing by parachute at the ... top of Seal Hill ...

A newspaper cutting relating to the *Magpie* dig.

Pilot Officer Noel Karl Stansfeld in front of a Hurricane.

The Stansfeld excavation underway.

The dig on the Isle of Sheppey for Hugh Beresford's Hurricane P3049. His remains were also discovered that day.

A portrait of Hugh Beresford in uniform.

The funeral of Flight Lieutenant Hugh Beresford at Brookwood Military Cemetery in November 1979. He was killed on 7 September 1940 and nearly forty years later his remains were discovered with his aircraft.

The grave of 27-year-old Flying Officer Malcolm Ravenhill is located in his home town of Sheffield, at the City Road Cemetery. On the tombstone there is an inscription, 'One of the Gallant Few'.

Above left: A portrait of Malcolm Ravenhill by Cuthbert Orde.

Above right: A carburettor manufacturer's data plate from Flying Officer Malcolm Ravenhill's Hurricane, P2815.

Chapter 5

LUFTWAFFE PILOT ULRICH STEINHILPER

WHILST I am tremendously proud of the pioneering role I have played in the early recovery of so many Battle of Britain aircraft, there is one which stands out with such poignancy it deserves to be exhibited in a white-walled gallery on its own as the ultimate representation of aerial warfare.

It is the charred, blackened and defeated carcass of a Luftwaffe Me 109E-4, which delivers such an intense and robust message about the brutalities of conflict, it is as powerful as any piece of sculpture which aims to alight the imagination of today.

Even as the digger lifted it from its deep grave in 1983, I knew it was something special. For not only did I find a truly vast quantity of historically important artefacts at the site including the Daimler-Benz engine, propeller, ammunition, machine guns and small weapons, but a story of the battle from the German perspective, which would emerge a little later when I met the pilot who had baled out in the nick of time.

But like all significant achievements in life, it's often a case of 'no pain, no gain' and finding this Me 109E-4 which had been flown by Oberleutnant Ulrich Steinhilper of Jagdgeschwader 52 had not been easy.

As I have mentioned before, we often had to rely on villagers' eyewitness accounts and maps. I remember going door to door, along with historians and aviation recovery enthusiasts Dick Lukehurst and Tony Parslow, in and around the areas of Sarre and Chislet in East Kent asking for information. We often came away disappointed after being sent on several wild-goose chases. Mr Y remembers a German floating down over there... or was it by those trees? Or Mrs Z recalled an aircraft with black crosses on its wings heading for the field just north of Mr So-and-so's farm. And on and on went these recollections of 1940, which were often true but somewhat vague on the exact location.

Of course, in the 1970s we had to think at least one or two people in living memory of the Battle of Britain had the absolute correct information. We were an optimistic group, so we had to have some confidence we eventually would meet someone who would help us pinpoint an exact location. We thought someone, somewhere really must remember. What I always aimed for though, were aircraft from which the pilot or aircrew had baled out. It was never my intention to deliberately seek out and discover human remains. We knew this particular Me 109E was last seen diving towards Chislet and Sarre and had been free of its pilot, as brief records had shown.

So, the search for Steinhilper's fighter aircraft began with Dick in the late 1970s, and for a couple of years I was among the group who combed the area for any evidence or artefact from the aircraft which might have risen to the surface in this marshy area. Eventually of course, we had a result and we went all out to raise the aircraft affectionately known to its pilot – we were to discover later – as 'Yellow Two'.

This dig really stuck in my memory. Not only because of the archaeological treasure but because of the enormous effort and years that went into finding it. As a boy, Dick Lukehurst grew up with the Battle of Britain raging overhead and had always felt motivated to locate crashed aircraft flown by his heroes. His intentions to dig were pure, and carried out with the utmost respect in honour of the aircrews. We had that in common.

The day we finally dug down deep enough with helpful individuals like Harry Wynch, we found 'Yellow Two' and saw bits of it sticking up out of the mud. I recall asking my boss, who owned the low-loader lorry I drove for my day job, if it would be possible to borrow it so we could transport the mangled remains of the aircraft, which weighed a few tonnes, from the field to a local museum. And what a weight! I remember having to drive the lorry very steadily over to the site and once the wreckage was placed on the back of the lorry, it was so weighed down I was concerned the wheels would get stuck in the mud! But with determination and slow, skilled driving, I managed to take the mangled heap which once flew high and proud in battle against the RAF 43 years ago to its new location, where it would eventually go on display to museum visitors.

That day I found myself in the honoured position of transporting the world's most substantial excavated remains of an Me 109E from the Battle of Britain. I think for sure this is well worth recording as one of those days in life when we feel we've achieved something that truly matters. I'd like to think most of us in the group felt the same. It had been a unique privilege of sorts to find the aircraft and let it breathe again. We were back there day after day collecting all the items from the wreckage. Even today, when I look at the remains of that aircraft still blackened and charred on a carpet of various gnarled and twisted relics with belts of bullets adorning its fuselage like a mad necklace, I take a deep breath. Its intensity, coupled with the memories of a long, hard dig, reminds me of the fact that nobody wins a war. I don't believe the display represents any sort of triumphalism at all. No doubt the academics enjoy debating such a concept.

When I met Herr Steinhilper in 1985, the once-young pilot of 1940 who had flown this amazing aircraft, I found he was an articulate, friendly and highly intelligent man. His acute story of the day he baled out from 'Yellow Two' added so much to the discovery and gave it a provenance so valuable and awe-inspiring. He had many memories to share.

In his book *Spitfire on My Tail* he describes how he flew across the Channel in the morning of 27 October 1940 with his *Rottenhund* (wingman), Feldwebel Lothar Schieverhofer, by his side among a formation of fighter bombers. He recalled how they were greeted by dark clouds when they reached Kent at a height of 9,600 metres. This memory of the weather conditions over the county is confirmed when checked in the local Air Raid Warden's diary, which states: '7.38 am – Large formation of planes were heard but visibility poor'.

Ulrich recalls how he looked up and saw – flying at about 1,500 metres higher – the RAF in Spitfires and Hurricanes, which could assemble at additional height with the latest Merlin engines. The German bombers began to shed their loads in order to turn back, and Ulrich recalled how the bitter cold was not doing the engine of his Me 109 any favours. Also, he dared not risk going any higher, as if the pilots of No. 74 Squadron didn't get him then the chill would attack the temperamental Me 109. The next thing he knew was the sight of the RAF coming at him from out of the sun and as he took a dive down 'just like a staircase', he noticed his wingman, Feldwebel Schieverhofer, was under attack.

As Ulrich levelled off at 7,000 metres, he heard a loud bang to the left side of his Me 109. Within a minute or two, he knew his radiator had been hit and when his engine went silent, he made a decision to bale out – better than be left to drown in the Channel. That day he was taken

PoW. His wingman, Feldwebel Schieverhofer, force-landed his own damaged Me 109 at Penshurst, Kent. He was captured unhurt.

A few decades had passed, when veteran Luftwaffe pilot Ulrich Steinhilper was seen picking his way across a tangled grass field in Kent. A chilly breeze ruffled his hair and tugged against his long coat as he flinched at the vastness of such a remote vista ahead.

Ulrich, then 67, had last seen this place, a cow field at Chislet, near Canterbury, on 27 October 1940 as a 21-year-old Oberleutnant of Jagdgeschwader 52, when his country was at war with Britain. Of course, at the time, as the Battle of Britain was in its last stages, he wasn't in the mood to check out the landmarks of east Kent. He was still reeling from the traumas and indignity of a dicey parachute descent, a badly injured leg and a wickedly comical sight of cows hightailing it towards the edge of the field as he plummeted with his canopy in full sail towards them.

Within seconds of hitting the ground, he saw a group of people running in his direction and yelling. One man had a shotgun. Ulrich was scared of the British. Scared – full stop! He thought he would be beaten up because of all the bombs the Luftwaffe had dropped in the area.

As a man wearing an armband approached, Ulrich tried to remember the English he had learned in school. The man called out for him to get up, from across the riverbank. 'I can't, my leg is hurt', Ulrich shouted.

He looked around again. He wanted to see what had happened to his Me 109E-4. It was only minutes ago he realised that his aircraft, his precious 'Yellow Two' had engine trouble. The propeller pitch would not reach the level he wanted and he wondered if the condensation of the cold October days had leaked into the pitch gear causing it to freeze. The high altitude and cloud did not help.

As he was coping with a failing engine and a 400-mph dive in retreat from Hurricanes and Spitfires in full attack, he heard a bang on the left side. Looking around, he saw no other aircraft. Ulrich attempted radio contact with comrades in Calais. He wondered briefly if he should ditch in the Channel and wait to be rescued. He thought the super-charger on the aircraft had blown. Oil was now leaking from the engine.

Flying beneath cloud at just 1,500 feet, he decided to turn off the engine to give it a rest. After gliding briefly, he started up the aircraft again but all he heard was metal grinding against metal before the engine seized up. He told me: 'I ran through all the emergency procedures in my head. Poor Yellow Two I thought, this is your last moment! I pulled the lever to jettison the canopy. I glanced at the altimeter and I was at 800 feet now. I forced open the canopy and the speeding wind snatched it away from my hand and it fell into the void below.'

What followed was a terrifying few seconds as Ulrich attempted to heave himself out of the diving aircraft cockpit without tearing his parachute. When the wind tore him from the aircraft he grabbed his parachute handle and yanked it full on. The parachute had wound itself around his leg and like a circus performer he spun around trying to free the canopy. He said, at one point he was hanging by his leg and the pain was immense. He managed to watch 'Yellow Two' hit the ground in the distance. By the time he landed face down, he could hear the ammunition from the aircraft exploding.

It was during that shock and silence on the ground he thought about the events of his life that had brought him to such a bleak and inhospitable place – this field in England. They say one's life flashes before one if anything death-defying happens to us. Ulrich was no different that day. His childhood, schooling, the day he joined the Hitler Jugend (which he'd been reluctant about because of the bully boys), his time at the compulsory labour service, which aimed to toughen up young German men, then the Luftwaffe pilot training, his work running the radio communications unit, his time spent as adjutant to Luftwaffe ace and Spanish Civil War pilot Adolf Galland, and ultimately his days as acting commander of JG52 at Calais. There's no question he had packed a lot into his 21 years!

Then in 1983, when he made a special pilgrimage from his home in Stuttgart, Germany to not only revisit the field of memories, but to later visit the wreckage of his aircraft in a museum, it proved an important moment in the history of aviation archaeology. I was there that day when the mature Ulrich stepped forward to check out a piece of twisted medal that was once a rudder bar. He, too, examined the battery and the radio we'd dug up, which were remarkably still intact. He remarked with a smile how he was glad he hadn't remained in the aircraft.

He looked closely at the engine, too, which had seized up on him in the cold October weather of 1940. Only minutes before that moment, as a young Luftwaffe pilot full of confidence and energy, he had heard the bang that caused him to lose speed and height.

In 1985 Yorkshire Television made a programme called *Churchill's Few* and in it, my friend Dick Lukehurst, who began the search for 'Yellow Two' appears in a room with Ulrich examining the remains of the aircraft.

Ulrich said: 'When I saw the debris, I remembered again and again just how lucky I was to get out of it. I saw the ammunition and stepped back. I think it is good to see that it is not a glorious sight and how it reminds us all there is death and blood and harmful things associated with this wreckage.'

However, I recall how nostalgic Ulrich was about 'Yellow Two' and he told me this Me 109 had been special in 1940, because it had been fitted with new MGFF type cannon in the wings. These, he said, gave it a formidable hitting power, and he hoped, a real edge when he needed it during a dogfight.

When the aircraft was delivered to him in the September of 1940, he discovered it wasn't factory fresh and had already been flown by another pilot in battle. 'Yellow Two' came with three stripes on the tail as confirmed victories. This was what made him feel it would be a good omen for him, as he would soon be adding his own stripes as the Luftwaffe gathered strength in its bid to beat the RAF out of the skies. In the months leading to him being shot down, Ulrich had claimed five British aircraft.

For most of the Battle of Britain he flew from Jagdgeschwader 52's base and tent village at Calais. In the early weeks of 1940 the men of JG52 found themselves operating in and out of Coquelles.

For most of the battle and the 100-plus sorties over France, Kent and London, he flew an Me 109E known as 'Yellow 16', which he admitted in his own autobiography, *Spitfire on My Tail*, served him reliably and well. As the proud owner of an Iron Cross First Class, he later questioned why he became so attached to his fighter aircraft as 'after all, they were only machines'.

Ulrich said: 'Pilots are notoriously superstitious, and I had done a lot in Yellow 16. I had also spent much time along with my ground crew tuning this aircraft to my personal taste and with that, I'd begun to imbue it with some of my personality. Certainly, I felt she'd responded to the odd kind word or the promise of a rest and a full service! But I had to move on, and Yellow Two was waiting for me. However, I do believe that after our last flight I said "goodbye" to "16" and gave her unyielding metal skin an affectionate and final slap!'

When asked how he felt about the British aircraft and crew he'd downed as an ambitious young Luftwaffe pilot, he recalled a Blenheim he had attacked and shot at twice. The Blenheim went down in the sea and from the air he saw two of the crew make it to a lifeboat.

'I was called up and asked if I wanted to visit them. I was told that a crew member had been killed and two men had been taken prisoner. I didn't want to go down there,' he recalled.

Talking to Ulrich during one of his book signings obviously proved tremendously interesting to me. I told him about how much we'd laboured to find his downed aircraft in the marshes of Chislet and he seemed genuinely overwhelmed about that. I learned a lot from him about his time in the Luftwaffe as he was happy to share that information with anyone he believed was genuinely interested. He knew I had dug his aircraft in 1983 and that I was one of the earliest-ever pioneers of Battle of Britain aircraft recovery and archaeology, and he welcomed the chance to reveal as much as he could.

It all helped with the provenance of what digging Battle of Britain aircraft was all about. Knowing and understanding who was flying and was aboard a particular aircraft made all the difference. It gave the rare and specialised job of aircraft recovery a reason and a definite purpose.

Ulrich said: 'When I joined the Battle of Britain, there were thirty-six experienced pilots in my JG52 Squadron. All of them had up to three years' flying experience but by the time I was shot down on 27 October 1940, there were only seven left of the original thirty-six. When I look back at pictures from the time, I realise by our pale, drawn faces how we weren't young men any more. We had shaky hands, and there came a time when everyone was talking about Kanalkrankheit (channel sickness), which meant that pilots wanted to go to hospital to have their appendix out just so they could get time off from flying! Then there were the cases of pilots facing court martial because they were faking engine failures and returning to base too soon. They were also reporting their aircraft having too high temperatures, radio failures, mechanical faults and things like that.

'My commanding officer at JG52 was Helmut Kuehle, who genuinely suffered from a searing earache and sinus problems, and when he was in too much pain to fly, command was passed to me.'

When Ulrich was interviewed in 1985, he was reminded about a raid on Manston Airfield in Kent. He didn't want to remember the time he strafed a fuel tanker and watched a man who was holding the hose to a fighter aircraft die. He said: 'This man had been hit. I could see that. It was the first and only time I was hitting a human being. Before that I had been solely concentrating on aiming for the aircraft.'

I did learn that during his visit to Kent in 1985 a meeting was arranged with former sergeant pilot, (later Pilot Officer) Bill Skinner, DFM, of

No. 74 Squadron, who is believed to have shot Ulrich down in 1940. There was no hatred between the two of them as Ulrich revealed he was just interested to meet the pilot who had changed the course of his life. Bill attacked 'Yellow Two' and other Me 109s as they made their way back to France after a heavy raid on London.

'I could see enemy aircraft coming at us from under the sun, and I called to my *Rottenhund* (wingman) to dive away into the clouds and when I looked at my rpm, they were terribly off so I had to come up again. Then I heard that bang... Just one bang!'

Bill recalled how on 27 October his flight commander saw him shoot at an Me 109, which then emitted a trail of black smoke and dived towards the sea.

He told Ulrich: 'I can only imagine that Wing Commander John Mungo-Park (1915 – 1941) got one of you and I got the other one. There's no way of telling all these years later.'

Both Ulrich and Bill discovered they had shared similar experiences during the war, including the battle for Dunkirk, the Battle of Britain, and later life as prisoners of war.

Bill parachuted out of Spitfire Mk I X4022 on 30 August 1940 and soon returned to duty. He was later promoted to pilot officer and was awarded the DFC. In 1941 he was shot down over France in his Spitfire Mk V W3208 and captured by the enemy and sent to a PoW camp camp then soon moved on to the notorious Stalag Luft 3. Bill was released from the RAF in 1946 as a flight lieutenant and later rejoined the RAFVR.

As for Ulrich, as a PoW he was sent to Neys, Ontario in Canada and became an artful escapee, breaking out of the camp on three occasions. The furthest he got before recapture was New York. After the war, he returned to Germany and like many of his generation, he started life again as a very different man. He said: 'Coming down by parachute in the Battle of Britain changed my life completely.'

Hearing these words from someone who had once been our enemy had a great impact on me, as it once again drove home the fact that there was very little difference between the humanity of the young aircrews of the RAF and those of the Luftwaffe. The only outward sign they came from a different country was their uniforms and the shape of their aircraft, as inside they were just as frightened, just as anxious and just as proud when it came to the ultimate dance with death in the skies.

Ulrich Steinhilper, who died aged 91 in 2009, had a great deal in common with those RAF veterans who had taken part in the Battle of Britain in that they all had memories of the friends who disappeared from their lives as quickly as they had arrived; the thoughts of unforgettable faces who haunted them in the dark hours of reflection, that special camaraderie was seldom repeated as they grew into their maturity.

Ulrich made many friends in England and was always happy to talk to pilots and historians about his war. His humanity certainly added a new dimension to my thinking whenever I turned out to dig an aircraft, especially if it bore the colours of the Luftwaffe. Speaking to Ulrich and many other veterans, I realised I was no longer the boy who thought scraps of a Luftwaffe aircraft were a prize because I shared a kinship with the victor who had shot down an enemy. I had gone beyond the simple childhood thoughts of friend or foe, and those convenient ideals etched in black or white. Chatting to Ulrich, reading his memoirs and hearing him talk about his days as a young pilot who thought only of flying and the speed of his Me 109E, confirmed in me another layer of answers whenever I was questioned over my need to recover the crashed aircraft of the Battle of Britain.

In contrast to Ulrich's experiences of the Battle of Britain is the story of Unteroffizier Fritz Buchner. In 1974 and 1984 there were two attempts to recover and identify an Me 109 and most importantly of course, the pilot. Firstly in 1975, I joined the Brenzett Aeronautical Museum group in an attempt to find this aircraft which had gone down at Shuart Farm, St Nicholas at Wade, Thanet on 26 August 1940.

This dig was not a great success owing to bad weather conditions; the mechanical diggers of the time hardly went below a few feet and nothing substantial was found or could be seen. Investigations at the time did reveal the *Werk Nummer* of the Me 109, which was 3874. Later this led to the identity of the Luftwaffe pilot who was killed when the aircraft was shot down by RAF fighters.

The remains of Unteroffizier Fritz Buchner were discovered in September 1984, when a new excavation was orchestrated by Peter Diamond. A larger, more far-reaching heavy equipment was brought in to plummet the great depths of the hole in which the wreckage had remained for more than forty-four years.

Even after forty feet down though, as Andy Saunders reports in his book *Finding the Foe*, there was still no sign of the engine. Then after another determined effort to beat the marshy soil and water-logged conditions that day in early autumn, artefacts began to come to light. I sat in the great hydraulic bucket as it plunged down deep to the bottom of that great hole, but as fast as I could look around, water was rising up on me. I dread to think what would have happened if the hydraulics had packed up on me that day.

Andy writes: 'The concertinaed wreckage was found compacted into the last few feet of the excavation, and apart from a tailwheel and crumpled fuselage panels, much of the cockpit area was also uncovered in this compressed mass.'

At this point, the remains of Unteroffizier Buchner were discovered by Andy, and Steve Vizard and operations ceased at once.

Andy continues his account: 'It was getting dark, I remember, when the two police officers arrived at the scene. The one acting as the coroner's officer took away the remains, and whilst definitive proof of the pilot's identity was still needed, we saw a torn handkerchief with the initials 'FB' on it, plus a piece of uniform tunic showing the rank of the pilot – Unteroffizier (Corporal).'

This excavation unearthed pieces of fuselage with traces of yellow paint and parts of an emblem of II/JG3. As Andy points out in his book, there was a small lucky charm in the form of a cloverleaf with the inlay of a red ladybird on it. The name 'Christl' and the date '4.4.1940' were stamped on the back. The date was the pilot's 24th birthday and was to play a huge part in convincing the coroner that Unteroffizier Buchner could be identified as the pilot of Me 109 3874.

At the inquest held in Broadstairs, Kent on 1 July 1986, coroner Rebecca Cobb learned how careful researchers had tracked down Unteroffizier Buchner's 80-year-old sister (a Frau Heumos), who was living in an old people's home in Augsburg, Germany. Later her son, Gunther, wrote to the leader of the 1984 dig, Peter Diamond, to thank him for finding his uncle after so long, and copies of Buchner's birth certificate provided even more evidence of identity.

An eyewitness to the crash in 1940 was 81-year-old John Marsh, who was a baker at the time. He was taking food and cigarettes to local troops on the day Unteroffizier Buchner met his death.

He recalled: 'In the August of that year I remember a Messerschmitt crashing. No parachute came down and it dived into the ground at Shuart's Farm, just leaving its mark on the surface.'

During the inquest, evidence and research was supplied by the Ministry of Defence Air Historical Branch representatives. It was agreed by many that the Luftwaffe pilot deserved a decent burial with full military honours at Cannock Chase.

On 31 August 1940 Oberleutnant Erich Woitke wrote to Unteroffizier Buchner's parents. Buchner had been a popular member of the squadron and had been known to fly his little dog with him on various sorties over Britain. He had also survived being starved of oxygen at a great height during battle and blacked out. He came round just in time, as his Me 109 began a noisy plummet to the ground.

Woitke wrote: 'On 26 August I took my group over Great Britain and we were advancing against southern England, when I think your son probably suffered some damage to his engine. This made an emergency landing on the other side of the Channel necessary.

'I don't think you should make too much about the safety of your son, as he was a skilled pilot and our expectation is that he can take care of himself. We all hope he made an emergency landing safely and I think that with his excellent flying skills, he will have managed that easily. Of course, once I have any further information, I will notify you at once. Yours truly, Woitke.'

When the popular Buchner failed to show up at the airfield in France, his little dog was sent back to the family in Germany. This much-loved pet was looked after for five years until he died in 1950. Sadly, it would be forty-six years before the Buchner family had definitive news of his master, Fritz's death.

Unteroffizier Fritz Buchner was buried with full military honours at Cannock Chase German Military Cemetery on 8 May 1987 with members of his family following the coffin.

One of his relatives, Helmut Dumberger, wrote: 'The recovery team have enabled Fritz to have an honourable burial and for us to know exactly what happened to him. It is a pity that his parents had not lived to see this. I can absolutely assure you it is what they would have wanted for their boy. We must thank everyone who made this possible, and feel that we should also offer these thanks on behalf of our Fritz who would surely be grateful for all the efforts made on his account. His lucky charm had not been so lucky for poor Fritz in the way that he had imagined, although many years later it would turn out very fortunate indeed that he had been carrying it that day.'

Oberleutnant Ulrich Steinhilper.

A portrait of Oberleutnant Ulrich Steinhilper as painted by artist and curator of Shoreham Aviation Museum, Geoff Nutkins.

Sergeant Pilot (later Pilot Officer) Bill Skinner, DFM, in the back seat of a car during a journey with squadron pals.

Terry, on the right, with his pal Harry Wynch during the dig for Steinhilper's Me 109, which went down near Sarre, east Kent. Both Terry and Harry are pictured here working on the removal of the fuselage. (Picture courtesy of Tony Parslow)

The recovered remains of Steinhilper's Me 109E-4. (Courtesy of Tony Parslow)

The search begins for the wreckage of a Spitfire flown by Flying Officer John Wintringham Cutts, who was shot down on 4 September 1940 by Me109s over Maidstone. His Spitfire, X4278, crashed and burned out on Amberfield Farm. The 20-year-old pilot was reported missing. When Terry dug the site of the Spitfire crash in 1972, a propeller boss and blades were found. In 1999 research revealed that a body of an unknown airman had been discovered at Amberfield Farm on 14 September 1940 and buried as such at Bell Road Cemetery in Milton, Sittingbourne, Kent on 28 September 1940. Evidence of an administrative mix up in 1940 revealed the 'unknown airman' was in fact John Cutts. A new headstone was rightfully placed on the grave with 20-year-old Flying Officer Cutts' name engraved upon it. Sadly, for John Cutts' family living just a few miles away in Bognor, West Sussex, they never got to know where he had been buried.

The excavation crew at the scene of crashed Spitfire R6690, which burnt out here near Kenley on 15 September 1940. The pilot was Geoffrey Gaunt of No. 609 Squadron, who was shot down during an attack on German bombers over London. Aged 24, Pilot Officer Gaunt was killed. He was later buried in Huddersfield, Yorkshire. The site of the crash was dug in the 1970s by a team that included Terry.

Chapter 6

KNIGHTS OF THE SKY

THE late Group Captain Johnny 'Kentowski' Kent, DFC, AFC, Virtuti Militari (1914 – 1985) was one of my heroes of the war and many years later, in 1982, I got to meet him at a popular pub used by Biggin Hill pilots – the White Hart at Brasted, Kent.

Group Captain Kent was a charming man and a sensitive soul with the watchful eyes of a poet. But long before I got to share a pint or two of beer with him, I knew how during the Battle of Britain he had led the now famous No. 303 Squadron of Polish airmen into the skies from RAF Northolt. By October 1940, his men were already experienced in the art of aerial warfare and became the highest-scoring squadron of the Battle having destroyed a massive 126 enemy aircraft, thirteen probables and nine damaged. This was an extraordinary accomplishment.

The Polish aviators were fearless; as was their Canadian-born leader, Group Captain Kent. When the Luftwaffe first darkened the skies of Poland, its national Air Force worked hard to beat them back but by early September 1939 the Poles were grounded and their aircraft destroyed – but the spirit of these pilots was not defeated. In their homeland, there was no chance for them against the vast numbers of Luftwaffe fighter and bomber aircraft attacking their country, and Hitler and his army marched in.

Following the invasion of Poland on the east by the Soviet Army later that same month, many Polish airmen were told to make their way to Romania and from there, go to France, where they were sure that their aerial skills and battle experience would be appreciated. At that time Romania was a neutral country in the conflict, but having witnessed the might of Nazi Germany, it was interning Polish flyers. Avoiding internment, or escaping from it, the pilots made their way via Bucharest to ports on the Black Sea. It wasn't an easy trip and many were left to fend for themselves with barely enough money to buy food. Using forged documents, they were able to board ships that took them to Marseille.

Having undertaken the arduous journey to France, these pilots realised that there wasn't the resistance to the Germans that they'd hoped for. Some Polish airmen were sent away to fly old First World War aircraft in Morocco, including fighter pilot Marian Pisarek, whose Battle of Britain Hurricane I was to dig out of the ground more than thirty years later.

Other pilots had barely finished their training on French fighters when France capitulated in June 1940. They determined to continue the fight in the air against the Nazis, and England was their last hope to unite against the aggressive enemy. Thousands of them made their way to the Atlantic Coast, where they were able to board ships for Britain. Others flew to French North Africa and made their way to Britain via Casablanca.

In the award-winning documentary *303*, written and produced by Tomasz Magierski and released in 2016, there is a clip of Winston Churchill declaring that the Poles and the British were to be 'united for life and death'. Churchill admired the fighting spirit of the Polish pilots, and their experience in aerial battle was eventually to prove a tremendous boost to the RAF. However, it was vital they learned to speak English. This was a hard and fast rule installed by the RAF, who insisted airmen should talk the same language if command was to be effective.

When John A. Kent arrived as a young flight lieutenant on 27 July 1940 to lead the Poles into action, he admitted in his memoir, *One of the Few*, being somewhat bemused. He wrote: 'They posted me to the Polish squadron. Lord knows why, and he won't tell me! The other boys are getting a kick out of it and laughing a lot right now. At present we have no troops, no Poles and no aeroplanes.' All there was apparently in the Mess at RAF Northolt was a book called *Polish Without Tears*. Of course it wasn't very useful, as it didn't include any of the phrases required for translation that related to aircraft and technical terms. 'Pass me the cake!' wasn't going to get the new squadron commander very far with his new crew!

The English lessons proved of help to the airmen who were mad keen to get into the cockpits of the Hurricanes and Spitfires around them. On 30 August 1940 they went into action and declared their first 'kill'. No. 303 Squadron was then deemed operational and they were able to let their fury loose on the enemy Luftwaffe, which had played its role in driving them from their homeland and destroying their country.

Flight Lieutenant Kent, known affectionately as 'Kentowski' by his Polish squadron, proved a strong leader to his men and even today he is hailed a true hero by Poland, having been awarded with the rare honour of a Virtuti Militari.

Like the Polish aviators who fought in the skies over Britain, Kentowski was an outsider. He was brought up in the prairies of Canada and had the skills of a cowboy. When the passion to fly seized him, he trained hard and gained his pilot's licence. His mother sold her jewellery in order to pay for his passage to England to join and train with the Royal Air Force in 1935. His courage was never questioned, and for two years from 1937 he was based at RAF Farnborough as a test pilot.

Much of this time was spent flying into balloon cables and risking his life time and time again. In 1939 he flew a Spitfire armed only with a camera for the RAF's Photographic Development Unit. Before long, he was flying Spitfires with guns and managed to shoot down his first Me 109 as the Battle of France was at its height.

His wonderful daughter, Alexandra Kent, who has written a foreword and epilogue to her father's famous memoirs, said: 'My father got on so well with his Polish airmen because like them, he was an outsider. He came from Canada and just didn't have the social codes of the British at that time. Just like the Poles, he didn't play cricket. I think in many ways those Polish aviators taught my father to fight. Like them, he didn't feel the need to glide in and around the RAF because of his social credentials.'

British women loved the Polish airmen, who had been christened 'true knights of the sky'. Their accents and courteous manners led to many romances. As warriors, of course, they were the bravest of the brave because they wanted their own country back.

During my long career as a Battle of Britain 'wreck hunter', I found myself in the rare position to be digging the one or two aircraft once flown by my Polish heroes. To be honest, I found this situation a great honour, as No. 303 Squadron were such high achievers when it came to defending Britain and helping this country in an extreme hour of need.

One day in the late spring of 1971, I received news about a group who were planning to dig up the wreck of a Spitfire which had gone down in a marshland area at Westbere near Preston and Stodmarsh villages near Canterbury, Kent.

I decided to help out and it turned out to be the worst thing I've ever had to do. I was not informed that the aircraft might still be 'occupied'.

Well, the aircraft had been flown by Polish Flying Officer Franciszek Gruszka, who was stationed at RAF Hornchurch, Essex with No. 65, 'East India', Squadron.

On 18 August 1940 he took off in Spitfire R6713 to intercept German bombers and was seen in dogfights in the skies over Canterbury and Manston and then he was spotted chasing a fleeing Me 109 as it made for the Channel. This was the last time Flying Officer Gruszka was seen alive, as he failed to return to Hornchurch and was later posted by the RAF as MIA (missing in action).

When I joined the dig for an aircraft on 28 March 1971, it was rapidly suspended because some teeth were found and reported to the official on site – a policeman – who wasn't quite sure in those days on how to proceed.

The excavation was then suspended and filled back in. I was certainly uneasy about what might be found, and yet was very unhappy about the thought that the remains of a pilot might still be there, his family never having had a chance to know what had happened.

The coroner dealing with the case at the time told the leader of the group that he was not qualified to identify whether the unearthed teeth were human or not. The question whether correct procedures had been followed after the human remains were found was referred to the Coroner's Court, and no further action was taken after the coroner was shown photographs which revealed police officers had been present at the original dig.

However, after rightful protests to the Ministry of Defence, the site was re-excavated on Monday, 15 April 1974 by myself and a team from the RAF. This was when the mortal remains of Flying Officer Gruszka were unearthed.

I went out on this second dig and I was using a spade to get deep into the wreckage, and suddenly all this cloth came out. It was a pair of trousers and a leg bone fell out of them. I was horrified and immediately said 'Stop, stop!' This was the revered ground where a hero had fallen. Out of deep respect, I ordered everyone to leave the site until the coroner's officer and his team had finished going over the area. We then had just half an hour to return and remove any pieces of aircraft. They made it clear to us that it was vital there was evidence that no one had been murdered and placed there in the excavation site in recent days.

Finding Gruszka's remains really backed up the argument for being sure to check the aircraft and to know beforehand what had happened to the crew before it went down.

In regard to the artefacts recovered from the site, I must point out how swampy ground and moist earth can provide protection from decay. Several of Flying Officer Gruszka's personal items were in good condition even after sitting in the ground for 35 years. His uniform was reasonably recognisable along with his Polish emblem and a wallet. I recall finding a device which pilots used to carry with them like a watch. This was a special gadget that told them the height and speed of the aircraft, which could be used if the instrument panel in the aircraft ceased to function. These items were to go on display at the Polish Institute and Sikorski Museum in London.

The body itself was identified by the discovery of a gold fountain pen with an engraved dedication to Flying Officer Gruszka from his fellow Polish airmen. Although he was just 30 years old at the time of his death, he was a highly experienced pilot, having first enlisted with the Polish Air Force in 1934. He was one of the first Polish airmen to arrive in Britain and was sent directly to a Spitfire squadron, where he was held in high regard by his colleagues and commanding officers. Flying Officer Gruszka was buried with full military honours in the Polish War Cemetery near RAF Northolt on 17 July 1975. I was delighted to discover his friends who stood by the graveside that day to pay tribute included famous Spitfire test pilot Jeffrey Quill.

Days before his death on 18 August 1940, Flying Officer Gruszka wrote in his memoirs:

Battle of August. I am starting to fight. Many Germans above and just twelve of us (only two Poles are me and Władzio Szulkowski). We attack bombers, German fighters attack us from behind. One of them is closer and closer. I make a sudden turn, get his tail, and send a series (burst of shots). He is going down to the clouds, inertial. I cannot go after him, because in the same moment two other 'Jerries' attack me. Have no chance, I hide in clouds.

When I look back on the dig for Gruszka's Spitfire, I am reminded of some of the darker reasons why some people are attracted to aviation digs. In fact, it is too macabre for me to think too much about and I did appear on an ITV documentary programme in 1996 called *The Graverobbers* to talk about some of the digs I've been on.

As I explained, if any human remains or personal items belonging to aircrew are ever found, I make sure the decent thing is done. The authorities are always informed, as well as the relatives. It wasn't often

I found personal items but if I did, I never, ever kept anything like that in my house. That's just not right.

The television programme was written and produced by journalist Jonathan Marland, who asked me if digging remains of aircraft was 'bizarre' or even 'ghoulish'.

I told him it was the sort of programme that needed to be made, as it raised the right questions over some of the negative aspects of aviation archaeology at the time. I'd like to think the programme helped clean up the ethics of the digging process and contributed to the placement of the correct formalities which must be adhered to on any dig today. I know my conscience is clear, as I trusted my instincts and have always strived to ensure morality came first. The Ministry of Defence brought in the Protection of Military Remains Act in 1986.

In the 1960s and 1970s, and even in the later decades, digging aircraft introduced me to some good, clever people who were just as keen to preserve the memory of 'The Few' as I was, and still am. One dig I recall particularly well was the time I met Winston Ramsey and his son, Gordon. (Winston Ramsey went on to compile with material generated from many digs involving myself and the early diggers, the magnificent *Battle of Britain: Then and Now*). Gordon was just a lad, when in the summer of 1976 we turned up at a house in Roding Road, Loughton, Essex, where for thirty-six years the wreckage of a Hurricane had remained buried in the backyard.

The aircraft had been located by leading aviation archaeologist and historian Tony Graves, who in those days ran the London Air Museum. The Hurricane had been flown by Polish fighter ace Flight Lieutenant Marian Pisarek of No. 303 Squadron.

That day in June when we stood in the back garden of that terraced property, it brought home to me once again the serious dangers of aerial warfare, which not only affected the aircrews but those residents in the small streets below. Innocently they'd struggle to live their lives on meagre rations and survive the war by taking each day at a time, and knowing the dogfights and raids overhead could result in tragedy, whether it was from bombing, gunfire or lethal incendiary devices. The sight at Roding Road made me realise everyone had been vulnerable, as life could be over all in a flash.

On 7 September 1940 an Air Raid Warden's diary noted: '11.29 am – The warning sounded and we were on Red 140. A few enemy aircraft observed. 15.50 pm Red 141 – The largest number of enemy bombers so far seen, passed over Ashford escorted by fighters and proceeded in the direction of London. Later it was reported that the largest and most concentrated attack so far had been made on the capital chiefly in the east and south-east and much damage and many fires had been caused.'

Gordon Ramsey, whose childhood interest in the Battle of Britain turned into a lifelong journey of research and knowledge, kindly allowed us to reproduce the following article from his collection:

'The full horror and tragedy of war was cruelly thrust upon the community of Loughton in 1940 when an event occurred in its midst which was horrifying in its nature and tragic inasmuch as it was caused by one of our own aircraft.

On 7 September 1940, a gloriously fine Saturday, the kind of day that is now synonymous with the Battle of Britain, Reichsmarschall Hermann Goering assumed personal command of the first great daylight attack on London. During the afternoon of that day a massive force of Dornier and Heinkel bombers from General Albert Kesselring's 2nd Air Fleet took off from their bases in Northern France and set course for the British capital. Soon afterwards a similar force from General Hugo Sperrle's 3rd Air Fleet climbed into the air from their airfields around Paris and also headed for London. Both bomber streams were escorted by swarms of Messerschmitt fighters led by the cream of the Luftwaffe's fighter force. Thundering over the French coast high above the Pas de Calais, the aerial armada was critically watched by the supreme commander and his staff. The Battle of Britain was about to become the Battle of London.

South of Orpington, part of the fighter escort broke away and headed back for France, short of fuel, while the stacked layers of bombers and their high escort bored inexorably on towards their targets – the huge complex of docks in East London.

At about 4.15 pm that afternoon, the air-raid warning sounded in Loughton, sending a 36-year-old architect, Mr Brockwell and his wife, of 40 Roding Road, to seek cover in a brick surface shelter which he had designed and built himself in his back garden. With a last anxious look at the sky, he shepherded his wife and her 60-year-old mother, Mrs Emily Minnie Gurden to safety.

Ten minutes later at Northolt aerodrome, No. 303 "Kosciuszko" (Polish) Squadron scrambled eleven Hurricane fighters to join the other twenty squadrons committed to the battle. Led by Flying Officer Paszkowski, they made contact at 4.40 pm with a *gruppe* of over 40 Dornier 215s returning across Essex from the capital.

From London to the coast, the returning bomber units were harried by terrier-like packs of British fighters snapping at their rear and flanks. The path of the battle was marked by plunging aircraft and blossoming parachutes.

Ernie Rule, who was then Fire Chief in Loughton, watched the skirmishing as it passed overhead. He saw a Hurricane make a diving attack on a Bf 109, setting it on fire and then fall victim to another Messerschmitt. The British fighter dropped rapidly, streaming smoke from aft of the cockpit.

Flying in the leading section of 303 was a pilot making his first operational flight over England. Flying Officer Marian Pisarek had served as an officer in the Polish Army since 1930, and in 1932 transferred to the Polish Air Force. During the 1939 September campaign in Poland he flew with the "Torun" Squadron, which received the Cross of the Virtuti Militari, the highest decoration a unit could receive for distinguished service. After the fall of France, he made his way to England where he joined No. 303 Squadron on its formation on 21 August 1940.

Rapidly overhauling the enemy formation, Marian Pisarek suddenly found that his two companions had sailed into the rear of the bombers downing one and turning their attention to the others. Immediately below him he spotted a fight in progress and dived to join in. At that point, a Bf 109E appeared in his sights and tacking himself on to its tail he gave it a short, but accurate, burst of fire. Flames burst from the Me 109 and at the same moment his aircraft staggered as it took a hammering from cannon and machine-gun shells behind the cockpit, delivered by another Me 109 in a beam attack. His Hurricane, pouring smoke, tilted towards the earth in a steepening dive.

At about 5.10 pm, Walter Bullen was on duty with an ARP Rescue Squad when he saw Pisarek's Hurricane diving over Lincoln Hall trailing its banner of smoke. He remembers that the aircraft altered course to take it away from the houses in Roding Road and out towards the playing fields by the river. Then he saw the pilot bale out.

Mrs Doris Steed at this time was watching events from her home at River Way. She, too, recalls seeing the pilot alter course to take his burning aircraft away from the houses before jumping clear.

Flying Officer Pisarek, struggling to control his mortally-stricken aircraft, saw the houses of Roding Road looming rapidly in his windscreen. Over six feet tall and endowed with exceptional strength, he now exerted every ounce of it to pull the plunging Hurricane away from the houses. Releasing his safety harness and removing his flying helmet, he prepared to abandon the fighter which had now passed beyond the vertical, when he found himself literally ejected from the cockpit.

The Hurricane, now in its death dive, spiralled back towards the houses where it finally crashed onto the surface shelter at the rear of number 40, practically demolishing it. A fuel tank ruptured and with a roar the contents ignited. Blazing high-octane petrol was cascaded into the shelter. Of the three occupants, Mr and Mrs Brockwell were killed instantly. Mrs Gurden died shortly afterwards with grievous burns.

Walter Bullen was at the scene with a rescue team within two minutes. Fighting their way through the flames, smoke and exploding ammunition, they strove to reach the shelter in the forlorn hope that someone could be saved. A complete wing was torn from the fighter and had landed in a garden a few houses away. Then came the struggle to retrieve the bodies. It was a scene, the details of which, they could never erase from their memories. Some of them, like Mrs Stead's husband, who was a member of an ARP First Aid Team, refused to tell their wives what they had seen at the shelter.

Meanwhile, Marian Pisarek was drifting across the allotments towards Alderton Hill at the end of his parachute. After being fired at by two Home Guards (who luckily missed) he reached the relative safety of a tree in the front garden of number 59. Disentangling himself from the parachute harness, he climbed down to find himself surrounded by a number of highly suspicious locals. Being tall, blonde and unable to speak much English, it was presumed that he was an enemy whereupon he was promptly arrested. At Loughton Police Station, after laborious questioning, his identity and more importantly, his nationality were established. Before he left the station to be returned to his unit he became extremely distressed on learning of the tragic aftermath of his escape.

Marian Pisarek eventually flew 47 sorties with No. 303 Squadron, during which he shot down four confirmed enemy aircraft and one probable, and was awarded the DFC. On 23 January 1941 he took over command of No. 315 "Deblin" (Polish) Fighter Squadron on its formation and led them until 18 April 1942, when on promotion to wing commander, he took command of the Northolt Wing. It was while leading the Wing on a "Circus" Operation over Desvres,

Northern France that he was killed while fighting a superior number of Messerschmitts and Focke-Wulfs. His ultimate score was 12 confirmed, 1 probable and 2 damaged.

On 7 September 1940 London's dockland suffered severely as a result of intensive and accurate attacks. Three hundred and forty-eight bombers escorted by 617 fighters had attacked Woolwich Arsenal, the immense Beckton Gas Works, the docks at Millwall, Limehouse, Rotherhithe, the Lower Pool, the Surrey Docks and West Ham Power Station. As a result of this and later attacks that night, 306 people were killed and 1,337 seriously injured within the capital. For the people of London's East End this was the first of many days and nights of terror. For the people of Loughton it was a terrifying introduction to the horror and tragedy of war.

In the running air battle over Essex, the Poles downed 14 enemy planes for the loss of 2 of their Hurricanes, 4 damaged and one pilot wounded.'

This graphic account of what happened that day illustrates the weight of responsibility the aircrews felt, not only in their waking hours but in their sleep too. We learn how distressed Pisarek was about the deaths of the three residents in the air raid shelter, and information like that must have sat deeply in his heart for the rest of his short life.

Extracts from Pisarek's own diary reveal a man of great sensitivity and observation. He wrote:

'7 September 1940
Take off from Northolt at 16.25 - 11 Hurricanes
Air battle at 16.40 hrs

Results:	Victories	Certain Probables
Do 215	12	2
Me 109	2	2
Losses:	Daszewski wounded, aircraft total loss	

Pisarek baled out " " "
four aircraft damaged

I took off for my first operational flight over England together with Paszko (Paszkowski - section leader) and Tolu (Lokuciewski). After a while I began to fear that the flight will be a fiasco, when suddenly I saw the bursts of artillery fire indicating that enemy aircraft were somewhere near. Paszko also noticed these signs, and to show that he was not only pious but also hot-blooded; he did not lose any time but waggled his wings as a warning to get ready for the attack and turned sharply to starboard towards the enemy formation attacking the end pair of Dorniers one of which soon burst into flames.

That left two of our 'planes and one Dornier and therefore nothing for me, but below us there was a fight in progress and I decided to join it. I soon had before me an aeroplane with swastika on its tail. With a height advantage there was no difficulty in making the attack. I had time to notice the flames issuing from the Me 109 when I, myself, received a burst from behind and my Hurricane started to smoke heavily, going into a steep dive. I released the belts and slipped off the helmet whilst trying to get the 'plane away from houses and into the open spaces but the Hurricane was already past the vertical line and I found myself literally ejected from the cockpit. It was not until I landed that I noticed the loss of one shoe which probably caught against some lever in the cockpit.'

Well, there is nothing more emotive than a solo shoe, be it discarded in the middle of the road in today's times or found abandoned in a wood or even tucked into a shop doorway. The sight of such a personal object always sets the mind onto an imaginative journey.

And I'd argue that one of the most incredibly poignant artefacts we discovered on that day in June 1976 was indeed Marian Pisarek's mangled brown shoe. This now sits on its own plinth under a glass case and belongs to my friend Gordon. It's a remarkable object and tells a story all on its own.

As indeed, when the *Sunday Mirror* got hold of the news that we'd found it while digging Pisarek's Hurricane, the story ran on page 31 in the edition of 13 June 1976:

SHOE THAT SAVED MAN OF COURAGE
'A size 9 shoe has led investigators to unearth the incredible story of a Battle of Britain hero. The shoe has been unearthed by Tony Graves with the wreckage of a Hurricane fighter that crashed after a dogfight on 7 September 1940.

The shoe was shed by Polish fighter ace Flight Lieutenant Marian Pisarek, as he struggled to free himself from the crashing plane.

For agonising seconds Pisarek's foot was trapped under the rudder pedal of the Hurricane, which was plunging to earth at 600 mph.

At last he freed his foot and parachuted to safety. Fortunately, he had not had time to put on flying boots before the order came to scramble... for the boots would have held him fast.

Tragically, his aircraft – from the RAF's No. 303 Squadron – crashed on an air raid shelter, killing the three occupants. The impact buried the plane's wreckage 16-feet under a garden, where it lay undetected for thirty-six years.

Group Captain Johnny Kent, who commanded the squadron and wrote its memoirs entitled *One of the Few*, said at his home in Harrow this week: "This is incredible. Pisarek was a quiet, pleasant young man who shot down twelve enemy aeroplanes. It must have been quite an ordeal when he was hanging upside down in the Hurricane, trying to free his trapped foot."'

According to witnesses of 1940 when Pisarek landed after baling out, he was most embarrassed to be missing that shoe, as his sock had a hole in it and everyone who ran over to greet him saw his big toe sticking out! It seems, even in times of great danger, Pisarek was a man of great dignity.

No one should forget the Polish airmen of No. 303 Squadron who clocked up the most victories during the Battle of Britain. Their bravery was stupendous. I was reminded of this even more so when in the summer of 2017 I visited the crash site of Sergeant Stefan Wojtowicz – one of Pisarek's esteemed colleagues. Sergeant Wojtowicz was 24 years old when he joined No. 303 Squadron at Northolt at its formation on 2 August 1940. The young pilot from Wypnicha, Poland proved fearless in the face of the enemy and went head to head with Me 109s over the Channel day after day. On 7 August he claimed two Do 17s, then on 11 August an Me 109 followed by another probable.

Sergeant Wojtowicz was killed on 11 September 1940 as he chased an Me 109 during the squadron's aerial defence of south London. I had heard from an eyewitness how the Polish fighter pilot's aircraft was seen to skim the top of some trees, which sent it cartwheeling across the field, killing him instantly. The Hurricane V7242 crashed and burned out on Hogtrough Hill, Westerham, Kent. As with many of his fallen comrades, Sergeant Wojtowicz is remembered on the Polish Air Force Memorial at Northolt.

One of the Polish heroes of No. 501 Squadron was Pilot Officer Franciszek Kozlowski, who took off from RAF Gravesend on 18 August 1940 to take on a hoard of Me 109s on their way over east Kent. When his Hurricane P3815 was shot down at Pean Hill, near Whitstable, Kozlowski baled out and as a seriously injured young man, he was admitted to hospital. By October that year he had been transferred to No. 316 Squadron and by 1942 had been promoted to flight commander.

On 13 March 1943, as he tackled the Luftwaffe in his Spitfire over the skies of Fesques in France, he was to brutally meet his death near Neufchatel. Aged just 23, he was buried in Dieppe Canadian Cemetery, France.

A little more than thirty years later in 1979, I had the honour to help locate and excavate the remains of Flight Commander Kozlowski's Hurricane which had plummeted into the soft ground of the Whitstable wetlands. On that dig we unearthed some extraordinarily important artefacts including a bent propeller blade and a complete example of armour plating which formed the back of the seat in the Hurricane.

The aircraft had been shot down by Oberleutnant G. Schöpfel of JG26 on 18 August 1940. The excavation unearthed a complete Rolls Royce Merlin engine with its propeller boss. It was recovered with the instrument panel, control column, maps and a copy of the *Daily Express* dated 9 August 1940. Items like the newspaper proved how the

cockpits of these stricken aircraft were fateful time capsules which would hold vital evidence of a history no one should forget. I also wondered if the newspaper we discovered had been used to plug up a draught or silence a noisy rattle in the aircraft or whether indeed an anxious Kozlowski had sat in his cockpit attempting to catch up on the news while waiting ready for an hour or two before given the all clear to take off?

Questions like this always occupied me during my digs with each and every one proving to be different in so many ways.

Flight Lieutenant Marian Pisarek of No. 303 Squadron.

Flight Lieutenant Marian Pisarek (right) with Johnny Kent (centre) and Flying Officer Zdzislaw Henneberg.

Terry and the team are joined by an interested cat during the Pisarek dig.

Tony Graves and team at work at the excavation on Pisarek's aircraft.

Tony Graves and John Tickner with artefacts from the Pisarek dig.

Above left: A shot of the top half of the control column of Pisarek's Hurricane of the famous No. 303 Squadron led by Group Captain Johnny Kent.

Above right: Terry and the control column he discovered during the dig for Pisarek's Hurricane.

Pisarek's battered shoe which was recovered from the wreckage of his aircraft many years later.

Polish hero Franciszek Gruszka of No. 65 Squadron, whose remains were discovered twenty-six years after his Spitfire R6713 was shot down at Westbere, near Canterbury, Kent. He is remembered on the Polish Air Force Memorial at Northolt and is now buried in Northwood Cemetery, Middlesex.

Chapter 7

'THEY FOLLOWED ME DOWN'

OF all the wartime aircraft crash sites I have dug and re-dug over the decades, there is one which stands out for the way nature has created a lasting memorial to the pilot.

Just outside the village of Hothfield, east Kent, there sits in a grassy field the stunning sculptural remains of an ancient redwood tree, which measure around thirty feet in height. This tree came from America and was planted in Hothfield Park as a sapling during the reign of George I. Exactly why it grew up so far from home in the garden of England is a mystery, but at the time it obviously seemed a wise idea and according to the current owner of the field, a history enthusiast and farmer by the name of John Coles, it was and is a rare tree to be in England at all.

The wide girth of the redwood indicates its 200-year-old history and the blackened holes inside the trunk suggests its troubles with a fire over the years, caused – I hasten to say – by accident when the farmer had a bonfire nearby in the 1980s. Plus, more seriously, the momentous occasion 76 years ago which saw burning debris of Hurricane P3053 sculpt it to its new-found shape and fatefully create an important memorial to the honoured 'Few' of the Battle of Britain.

Its hallowed identity as to what now should be a recognised tribute of the greatest aerial battle the world has ever known, was established on 29 October 1940. That morning it stood as tall as a castle turret, 100-plus feet high, and boasted a strength that had outwitted many a good storm over its long, expansive history. It had survived wars before, remember! Its roots were unshakeable and it stood alone as a king of trees surveying the land around it with an empiric majesty.

But by the afternoon of that cold, rainy October day, this swarthy old redwood had been broken in two. Its top half, around 40 feet of trunk, had been shorn off by a burning RAF fighter aircraft as it hurtled towards the ground. The pilot, Sergeant Herbert 'Bert' Black of No. 46 Squadron had baled out seconds before the stricken aircraft hit the trunk and ploughed itself deep into the damp, dozing autumn earth.

Pieces of the aircraft went everywhere on impact, of course. Imagine the crunch and the noise as wood snapped and boughs crackled, as the burning, still-spinning propeller tore through the heart of the tree. The field was littered with every single sort of Hurricane Mk I fragment, as you can imagine.

The Ashford Air Raid Warden's Diary for 29 October 1940 noted: '12.20 pm – Large formations of planes flew inland and intercepted by our own fighter planes. 14.16 pm – A great deal of fighting took place over the Ashford area. An RAF pilot baled out and was protected by Spitfires. He landed at Chart (NB: the handwriting is hard to read but the next word looks like 'Rocks'. Of course, he may have been referring to the final destination of Sergeant Black's parachute descent.)

Turning the clock forwards forty-five years, and I was there at Hothfield Park to help my colleague, aviation historian Andy 'Cressie' Cresswell, to look for important remnants and artefacts of the Hurricane in which Sergeant Black had so valiantly charged into action against a marauding pack of Luftwaffe Me 109s during the Battle of Britain.

That day a teenage Gordon Ramsey and his father, Winston, joined us and it wasn't long before we organised the best place to set the digger to work with the full permission of the farmer, Mr Coles senior, who owned the land. He was a lovely person who, like his son John today, seemed refreshingly interested in us finding the wreckage. We set to work in the full knowledge of the history of the crash and as we removed the earth, we thought about the story of Sergeant Black, who died of his injuries on 8 November 1940 – ten days after baling out.

The full horror of the pilot's experience at the mercy of the Luftwaffe had been revealed in Winston Ramsey's book *The Battle of Britain: Then and Now*, which was first published in 1980.

Five years later, in 1985, just below the top layer of the soil at the crash site all sorts of pieces of wreckage could be found. Tiny lumps of fuselage, cockpit, propeller. And deep down there was the engine, pretty smashed up and we found many fragments scattered yards and yards away. When an aircraft hits the ground at 500 mph and is on fire, then what remains are pieces which could form a giant three-dimensional jigsaw puzzle that could never, ever be completed.

Andy Cresswell brought a truck along that day, and when we found the smashed remnants of the Hurricane's Rolls Royce Merlin engine, we loaded it up, along with all sorts of larger pieces of the aircraft. We spent two days clearing as much as we could from the field and I recall that a few months later we returned to uncover even more.

(Today, Andy is much missed. He was murdered near his work place in Pluckley, near Ashford, Kent on Armistice Day, 11 November 2008. His amazing collection of artefacts from the many, many Battle of Britain and First World War digs he took part in were donated to the Lashenden Museum at Headcorn. Police are still looking for his killer.)

When I stepped back into the field for the second dig a few months later, I noticed the old tree then. It gave me the shivers sitting there watching us scrabbling around near its roots and within the vicinity. The sheep had scattered and left us to our digging, friendly banter, flasks of tea and sandwiches. What I found that day was the prize! The control column of the Hurricane was sitting just inside a tyre and it might have been placed in there for collection on the first dig. I showed this to the teenage Gordon and I didn't realise what an impact the story of Sergeant Herbert 'Bert' Black had had on him.

Gordon had met Sergeant Black's wife, Gwen, at the launch of *The Battle of Britain: Then and Now* in July 1980 and for many years he kept in touch with this remarkable woman by letter and telephone. They corresponded up until her death in 1990. The letters, which are full of stories about Bert and Gwen's happy memories, are among the treasured possessions Gordon covets and he is the proud owner of Sergeant Black's medals, logbook, and display cases showing parts of his hero's Hurricane which we found back in the 1980s. His enthusiasm to learn as much as he could about the Battle of Britain began in childhood and today he has a fascinating collection of artefacts from both RAF and Luftwaffe aircraft and aircrew.

With Gordon's permission, here is the full story of what happened to Sergeant Herbert Ernest Black on 29 October 1940, and the events leading up to that day:

'I remember well the *Battle of Britain: Then and Now* book launch in 1980. Our guest of honour then was Mrs Gwen Black, the widow of Sergeant Bert Black, shot down near Ashford, Kent on 29 October. She contributed our moving foreword, and it is typical of her character to have minimised her own suffering at the loss of her husband. She and Bert had been childhood friends born in Leicestershire within six weeks of each other. When I met Gwen, she was a retired headmistress living in

Coalville, Leicestershire and had never remarried but dedicated the rest of her life to her school and its children.

Bert, as she always called him, was born in Measham and moved to Ibstock, five miles away, when he was five. There he and Gwen grew up, going to the same village school and attending the same church. It seemed to Gwen she had never known Ibstock without Bert. On leaving school, he attended a course at Clarks College in Leicester but later took up training as a weights and measures inspector while Gwen began a career in teaching. She followed his keen interest and participation in sport, especially cricket and hockey and when he joined the Royal Air Force Volunteer Reserve in August 1937, his enthusiasm for flying knew no bounds. "Gwen you can't imagine what it's like up there, belting around the sky. I've got to take you up." But there never was time – it was the one thing they were never able to share.

On 1 September 1939 he was called up to complete his training and was sent to France early in 1940 to join No. 226 Squadron flying Fairey Battles. By May that year he was in action in France against the Luftwaffe and after the evacuation at Dunkirk he flew back to England. By mid-June he had volunteered to join Fighter Command and was posted to a training unit to convert to Hurricanes.

Soon after, he had some leave and he returned to Ibstock... and Gwen... and at seven o'clock in the morning on June 17 threw a stone at her bedroom window to wake her. The same afternoon they were married in St Denys Church. Gwen had wanted a quiet service but news of Bert's return from France spread throughout Ibstock and there were crowds at the church when they arrived, all wanting to share the happiness of the young couple. After an all-too-short honeymoon at Matlock, Bert went back to war while Gwen returned to work. By September 3 he had joined No. 32 Squadron at Acklington.

She was at Caldecote Road School, Leicester, tying a little boy's laces on the last day before half-term, when Bert was fighting a losing battle with Messerschmitt fighters over Ashford, Kent. Earlier, Bert had booked a room in Abridge, close to his base at Stapleford Tawney, Essex, where they could be together for a few days. Although they had been married for four months, they had only been together for nineteen days and half term brought the chance to snatch a few more.

Rushing home to pack, it was there she received the phone call... The one that told her to come to Ashford not Abridge... To the hospital not a hotel... And that Bert was lying grievously wounded with burns and gunshot wounds.

In wartime England, journeys in blacked-out trains seemed to go on forever and it seemed like ages to Gwen before she reached his bedside. Bert managed a smile and slowly, little by little she learned what had happened. Scrambled from Stapleford Tawney with the squadron he hardly knew, (he had transferred to No. 46 Squadron to enable two Polish pilots to stay together in No. 257) flying a Hurricane he had never flown before, his aeroplane had been set on fire. The cockpit hood had jammed and only after a great struggle had he managed to open it and fall clear. His parachute had opened and two other Hurricanes had circled him to keep away enemy fighters. "The boys followed me down, Gwen", he told her with gratitude, and it was something that stuck with him to the end; the way they had protected him from marauding enemy fighters, some of whom were not averse to machine gunning pilots helpless on the end of their parachute.'

Such a situation which provoked the enemy to act so ruthlessly towards a fellow human so vulnerable to attack is astonishing. The idea that just RAF aircraft were the target was only half of the plan for some Luftwaffe, who had brutal ambitions to finish off the aircrew as well during every battle.

This attitude to the plight of RAF parachutists did not seem to faze Head of Fighter Command Air Chief Marshal Hugh Dowding, who understood the enemy's fight-to-the-death attitude. But surely, we ask, the pilot should have a second chance after the horrors of baling out?

Fortunately for Sergeant Bert Black in 1940 and his RAF comrades who served during the rest of the war, Air Chief Marshal Dowding's somewhat benign opinion on strafing parachutists was not known until a year after the end of the war in Europe when *The London Gazette* published his despatch on 11 September 1946:

'Germans descending over England are prospective Prisoners of War, and, as such, should be immune. On the other hand, British pilots descending over England are still potential combatants.

Much indignation was caused by the fact German pilots sometimes fired on our descending airmen (although, in my opinion, they were perfectly entitled to do so), but I am glad to say that in many cases they refrained and sometimes greeted a helpless adversary with a cheerful wave of the hand.'

Despite this opinion, it remains difficult to justify Sergeant Black's deadly injuries as the enemy's 'entitlement'. However, war often transcends all sense of morality, and any idea of fairness has long perished in the flames of destruction sparked by deluded, power-crazed dictators like Adolf Hitler.

Before Sergeant Bert Black died, his wife, Gwen, stayed with a local butcher, and his neighbour gave her meals. Bert could eat nothing but she was desperate to give him something. She believed some Champagne might help but it was outside of opening hours. A kindly nurse told Gwen to knock on any door: 'Just say you're the wife of the British pilot shot down – anyone will help you.'

Throughout that week and into the next, Gwen stayed at his side, only leaving when the morphine dulled his agony. It was Friday, 8 November, and ten days since he had been shot down. That night she was called back to the hospital. Gwen said: 'I was at Bert's bedside in the early hours of Saturday morning when he died.' He was 26 years old. Gwen continued:

'I was immediately given a sleeping draught and put to bed in the hospital. When I awoke, I was told that Bert could be buried at Ashford but I insisted that I wanted to take him back to Ibstock. After much discussion, when they realised I was adamant, they told me to make the arrangements for the time, date and place of the funeral and they would pass them on in code to Desford aerodrome (Desford is about six miles from Ibstock). I was instructed not to mention the funeral time and place over the phone and I did exactly as I was told. I chose the afternoon of Wednesday, 13 November because Wednesday was half-day closing in the village.

I was also told to obtain the death certificate. Unfortunately, when I left the hospital, the Registrar had closed his books for the week. I desperately wanted to return to Ibstock that afternoon but of course could not. The British Legion came to my rescue and asked if the Registrar would meet me on the Sunday and this he did.'

At this point in Gwen's heart-rending story, as if the 26-year-old woman had not suffered enough, an almost unbelievable state of affairs took place:

'At the hospital they promised me that Bert's body would be dispatched on the Monday,' Gwen continued 'so I got an early train from Ashford in order to be in Ibstock, Leicestershire before it arrived. I was instructed to make arrangements for the collection of the coffin at Coalville station. When it had not arrived on the Monday evening, I expected it all day Tuesday and thought it had been delayed en route. When the time came on the Wednesday, Coalville railway office still could not say how far it had got or where exactly it was located.

'We were inundated at my home with floral tributes, some seventy-odd arrived and were placed by the undertaker in the drive and front garden. Also, in the village, streets were lined with people and the church full. It became imperative that something must be done to disperse the crowds, and make the necessary arrangements for the flowers, so I rang the rector and we decided to have a short service and to take the flowers into the church for the night.

'I picked up my own tribute – red roses – and insisted on carrying them to the service. I must have been very overwrought at the time and what I did must have distressed others I'm sure, when I look back on that action of mine. After the service on the Wednesday afternoon, the Chief Inspector of Weights and Measures of Leicestershire promised me he would see the Chief Constable and ask him to find out what had happened. That evening the Chief Constable of Leicestershire spoke with the Chief Constable of Kent and the delay was explained. We were assured the body would leave Ashford in time for the burial at St Denys Churchyard, Ibstock, now fixed for Thursday afternoon.' Sergeant Black's body arrived in the late morning and the funeral took place at the same time as it should have done on the previous day. 'I was told the delay was because it was not known who would pay for the journey from the hospital to Ashford Station, but I hasten to add, I never received any account for that when it was all sorted out.'

'I have always thought it was a slip best forgotten,' says Gwen magnanimously. 'I was uplifted by the thought that Bert had a known grave and one to which I could go and see each time I went to church – that was my comfort during the rest of the hostilities.'

Gwen's strength during such a time of heartache and loss is admirable. For not only was there the overwhelming grief to endure but the dismal confusion and dysfunction relating to the practicalities concerning the burial of her husband – a man who was one of the heroic 'Few'. It was a situation which she should absolutely not have been made to suffer.

It would be thirty years before I visited the crash site of Sergeant Black's Hurricane again. I can't really class it as a 'dig' though. More like a gentle look around beneath the surface of the grass. At first, author Melody Foreman had contacted me about the sight of the old redwood tree and I told her I remembered the excavation from the 1980s. She said the farmer (John Coles) who now owns the land knew all about Sergeant Black and he would be happy for us to have another look around with a metal detector. Mr Coles had already found a few pieces of the Hurricane over the years but always wondered what had happened to the engine label.

Whilst we know the Hurricane was P3053, the official records do not reveal the engine number. This was not that unusual, as more often than not the aircraft had been repaired and parts from others were fitted here and there as the need for equipment increased by the minute.

It was a mild but rainy day in September 2016 when we strode across the field and watched the sheep scatter. The climate was a little brighter than that experienced by Sergeant Black and his comrades seventy-six years earlier – they had taken off on 29 October 1940, which was reported to have been a chilly morning with the sky an uncompromising grey in colour, even portentous of impending doom.

I got out my metal detector. We were joined at the crash site that day by author Melody Foreman and my archaeology friends Mark Kirby and Adrian Crossnan. (Mark is a seasoned recovery specialist and had already played a significant role in the discovery of missing pilots over the years, and while working with grieving relatives of 'The Few', he has taken on the might of Britain's starchy officialdom at the highest level – and won.)

As we trod around the tufty grass beside the looming presence of the old redwood tree, we marvelled how it was the only surviving witness to know and suffer first-hand the carnage delivered by the crash that day in 1940. Then overhead and quite by chance came the sound of a small aircraft engine. We looked up and saw a Tiger Moth making its way towards the Channel. We'd like to think it was a spiritual sign we had Sergeant Black's approval for our endeavours.

We'd only been in the field for a few minutes when loud bleeps from the metal detectors went off and various artefacts from Hurricane P3053 were removed from the earth, dusted off and examined in full daylight.

One of the largest items was a piece of airframe bracket recovered by Adrian, and then Mark dug up some small piece of undercarriage. I found a chunk of the brown Bakelite aerial measuring around three inches with the round, rusted clasp still in fastened position. I knew it was a piece of the aerial as there was a hole running right through the Bakelite to suggest a wire had once run through its centre. Within an hour, we had filled two small boxes of remnants to show the farmer. There was still no sign of the engine plate but as the afternoon drew to a close, we decided there was every chance we would return to excavate the area again on a grander scale. Indeed, any visit to this place (with the permission of the farmer) is sincerely meaningful, as not only is there the most rare and natural monument to the Battle of Britain in the form of the carcass of the old tree, but it's a place to pay tribute to Sergeant Herbert Black, who died fighting for our freedom.

It is safe to say that the majority of farmers I have met during the course of my aircraft excavation career have been as compliant and helpful as Mr John Coles. Farmers will only become irritated if people go out on their land with a metal detector without asking permission. There were, I am glad to say, more farmers pro-digging for aircraft than against.

At Godstone, one farmer was delighted to learn we knew there was a Hurricane on his land. They do say it went down in a tragically similar fashion to a Spitfire flown by pilot Peter Chesters (see Chapter 11). The Hurricane pilot, Sergeant Stanley Fennemore, lived down the road in Bliney Heath, Godstone. Anyway, during the Battle of Britain, full of excitement having just shot down a Luftwaffe aircraft, he is supposed to have flown over the family house and done a victory roll and ploughed straight into the field we dug twenty or so more years later. Apparently, his wife and parents watched the accident which killed him. I guess the morale of the story is, 'Don't show off when operating aircraft!'

The farmers and landowners needed to be treated with respect, but I found that as long as you explained the situation, they were fine. I also had to make sure I did a good job putting the soil back into the hole. If word got around among them via *Farmers Weekly* magazine that any of us did a poor repair job on the field, then reputations were ruined.

Many farmers got very interested and involved in the story around the aircraft. They'd often appear asking questions like, 'Have you found anything yet?' And if you hadn't, they got disappointed.

I can't mention the east Kent village of Hothfield without thinking of the time in the 1980s I arrived at the nearby Cowleas Farm, Kempton Manor, just off the A20. For it was here I dug up a propeller hub and unearthed a few tiny fragments of bone from the crash site of Sergeant

Pilot Geoffrey Wilberforce Pearson, who was killed at just 21 years old when his Hurricane P3516 was shot down in combat at 9.00 am on 6 September 1940.

The Ashford Air Raid Warden's diary noted: '12.44 pm – Red 138 warning. Definitely the most exciting day we have had to date. Hundreds of planes fought over Ashford, large formations of bomber, with strong escorts which were intercepted by our fighters. Many planes were reported as going down.'

Sergeant Pearson of No. 501 Squadron was last seen over Ashford in action against the Luftwaffe on that warm early day of autumn. Suffering the same violent attack from the marauding Luftwaffe that morning were two of his comrades from the same squadron; Pilot Officers Hugh Charles Adams, 22, who crashed at Elham near Folkestone, and Olivier Vincent Houghton, 19, who was shot down over Charing, near Ashford. Both were killed.

The story of Geoffrey Pearson's flying career began in December 1938 when he joined the RAF as a trainee pilot. He was called up on 1 September 1939 and finished his training at No. 2 Flying Training School at Brize Norton – not far from his home – on 3 August 1940. From there he was transferred to No. 7 Operational Training Unit at Hawarden and on 10 August converted to Hurricanes. By 27 August he was among the men of No. 501 Squadron at RAF Gravesend and it was from here he took off on the morning of 6 September only to meet his death minutes after climbing into the cockpit.

Finding Sergeant Pearson's Hurricane had not been easy in the 1980s as the eyewitness reports were vague but I was hopeful the metal detector would guide me to the exact location of the site which today, as with so many, has now been built on.

If you remember, earlier in this chapter I described the pitiful bureaucratic dramas surrounding the transfer of Sergeant Black's body from Ashford to his home town in Leicestershire. Well, for Sergeant Pearson's family there was a similar horror in store; only this time all means of his identity were lost in the most appalling 'mix-up' of records. For several days, Sergeant Pearson's remains lay on a table in Hothfield's village hall (now the site of a house) and no one knew who he was. I was reminded of this harrowing fact by my great friend and leading aviation archaeologist Tony Graves, who for more than fifty years has researched and dug aircraft of not only the Battle of Britain but the aircraft which went down in Normandy, France during and after D-Day.

According to Tony, there was so much confusion over the mystery body, that after four days someone decided it would be more convenient to bury the young pilot at St Stephen's Churchyard, Lympne, Kent as an 'Unknown Airman' than to investigate thoroughly and find out for sure who he was, out of respect for him and his family! And there Sergeant Pearson, one of the heroic 'Few', lay for forty-two years, until in 1982 his sister and brother-in-law, Richard Griffiths, went all out to defy the various obstructive authorities and prove the grave was indeed that of the young pilot.

Thanks to their lengthy research and determined efforts, his headstone was promptly corrected and the family of Sergeant Geoffrey Wilberforce Pearson had some sense of closure at last. I think you'll agree it was shameful they had to wait forty-two years though, to find any sense of peace. Sadly, it seems the bungling actions of those in so-called officialdom and 'mix-ups' of paperwork were not uncommon in wartime. I've also learned, to my horror, how 'cover-ups over the whereabouts of missing pilots' are and were much more convenient and less politically humiliating to administer than the pomp and ceremony of a costly military funeral. It still shocks me how often I learned that the family of a loved one who had died in battle was sent their mess and bar bills to pay soon after they were deemed 'missing in action'. It's a pitiful slap in the face for those whose loved one died defending Britain – many of whom never even had a known grave. Yet another reminder that war is just business and 'not personal'!

During the 1970s and 1980s I was to join Tony Graves on many digs. It was Tony who located the most unusual Battle of Britain aircraft I got to recover and that was a twin-engine Bristol Beaufighter, which was christened 'Whispering Death' by the Japanese. This lovely old aircraft was often used as a night fighter and could carry torpedoes, too. It also had the latest and most secret radar detection equipment on board and in its day, was much favoured by the Fleet Air Arm. It was introduced to the RAF in July 1940 and yet for most of that year, its presence in various squadrons was hush-hush, probably due to its role in enemy aircraft detection. I wonder if it was this mask of secrecy that led to the crash of Beaufighter R2071, which went down at Edenbridge, Kent on 13 November 1940. It belonged to No. 219 Squadron, based at Redhill, Surrey.

In the 1970s I believe Tony and I were the first to seriously dig this aircraft crash site which of course had been attended to by the RAF and local residents during the war.

On the day of the crash, Beaufighter R2017, an Mk1 F, had two crew on board – Pilot Officer Thomas Birkett, aged 26, and Sergeant Colin Ewart Patrick Castle. An eyewitness account, given by a Don Whiffen and recorded on the excellent *Edenbridge in the Past* website, states:

'It was an overcast day and I was just leaving home at Four Elms to go to afternoon school, it was about 2.00 pm. Suddenly this aircraft came out of the low clouds in a steep dive, there was no sound, I assumed that the engines had stopped, the aircraft disappeared below the treeline and shortly afterwards a column of smoke arose from the direction of Edenbridge. Later, I had found that the aircraft had come down in (Town Field), next to the bridge in Edenbridge the aircraft was shattered into small pieces.

My mother, who was in the local St John Ambulance Brigade, was on duty at the first aid post (now the WI Hall). She had to go to the crash scene to place blankets over the bodies that were found. One book states that it is believed that another night fighter shot down this aircraft by mistake. I do not think this is true, as it was daytime and I did not hear any cannon fire. It was not until some months later that this aircraft was declared to be a Beaufighter and it had been previously put on the secret list.

The rear wheel is on display at the Eden Valley Museum. We learned how the pilot, Pilot Officer Birkett had previously survived three forced landings in Blenheim Bombers during his service with No. 219 Squadron.'

Another account comes from Albert Jeffrey, who was a schoolboy at the time the Beaufighter went down. He recalls the following:

'We were in the playground in Croft Lane on Wednesday, 13 November 1940 and some of us had been home to lunch. We were waiting to go into the classroom at 1.00 pm. These were exciting days and the Battle of Britain had not long been fought overhead. When a new type of aircraft put in an appearance, we somehow found out what it was, usually with assistance from members of the local Royal Observer Corps situated at that time on Hever Road.

On this day in question, we had observed a Bristol Beaufighter flying to and fro as if on patrol and were quite excited as it was a new type of aircraft. We were watching it fly when we heard its engines splutter as it came overhead. Its wing dropped and it started a vertical dive twisting once as it did so. The Beaufighter bore a close resemblance to the Luftwaffe Junkers Ju 88 and I thought "My God, it isn't a Beaufighter after all; it's a German aircraft and it's going to dive bomb Edenbridge."

Well, its dive continued on and I could see there wasn't time for it to pull out as it disappeared behind the houses in Church Street. It went down vertically into the ground near to the North Bank of the River Eden. It was fortunate there were no civilian casualties but alas, the crew died with the aircraft that day.

I recall a loud explosion and a fireball, then a large pall of black smoke, and live ammunition exploding. Soon we all ran over to the bridge to see the crash site, which was packed with spectators. The Tanyard foreman, Mr Budden, was first at the scene and yet there was no time for the crew to get out. That aircraft went down at 12.50 hours and at 13.16 we had an air raid warning and at 13.41 a Junkers Ju 88 was seen twice.

The cause of the crash will never be known for sure but in an article published many years later in the Royal Observer Corps aircraft recognition journal, it said it had been a case of mistaken identity and it had been shot down by friendly fire. The fact is, no gunfire was heard by me that day and I would know. The official RAF version of the loss states how Beaufighter R2071 was probably shot down by another night fighter. The large crater where the nose and two engines buried themselves was full of water the next day as the river was well high.'

The wreckage of the Beaufighter was hauled onto a back of a lorry later that day and taken to an unknown destination.

When I went to the site some thirty-odd years later, I managed to dig up an engine and a propeller boss. I understand that a person called Dennis Leigh, who was thirteen at the time of the crash, had visited the site in 1940 and found a few artefacts, including an oxygen mask which is now on show in the Eden Valley Museum. A digger arrived with me but the driver was concerned about getting stuck in the hole so we left the heavy props and hubs. Tony Graves then went back to the site and collected them for his museum.

There is also the tragic story of a Spitfire pilot who suffered oxygen failure, which then also led to the deaths of residents on a busy street. My friend and fellow historian Tony Webb has kindly agreed to us telling the following story, which first appeared in his book *Battle over Kent: Maidstone 1940*. I remember visiting this difficult wreckage site. It was the first time I had been called to a dig which was in a narrow pathway along a busy road.

Few people travelling through Maidstone on the A249 notice Coronet House, a new office block amid the century-old terraced houses in Albion Place; even fewer know the tragedy that happened there in the closing weeks of the Battle of Britain in war-torn Kent.

To obtain a full appreciation of this occurrence, we must go back in time to Cambridge, September 1931, when Harold Henry Allgood, aged 16, had just left the city's Central School and joined the Royal Air Force as No. 565462 Aircraftsman Apprentice (metal rigger).

This was at the time of an industrial depression, and for a young man of ability and education, the future offered by the Royal Air Force held better prospects than the field of industry and commerce. Young Harold Allgood spent the first years of his apprenticeship at RAF Halton, near Wendover, Buckinghamshire, and soon took full opportunity of the sports facilities there. He won the Barrington/Kennett trophy for swimming in 1932, and had success in senior events in 1934.

On completion of his apprenticeship, he served on several RAF stations, but with the gathering clouds of war and the declining political situation in Europe, the Government decided on a massive strengthening of the RAF. On 19 July 1934, plans were announced to increase the total number of squadrons from 75 to 116 in five years, and to enlarge the homebased front-line strength of aircraft from 488 to 1,304 in the same period.

It was during this phase that Aircraftsman Allgood was posted and attached to various fighter units, resulting in him being recommended by the AOC (air officer commanding) for training as airman pilot on 13 September 1938, and subsequently attending No. 11 Fighter Training School at Shawbury, Shropshire, from 25 September 1939 to 6 April 1940.

At the outbreak of the war on 3 September 1939, Harold Allgood had completed eight years of service in the RAF, and within a few months, gained his wings. Early in 1940 he was promoted to sergeant pilot.

On 14 May 1940, he embarked overseas with other personnel to reinforce No. 85 (F) Squadron 'British Air Component' stationed at Lille-Seclin, France, to fly Hawker Hurricane Mk 1 fighters. Thus, he gained his first experience of aerial combat while engaged in giving air cover to the hard-pressed British Expeditionary Force in their retreat to Dunkirk.

A *Daily Express* news article of 27 May 1940 quoted an Air Ministry communiqué dealing with fighting over Northern France: 'At least 20 German bombers and fighters were shot down, and another twenty put out of action; these operations lasted from 5.30 am until 9.30 am, and in these there were only five British casualties.' Optimistic propaganda of the era and consumed by the British public over their breakfast tables!

110

Records show that No. 85 (F) Squadron returned to England on 21 May 1940, arriving at Dover at 3.00 pm. Many ground crew and some pilots from this and other squadrons were unable to rejoin their units before the middle of July, having travelled by various routes and means to British ports.

The last six Hurricane squadrons returned to England from France on 17 June 1940, Sergeant Allgood being officially documented back on 22 June 1940. He was then granted a period of leave owing to a damaged collarbone, the result of being shot down (possibly by Oberleutnant Bolz of 5/JG52) during aerial combat towards the latter part of the Battle of France. While home on leave, it would have become apparent to him that any impending aerial conflict with the Luftwaffe would depend on him and his fellow regular pilots and ground crews, backed up by the mobilisation of the weekend flyers of the Auxiliary Air Force and Volunteer Reserve. On 22 June 1940 the armistice between France and Germany came into effect. Britain now stood alone; the cards had been dealt. This was the prelude to the Battle of Britain.

Sergeant Allgood rejoined No. 85 (F) Squadron early in July of that year with the squadron now being based at Martlesham, Suffolk, under Squadron Leader Peter Townsend, DFC.

On his arrival, the squadron strength was twenty-one pilots, with an aircraft availability of eighteen Hawker Hurricane Mk 1 fighter aircraft, of which four were temporarily unserviceable owing to combat damage.

On Sunday, 11 August 1940, at 11.30 am, Squadron Leader Townsend was engaged in protecting a convoy of shipping (Convoy Booty) with Yellow Section of No. 85 (F) Squadron off the Harwich/Clacton coast in Essex, during which they encountered 20-plus German Me 110 aircraft. A short aerial battle followed, but owing to a previous skirmish, it left Yellow Section low on fuel and with very little ammunition, thus resulting in their return to forward base to refuel and rearm.

Squadron Leader Townsend recalls in his book *Duel of Eagles*: 'I had, of course, been clamouring loudly to Hornpipe (Ground Station) for help to get the rest of the Squadron over Booty. Six of our Hurricanes were there when Erprobungsgruppe 210 attacked; they sent two Me 110s into the sea.'

The summary of events for that day from No. 85 (F) Squadron's archives reads as follows:

'At 1200 hours Pilot Sergeants Allgood and Hampshire were engaged by seven Me 110s at 5,000 feet; the former dived on one Me 110 well below him and gave him a three-second burst; the

111

enemy aircraft dived into the sea, sinking almost immediately; the latter attacked another Me 110 below him and gave him one long continuous burst, and the enemy aircraft went into a steep dive; he followed it down firing until all his ammunition was used; he observed bits falling off the enemy aircraft before breaking off. This was a mere skirmish in the wings; heavy fighting was going on down South, a dress rehearsal for Adler Tag [13 August 1940 – Eagle Day – an all-out air assault by the Luftwaffe] which still hung fire because of the weather.'

The following day, Air Chief Marshal Sir Hugh Dowding ordered the squadron to be moved from Martlesham to Debden, near Saffron Walden, Essex, for fear of destruction of the coastal airfield by the Luftwaffe. The squadron's stay at Debden was only of short duration and on 19 August 1940 a signal was received to fly out the squadron's aircraft at 6.30 am, and proceed south to Croydon, to take over from No. 111 (F) Squadron.

It is important to point out that the bloodiest days experienced by the RAF during the Battle of Britain were at the end of August, as reflected by events at Croydon on 31 August, when scrambling for interception at 12.55 pm No. 85 (F) Squadron narrowly missed being caught in a string of bombs.

The Hurricanes ascended from the runway through a cloud of dust and debris. Sergeant Allgood, with 'A' Flight and piloting Hurricane VY-H, caught up with the German formation over Tunbridge Wells, Kent. A bitter combat took place during an attack on an escorting Me 109 formation, resulting in Squadron Leader Townsend being shot down and wounded. Baling out over Hawkhurst, he fell among some young pliable fir trees, having avoided a dense wooded area of solid English oaks. Pilot Officer Pyers Arthur Worrall from 'B' Flight also abandoned his Hurricane and parachuted to safety, landing at Benenden. The remainder of the squadron returned to Croydon at approximately 1.45 pm. That day the RAF lost a total of thirty-nine aircraft in combat. Sergeant Allgood accompanied the squadron north to Church Fenton, South Yorkshire, for a rest period on 5 September 1940, and was detailed to take Hurricane VY-E. On arrival, the squadron was grounded for two days' complete rest, after which the only activity undertaken was air drills, dusk landings and formation flying.

RAF records reveal Sergeant Allgood was practising dusk landings on 9 September when he crash landed. He was unhurt, although the Hurricane he was flying, P2827, was in need of repair.

On Battle of Britain Sunday, 15 September 1940, Sergeant Allgood and Sergeant Thomas Berkeley (who had joined the squadron on 2 September 1940) made two local reconnaissance flights, each of an hour's duration, with Miles Magister J9827. The following days were engaged in the ferrying of various aircraft to different airfields, as on 16 September 1940, when Sergeant Allgood flew out Hurricane TP-B – an aircraft belonging to No. 73 (F) Squadron – to Debden with an overnight stop, returning to Church Fenton the following day co-piloting a Blenheim Mk 1 fighter.

On 28 September 1940, Sergeant Allgood was posted to No. 253(F) Squadron, whose home base was Kenley, Surrey, under the command of Flight Lieutenant Raymond Duke-Woolley. This squadron had suffered heavy losses during September, resulting in ten Hawker Hurricane Mk 1 aircraft being destroyed, with four pilots killed and three injured. Such was the pressure of operational requirements that Sergeant Allgood was on combat duties two days after joining his new squadron, flying Hurricane P3537 on an interception mission at 4.40 pm.

The following two weeks of October were full of activity with operational flights each day, with the exception of 3 October, when no flying duties were undertaken by the squadron. This provided a welcome respite.

Nine Hurricanes took off from Kenley on 10 October 1940, at 3.20 pm, with Sergeant Allgood flying Hurricane Ll928. Shortly after takeoff, the flight took up formation over the Surrey/Kent border, Sergeant Allgood taking the position of tail-end Charlie.

Some thirty minutes later the formation was on patrol at 20,000 feet over the eastern outskirts of Maidstone, when with no apparent warning, Sergeant Allgood's Hurricane broke formation and went into a steep dive, with the engine screaming at maximum revs. As the aircraft broke through the carpet of autumn cumulus clouds, it reached a speed far in excess of its normal maximum performance.

From the ground, the aircraft was seen to appear from the Vinters Park area, narrowly missing some tall trees and heading straight for the outskirts of Maidstone. Within seconds, the Hurricane sliced through the roof of number 63, Albion Place (Albion Stores, owned by Mr E. H. Woodhouse), and cut its way through numbers 61 and 59, with the engine finally embedding itself in the cellar. The Hurricane immediately burst into flames, killing Sergeant Allgood and two families; three women and five children. A neighbour living opposite said: 'A little girl who every day sat in the window playing with her dolls is believed to be among the victims.'

113

The time was now 3.55 pm and within minutes, the emergency services arrived. The area was a scene of devastation, marked by a column of black smoke which rose to a great height and could be seen from miles around. There was little the rescue services could do except extinguish the fire and recover the victims.

The work of rescue squads was further handicapped by the presence of aviation fuel fumes in the basement of the house; once, when some men were working on the scene, there was an explosion and they were badly shaken. At about 5.00 pm, the body of Pilot Sergeant Allgood was located in the cellar, together with his parachute and parts of the aircraft engine. Such was the task that it was not until the following afternoon, on 11 October, that the recovery operations were completed.

Names of the civilian casualties were given as Mrs Doris Woods and baby daughter of number 61, Albion Place, together with her mother, Mrs Elizabeth Wooding, four sisters and a brother, who had been accommodated at number 61, since their own home in nearby Astley Street had become severely damaged during an air raid on 2 September. Both of their husbands were at work when the crash occurred.

The physical strain on pilots flying at high altitudes on standing patrols to oppose the threat of the high-flying tactical policy of the Luftwaffe became apparent during October. It was later discovered that Sergeant Allgood had suffered oxygen failure (anoxia) resulting in his tragic dive, echoed in a statement by Mr Tom Medhurst of Maidstone, an eyewitness on the day. He recalled the Hurricane speeding towards the ground, the pilot apparently unconscious. However, the plane pulled out, making Tom think the pilot came round for a while, but then it pitched forward, burying itself into the cellar of the terraced houses.

Sergeant Harold Henry Allgood was buried at St. Mark's, Newnham, Cambridge, on 22 October 1940. Added to the headstone some two years later was an inscription dedicated 'To the memory of his elder brother who has no known grave, Flight Sergeant Edwin A Allgood, killed in action over the North Sea, 28 May 1942'.

A week after the crash, RAF investigation officers examined and removed the aircraft's wreckage. Local contractors backfilled the cellars of numbers 61 and 59, Albion Place with rubble to street level, and the site remained an open plot between the adjacent properties. During 1941 a purpose-built blast-proof Civil Defence control block was constructed upon the site and remained operational twenty-four hours a day until the end of hostilities in 1945.

The early post-war years gave way to the block being converted into dwelling accommodation by the Maidstone Borough Council, and it remained occupied until the late autumn of 1977, when the area was to be demolished prior to redevelopment and the construction of a modern office complex. Following demolition of the former blast-proof block, it was not until January 1978 that the site was cleared and the area was levelled, leaving only the concrete base, which in turn had to be broken to establish foundations for the new project.

Upon opening up the base, it revealed a mass of loose backfill of rubble and timbers which had lain undisturbed for almost 40 years. This necessitated removal and additional excavation two metres below the cellar floors to lay the new foundations.

It was not long before workmen on the site reported seeing some of the twisted alloy wreckage of the ill-fated Hawker Hurricane L1928, which resulted in the Kent Battle of Britain Museum Trust being given permission by Rush & Tompkins Ltd. of Reigate (Main Contractors) to research the site.

Subsequent hand digging at weekends, and observations of site progress resulted in a conclusion that the aircraft, having sliced through the roof of No. 63 jinked abruptly through and down the bedroom, dining room and into the cellar of No. 61, shedding its alloy and wood-constructed airframe in the process. The engine and propeller boss deflected off the cellar floor and breached the dividing wall to No. 59, upon which it disintegrated with both properties collapsing into the cellars.

The resultant fire, aided by the aircraft's aviation spirit and fuelled with house timbers and combustible furnishings, became deep seated, and penetrated through and across one-third of the floor joists of No. 57 before being extinguished.

Eventual site progress revealed the empty Kentish Ragstone cellars of numbers 61 and 59; both were badly scorched and blackened by fire.

Merlin engine casting fragments were found embedded in the walls, together with a bulge in the dividing wall between numbers 59 and 57. Throughout the demolition, silver painted airframe tubes and struts were found amid the rubble as well as stressed alloy skin from the nose cowling and underside of the aircraft, depicting a dark green, brown and sky camouflage scheme. The largest pieces to be discovered were part of the high-tensile steel spar's 'centre section' and radius arm of the undercarriage; all found in the cellar of No. 61.

While sifting through other wreckage, the crumpled nose ring of the pilot's oxygen mask was found. Within a few days the cellars were demolished and passed from sight forever.

During the summer of 1983, Charles Herbert Woods, husband of Doris, then in his mid-seventies and still residing in the town, gave his account of that tragic day. 'Having arrived on the scene shortly after the crash from my place of work in the town,' he said, 'I found my home had been reduced to a mound of burning rubble. Instantly I recognised my wife's coat still hanging on a remaining wall section. I urged a group of firemen who were fighting the fire to start searching for the family, but there was no response. Together with a civilian bystander I desperately attempted to effect a rescue via the coal chute of number 57, the house but one from my own.

'Having removed the iron grille, the cellar was found to be partly filled with water, which appeared to be alight upon the surface. The gas supply to the property was broken and burning like a blow torch, accompanied by the muffled sound of exploding ammunition from the aircraft. For a second I thought there was movement in the dim light of the cellar; then I collapsed and was hauled from the coal chute, unconscious.' At this point, Mr. Woods paused – thought awhile – then said. 'It was all a very long time ago.'

Mr Woods died in September 1987 after a series of heart attacks left him bedridden and depressed.

Today, Albion Place is changed beyond recognition. Few of the terraced properties remain, and commercial buildings dominate what was once a residential area. A short distance away, Astley Street, former home of the Wooding family, has long since disappeared. Below the junction of Albion Place and Union Street stands Coronet House, its main entrance being the exact location of the incident, yet revealing nothing of its tragic past to those who pass within its shadow.

It was in 1970 that public records were released from the statutory thirty-year ban relating to the Battle of Britain, giving students and historians hitherto unavailable facts and data. Resulting from this, there followed a selection of well-informed publications, together with an upsurge of general interest in the epic struggle for air supremacy in 1940.

During 1970, a new term was created, 'Aviation Archaeology' – the exploration of former crash sites, both British and German, which involved the excavation and recovery of war-torn remains of aircraft in both rural and urban areas. Souvenirs and memorabilia were also soon to be very much sought after, with enthusiasts seeking out such items hidden in attics and garden sheds for three decades or more.

Towards the end of the 1970s, commissions were awarded to artists who faithfully depicted aerial combat on canvas, with signatures of surviving participants of the Battle. In retrospect, it was inevitable that this sequence of events had been pre-empted in the mid-1960s, with the issue of postage stamps commemorating the 25th anniversary of the Battle of Britain, followed by the epic film of the same name.

All this helped to create a base for an in-depth documentation of incidents, most of which would have been forgotten forever otherwise.

Sergeant Pilot Herbert Ernest Black.

Herbert's Tree at Hothfield in East Kent. On 9 October 1940, at the age of just 26 years old, Sergeant Herbert Black was shot down in combat with Me 109s. He baled out, badly burned and his Hurricane crashed in Hothfield Park, near Ashford. His wife Gwen was at his bedside when he died in Ashford Hospital on November 9, 1940. The giant Redwood seen here was the actual tree which took the full force of the burning, empty Hurricane. In 1940 the height of the tree would have measured around 100 feet. Sergeant Black landed in the field in the distance. The aircraft's last flight path – around 450 mph – was therefore towards the camera.

117

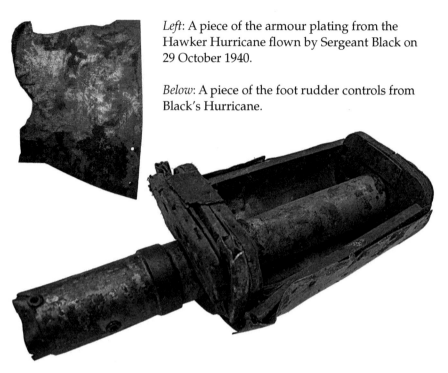

Left: A piece of the armour plating from the Hawker Hurricane flown by Sergeant Black on 29 October 1940.

Below: A piece of the foot rudder controls from Black's Hurricane.

Left: Terry with a piece of Herbert Black's Hurricane, pictured by Melody Foreman.

Right: Wreckage of Herbert Black's Hurricane recovered from the crash site by Terry.

Above: The tailwheel recovered from the crash site of Birkett and Castle's Beaufighter.

Right: Pilot Officer Thomas Birkett.

Another Battle of Britain excavation underway, in this case the location of Hurricane P2967 at Bluetown, Mintching, Sittingbourne, Kent. The aircraft was shot down on 20 September 1940 and had been flown by Flying Officer Michael Homer, DFC, of No. 242 Squadron, who died aged 21 that day.

Pilot Officer Michael Homer, DFC.

The excavation team at the crash site of Hurricane N2617, which was shot down at Dargate, Whitstable, Kent on 18 August 1940. Its pilot, Sergeant Donald Alistair Stewart McKay, DFM*, of No. 501 Squadron, baled out but suffered from burns. His aircraft had been shot down by Oberleutnant Schopfel of JG26. McKay served with the RAF until 1947 and then joined the RAFVR until 1953. He died in 1959.

Chapter 8

'WHO IS THIS SHADOW OF A HERO WE HAVE OVER US?'

IN recent years I have had the honour and pleasure of meeting the relatives of several aircrews who died in action during the Battle of Britain. It is they who are left with the ghosts of the past and the torment of unanswered questions sparked by the dreaded 'missing in action' telegrams. From them I have learned how heartache is passed on through blood, which flows on through each new generation of the family. I learned from them how the shadows of war loom far and wide in the form of inherited memory.

Widows, sons, daughters, grandchildren and cousins of 'The Few' have come to me wanting to know more about life in the war-torn Europe of 1940 and information about the aircraft I've dug out, which were flown by both the RAF and the Luftwaffe. They are keen to hear about the bravery experienced by 'The Few' and I do my best to help encourage a sense of pride in their hearts.

For those relatives of the aircrews killed in action, there came and still come vast waves of grief, often hidden and yet layered with confusion, frustration and despair, especially if their loved one has no known grave. More often than not they can't understand the attitude of the British authorities, which, unlike post-war governments in Germany, the United States, France and Russia, appeared to have no definite policy for recovering the remains of those men who had died for their home country. In Britain, the attitude was (and often still is) all about it being an honour for stricken aircrews to remain where they had fallen. That was the 'blessed fate' of all 'real' warriors – or so the grief-stricken were led to believe... There was also the expense for the government of a military funeral to consider!

And for those brave airmen who survived the war and wished to stay in the RAF, there were serious pressures to bear. For many, victory brought no bowl of cherries, as there were a multitude of social codes to abide by, the dismissal of genuine nightmares of past battles in the sky, memories of long-lost friends who many of the surviving 'Few' describe as the 'real heroes', and the ruthless attitude of a new British government with its chilly attitudes of denial and 'stiff upper lip'.

During and after the Second World War, there was no counselling for post-traumatic stress disorder of course. Was it any wonder many unhappy men and women sought solace in alcohol to blot out the gruesome memories? After all, it had often provided the all-essential Dutch courage before and during battle when adrenalin was high. When the war was over, that unforgiving compulsion to fly and to fight was not required any more. Full stop. It was an abrupt ending to life on a knife edge. We had 'won' but at what cost? Was it any wonder it took its toll on those struggling to regain a sense of purpose? (*The Deep Blue Sea* is an exceptional play by Terence Rattigan which explores such a post-war story of a former Battle of Britain fighter pilot's struggle for survival.)

One family who wished to share their story with me arrived in east Kent from their homes in France and Belgium in early September 2016. I was among the excavation crew who dug up the engine and parts of their relative's aircraft out of the River Stour at Bilting, near Wye, Kent in 1991.

Author Melody Foreman also witnessed the visit of these lovely people and wrote the following:

'As we gathered to honour the memory of a Battle of Britain hero on the exact seventy-sixth anniversary of his death, a freakishly hot sun of early autumn disappeared for a minute and a ghostly breeze blew through a crowd now still and silent.

And, if we thought this mysterious shift of cloud was a sign Pilot Officer Albert Emmanuel Alex van den Hove d'Ertsenrijck had joined our crowd, then who could blame us? For the whole of our 15 September at a Kent museum belonged to him that day and it's where seventeen members of his family, including his daughters Adrienne and Rosemary, joined in dedication prayers led by Reverend Ian Campbell and watched the special unveiling of a Merlin engine which once powered a Hurricane Mk 1, P2760, which he had flown on the day of his death in 1940.

The patriotic Belgian aviator, who months before had fled his home country to join the RAF and take up arms against the invading Luftwaffe, had been on patrol with No. 501 Squadron just before noon after taking off from Kenley on Sunday, 15 September, when he was shot down.

Pilot Officer van den Hove d'Ertsenrijck died on a day which became known as "Battle of Britain day". The Hurricane (which had been regularly flown during the conflict by long-standing No. 501 Squadron hero Sergeant Pilot Paul Farnes, DFM) went down in the River Stour at Bilting, near Wye, Kent and that's where it remained until 1991 when it was recovered by aviation archaeologists who included Andy Saunders, Steve Vizard, Terry Parsons and Mark Kirby.

More recently the pilot's family, who travelled to the ceremony from their homes in France and Belgium, funded the engine's restoration to exhibition standard – work which was carried out by the Medway Aircraft Preservation Society led by Lewis Deal MBE.

The engine is now on permanent loan to the museum, courtesy of Mr Vizard of Airframe Assemblies. The dedication ceremony included a eulogy by Robert Maylam, whose family farm the land next to the crash site – land upon which sits a plaque dedicated to the memory of the 32-year-old Belgian who gave his life fighting for freedom in 1940.

Not long after Mr Maylam's address to the crowd, the Hurricane Mk 1 AE977 from Biggin Hill Heritage Hangar tore across the sky in salute to our hero, and by then the sun was beating down on us all as we marvelled once again at the courage of all the aircrews of 1940 who took part in the deadliest aerial battle ever known to mankind.'

Phillippe Lecoeuvre said:

'My wife, Adrienne, was a tiny child when her pilot father Albert was killed, so she didn't know him at all and yet now after this service everyone in the family knows who Albert is, what he did and why he did it. His life was a mystery to us for many years until I began to research his story in 2009.

Nobody knew much about him and what they did know was so little that I said one day I would like to know, and know a jolly lot more. I was curious and eventually I managed to track down Lewis

Deal MBE and from there on we found more about the young pilot who was my wife's father. It took my whole heart and soul to find out more and more.

I have known Adrienne for forty-five years and I was always thinking, "who was this man – this shadow, this hero we have over us" and I am happy because now she knows about her father, she has changed, too.

It was important for her to know about him, as for much of her life she was bitter because she thought he had just disappeared and left the family in 1939. But his reasons for that have now become clear to us all. When you have a hero in the family, you need to know. People here at this ceremony today have been so wonderful and shown us along this path towards Albert. In England, I found all the records I needed about his flying career, his friends and his squadrons, and I have met some wonderful British people who cherish the history of their country and thanks to them, our family have learned so much more about the hero who is Albert.

We have been waiting for seven years for a day to honour his memory with a ceremony like this and now finally the engine, this memorial to him is rightfully on show at a place which sets out to honour the lives of Battle of Britain aircrew.'

The Medway Aircraft Preservation Society's managing director, Lewis Deal MBE, said the story of Pilot Officer van den Hove d'Ertsenrijck was one of the most memorable he had known during his long career in vintage aviation. Mr Deal added: 'The engine is truly a lasting memorial to a hero of the Battle of Britain.'

On 14 July 1940, Battle of Britain pilot Albert van den Hove d'Ertsenrijck wrote to his wife, Laure:

'When you receive this letter, I shall not be any more of this world. But I want you to know that I did my duty to the end and that you can be proud of your husband. Being in France at the time of the Franco-German armistice signing, I refuse to obey the capitulation order of the Belgian government in France, having estimated that my duty was to defend the allied cause presently represented by Britain. I have since succeeded in enlisting in the RAF after a voyage of one month.

I can completely assure you, I died as a Christian, my conscience being clear and quiet, in defence of the good cause.

124

When I took the decision to see my native country and my home again only after the victory of Britain, I did not forget you, my loving Laure, I did not forget my two loving daughters, Adrienne and Rosemary.

I was where duty was calling me and I did consign you all to the Divine Providence and more particularly to the Virgin Mary, who never refused me anything. I have asked her to look after you in all respects, being convinced she would do it better than I, and I am gone to my destiny with a conscience clear. I ask you to forgive me for all the sorrows and disappointments during the six and a half years of marriage we had together. I have not always been kind to you; I did not cherish you as I should have. I beg your pardon for it.

Goodbye my dear Laure. Goodbye my two loving daughters, I shall pray for you all in heaven and I shall wait for you.'

Albert, as one of Belgium's greatest aviators, arguably wrote the missive fully believing the Belgian Embassy would have no need to send it on.

Previous letters to his wife, Laure, always enthusiastically mentioned how his 'lucky star' was with him, and how during the German bombing raid on his squadron aerodrome in Schaffen, Belgium, he got through it all with 'a smile'.

Indeed, in 1933, with just two years' experience as an aviator with the Belgian 'Thistle' squadron, he was forced to bale out of his Fairey Firefly after an accident. The aircraft was a write-off but Albert escaped unscathed and, just ten days later, at the end of September, he was in fine form to marry his fiancée, the Countess Laure Gaspard Marie Josephe Ghislaine Cornet d'Elzius de Peissant Beyghem.

Albert was of aristocratic birth. He was born in 1908 in Charleroi, Belgium. His mother was Baroness Margueritte-Marie Coppens, and his father, Joseph, was a senior official in the military. Albert's new wife was to learn all about his aviation adventures, plus the aeronautical work with the noble Observer Corps and other important training sessions.

Albert's record as a pilot was an admirable one, with his commanding officer describing his skills as 'always completely satisfactory' and him as someone who had the aptitude and necessary 'zeal' to lead a squadron.

Memories and records of him recall a courageous, big-hearted and vivacious young man who earned the nickname 'Hole' (or 'trou' in French) because he had once won a beer drinking competition.

His commanding officer said Albert had the capacity of a hole. The name stuck and whenever people were looking for him they'd holler, 'Where's Hole?'

When returning from a mission on 2 March 1940, Captain Albert 'Hole' van den Hove was forced to crash land his Hurricane No. 39 because of problems which developed with its two-bladed propeller.

The aircraft tipped over after a wing had caught the ground at Bierset, Liege aerodrome and was a write-off. Albert tried to land in a nearby field to soften the blows but he suffered minor injuries and was taken to recover in the local hospital.

Within weeks, on 10 May, the 'Thistle' squadron base at Schaffen was bombed by the Germans. Pilots, including Albert, were scrambled to defend the skies overhead, and in Hurricane H23 he helped destroy a Heinkel and took shots at several Dornier 17s heading straight for him. Albert landed his bullet-ridden Hurricane at Beauvechain. Squadron Leader Captain Guisgand wrote:

'My Gloster Gladiator is in the sky waiting the arrival of the fighting group. I arrive alone, then there's a Hurricane, this is Jacobs... Here, another Hurricane! This is Captain van den Hove - "the vivacious Hole" a true fighter. He attacked alone a bomber formation. He came back disgusted "I think he took a hit," he tells me, "but the pig did not move and continued on course with no sign of a hit."'

The morning of 10 May was shrouded in fog, and in the confusion, Albert claimed he attacked a Do 17, although reports refer to an He 111.

Let's forgive 'Hole' if he got a little confused, as both aircraft are twin engine bombers, and also he had been up until 3.00 am the night before, partying with the British protection unit which had arrived under the command of Captain Gerard.

There is a wonderful picture of the 'morning after the night before', showing Albert wearing his dinner attire underneath his flying suit! This depiction of 'the vivacious Hole' is like something out of a James Bond film.

The adventures continued, but within a few weeks the heroic Belgian fighter pilot was being labelled a thief and a traitor by some of his fellow countrymen. Along with a few friends from 'Thistle' squadron, he had gone missing and his family had no clue where he was.

However, Albert was busy doing his best to escape life as a PoW as the Germans arrived in Belgium. He refused to surrender, and commandeered a car, hoping to escape to Spain and get to Britain. He mentions this in his 'farewell letter' to Laure, which he hoped would never be sent, because he was determined he would see her and their daughters again. Eventually, he got to Gibraltar and boarded a ship heading for Liverpool.

For nineteen weeks, Albert had just 'disappeared', leaving friends and family fearing the worst. From June to September 1940 he wrote three letters to Laure, but she didn't receive them until months after his death. In one of them, he lets her know he has joined the RAF in England, and he apologises if she has suffered because of the German invasion of Belgium.

Shortly after his determined arrival in Britain, Albert was assigned to No. 43 Squadron at Tangmere, West Sussex, where he proved a serious foe to the Luftwaffe.

On 4 September he wrote to his friend, Pilot Officer Georges Doutrepont, and said he had shot down two Me 110s, although a third aircraft he was aiming at put a bullet through his engine, and oil sprayed all over his face forcing him to land quickly. Doutrepont died on 15 September, the same day as Albert.

On that day – the day which was to go down in history as marking the British victory in the battle of the skies – Albert was with No. 501 Squadron based at Kenley. They were scrambled into action, and at 11.30 am Albert was last seen at 20,000 feet, under fire from the enemy.

Young Don Key was fishing by the East Stour River near Wye, Kent that day, when he saw Albert's Hurricane P2760 in trouble. He recalled a trail of smoke coming from the engine as the aircraft headed for a field. He saw Albert try to clamber out of the cockpit at around 200 feet to perhaps jump into the river, but the aircraft came down too fast, hit some trees and landed in the water. Don ran towards the wreckage and saw Albert floating face down. He had died when his head struck the trees.

Pilot Officer Albert van den Hove d'Ertsenrijck was buried in Lympne churchyard, Kent. In 1949 his remains were removed and re-buried in Belgium with full military honours.

The details of what happened to Albert on the day of his death are as follows: At 10.50 am on 15 September 1940 radar detected enemy aircraft amassing over the Channel and ten minutes later, Nos. 501 and 253 Squadrons were placed at readiness. No. 501 Squadron, comprising thirteen Hurricanes, took off from RAF Kenley between 11.15 and 11.20 am with orders to patrol Maidstone, Kent with No. 253 Squadron.

Not long into their patrol, 'bogies' were spotted and identified as twenty Dornier Do 17s at 16,500 feet, some 2,000 feet higher than the Hurricanes. No. 501 Squadron climbed to engage the bombers that were in a wide V formation and formed part of a stepped formation of 250 enemy aircraft flying between 15,000 and 26,000 feet crossing the coast between Dungeness and Ramsgate. The enemy were heading straight towards London. On seeing the Hurricanes, the bombers climbed to make their attack more difficult. Meanwhile, as No. 501 Squadron flew over Ramsgate, some fifty Messerschmitt Bf 109Es dived down and attacked and then climbed back up again. Green and Blue Sections claimed two Dornier Do 17s and two Messerschmitt Bf 109Es as destroyed, and a third as damaged.

Feldwebel Theodor Rehm, a navigator in one of the Dornier Do 17s of Kampfgeschwader 76, later described the attack by the Hurricanes of No. 501 Squadron; 'Their thrusting attack took them right through our formation. Manning the nose gun, I dared not open fire for fear of hitting our own aircraft but the Hurricanes flashing close by passed us and did not do much firing either, and we came out of the attack unscathed.'

Feldwebel Wilhelm Raab was a pilot of one of the Dornier Do 17Zs from Kampfgeschwader 76 and on his forty-fourth combat mission of the war. He wrote: 'They came in fast, getting bigger and bigger. As usual when under attack from fighters, we closed into a tight formation to concentrate our defensive fire. Four Hurricanes scurried through the formation. Within seconds they passed us. Then more black specks emerged from the bank of cloud in front, rapidly grew larger and flashed through the formation. They were trying to split us up, but neither attack had any success. Our formation remained intact.'

It was during this combat Squadron Leader Harry Hogan force-landed his damaged Hurricane, V7435, at Sundridge, Kent and Pilot Officer van den Hove d'Ertsenrijck was shot down and killed. The remainder of the squadron returned to Kenley between 12.25 and 12.45 pm. Squadron leader Hogan wrote the following in his report:

'Pilot Officer van den Hove d'Ertsenrijck arrived at Kenley on 14 September. He seemed to have plenty of experience and had done very well when he was in No. 43 Squadron. As he was anxious to fly with our squadron as soon as possible, he came with me next morning and flew in my section. We carried out our head-on attack on a large formation of about twenty Dorniers escorted by numerous fighters.

After breaking away from the attack, I did not see him again. From the information I have received, it appears that he tried to make a forced landing. His aircraft had probably been shot in the coolant, which caused the engine to overheat and it burst into flames when he was at 200 feet, and that van den Hove must have tried to put the aeroplane into the river to avoid fire. This must have required great presence of mind. If the accident happened this way, I believe that it did, such an accident was extremely unfortunate.'

There are many times in every year that farmer Robert Maylam makes his way across the wide green fields of Bilting to the riverbank where Pilot Officer Albert van den Hove d'Ertsenrijck fell to his death after aerial combat during the Battle of Britain.

On 15 September and on Armistice Day, 11 November, Robert places a wreath at the special memorial plaque honouring the memory of the Belgian fighter pilot. 'I reckon it hasn't changed much around here since 1940,' said Robert as he led the way to the crash site.

It's summer and the trees and fields around us are in full hue, and the East Stour river glides by just as calmly as it did when Albert was scrambled with No. 501 Squadron to intercept Dornier bombers over Ashford.

'I grew up always knowing about Albert,' says Robert. 'As a boy in the 1970s, I remember the engine of Albert's Hurricane sticking out of the river, and I recall the day the Army arrived to remove pieces of the aircraft. My father (Peter) always told me why this place was special, and I remain friends with Don Key, who saw Albert's aircraft go down that day in 1940.'

Robert described how Don, a teenager then, ran over to Albert and dragged him away from the wreckage. But it was too late, as the pilot was already dead.

'Don says Albert tried to level off the aircraft to follow the river at about 200 feet. Perhaps he was thinking of force-landing it in the field a few yards ahead. Anyway, he seemed fine when he stood up in the cockpit as if to jump out of the Hurricane but because he let go of the control stick, the aircraft turned sharply to the left, hit a big old oak tree and did a 360-degree turn. Albert was thrown out and died instantly of head injuries,' says Robert.

Then showing me an oak tree which might have caught the Hurricane on its way down, Robert recalls the day Albert's daughter Adrienne first visited the site. 'When my father and I showed her exactly where Albert had died, she was overwhelmed and gave me a big hug to thank us for placing the memorial plaque there. I will never forget it when she said, "You've made me love my father again." Apparently, she had spent years of her life feeling hurt and angry with him for abandoning her, their mother, Laure and sister, Rosemary.'

Robert said Albert wasn't flying his usual Hurricane on the day he died.

'There's a story told by Wing Commander Paul Farnes, who arrived back from R&R to No. 501 Squadron on 15 September, only find his aircraft missing. He asked where it was and was told P2760 was in pieces in the East Stour River at Bilting,' added Robert.

When I arrived to help remove the engine from the riverbed in 1991, it was a time for one of our team (Mark Kirby) to dress in the full

scuba diving gear. We organised for a crane to help us remove the huge old Merlin engine, and I remember we salvaged a lot of small pieces of the Hurricane from the bank and the riverbed.

When I met the pilot's daughters, Rosemarie and Adrienne, in 2016, I was honoured to present them with some photographs I'd taken of the excavation. They said, 'We cannot thank you enough for helping us to remember our father and his heroism during the Battle of Britain. We know his motivations to fight the enemy were righteous and pure and he paid the ultimate price for our liberty.'

Pilot Officer Albert van den Hove d'Ertsenrijck in 1939 – a proud Belgian who fought his way to Britain to join the RAF in a bid to drive the invaders from his homeland.

Above and below: The diver and excavation team get to work on the recovery of the engine from van den Hove's Hurricane, which had been shot down on 15 September 1940.

The Merlin engine from van den Hove's stricken Hurricane being lifted out of the water of the River Stour.

Gradually, the Merlin engine is hauled out of its watery grave.

Terry and the dig team check out the prop hub of the engine. Note the remains of the wooden propeller blades, which are split and ragged.

Pieces of wreckage; van den Hove's aircraft being examined during the recovery project.

A plaque placed at the side of the River Stour honouring the memory of Pilot Officer van den Hove d'Ertsenrijck.

Terry presents Adrienne Lecouvre – the daughter of Pilot Officer Albert van den Hove d'Ertsenrijck – with a framed collection of photographs he took during the dig of her father's Hurricane.

Chapter 9

GOOD RELATIONS

WHEN I first met 25-year-old Ian Trueman on a summer's day in 1999, I was struck by the strong resemblance he bore to the heroic grandfather he'd never met. Tall, dark haired, strong limbed and sharing the same chin I'd recognised from 1940 photographs of Flying Officer Alec Albert Gray Trueman, there was little doubt they were related.

Indeed, fine looks and physique were not all they had in common. Both had left their homeland of Canada to reach England out of a desperate need for answers.

Alec, in March 1938, was a bright intelligent young man with a conscience, a desire to fly and a determination to defend the skies of Britain against the Luftwaffe. He joined the RAF on a short service commission. First he trained as a bomber command pilot, and he had a miracle escape from death when a huge four-engine Hampden he was taxiing along a runway suddenly broke up carrying a full bombload.

By June 1940, recently married, he volunteered to join Fighter Command and was posted to No. 253 Squadron at Turnhouse, Scotland. During a sortie on 2 September he damaged an Me 109. Two days later, on 4 September, the young Canadian was shot down and killed in combat over Kenley, Surrey just after 1.00 pm. His Hurricane, serial number V6638, crashed in nearby Tudor Close (Nork Way), Banstead.

At the time, Alec's young wife, Ethel, was exactly eight weeks away from giving birth to their twin sons, who arrived on 4 November 1940 – one of them of course would eventually become Ian's father. A newspaper cutting from the time is headlined 'Twins Born After Flier Father's Death'. A photograph shows a young Mrs Trueman and her own twin sister, Margaret Hilda Lord, cradling the twin babies in their arms, and a caption reveals they had sailed from Liverpool to New York on the liner *Samaria* on 24 September. The ship, which arrived safely on

3 October, had taken part in the evacuation of children under the CORB (Children's Overseas Reception Board) scheme.

The proud, smiling young mother and two infant sons were photographed just weeks after the beloved Alec at the age of 26 was buried in St Luke's Churchyard, Whyteleafe, Surrey. Who knew the depth of the grief she kept hidden behind that smile? Her young husband, once so full of plans, and the life they'd have together now lay in the cold earth in the heart of Surrey, England and not far from where he died – a beloved father and one of the honoured 'Few'.

More than fifty years later his grandson Ian would be standing in a hole twelve-feet deep next to the pieces of the Hurricane Flying Officer Alec Trueman was shot down in. Ian hoped his grandfather would appreciate this homage, this important visit and his taking part in an excavation of the 1940 crash site, which had been sensitively organised by Hawker Hurricane Society's Colin Lee. Official permission to dig the site had been granted by the Ministry of Defence and the landowner.

For Ian, a young man about to become a father himself for the first time, it was an emotional experience to be at the place his grandfather Alec fell. It was also the day Ian felt he had finally got to meet the kin who the Trueman family rightfully cherished as a hero – a pilot who fought with valour in the Battle of Britain. I was awestruck by the love and respect Ian showed for his grandfather who died in the name of freedom. I can only guess Ian's father, who in 1940 was the baby son Alec never got to meet either, felt the same.

So, what did we find that day in 1999? Quite a lot of artefacts is the answer, although it was quite a tough dig, as it was summer and the ground was quite dry. Photographs of the propeller hub and other items we found can be seen at the end of this chapter. Although Ian is smiling in the shot down the hole with a large part of the Merlin engine which once powered his grandfather's Hurricane, he was quite understandably overwhelmed with a mixture of feelings.

I think all of us at the site that day, including Ian's pregnant wife, Jackie, were imagining just what was going on in the skies of 4 September 1940.

The following report marking a day of intense and deadly action reveals all, and shows just what faced every young man in the skies over the South East during the height of the Battle of Britain.

WEDNESDAY, 4 SEPTEMBER 1940
Weather:
Over the southern half of England it was expected to be fine and warm. Skies mainly clear with occasional cloud. The Channel

areas fine with good visibility. The north of England and most of Scotland was expected to have rain periods with some heavy falls and strong winds could be expected.

Operations in Detail:

0830hrs: Formations of enemy aircraft were detected coming across the narrow part of the Channel between Dover and Folkestone. But again, formations were divided as another had been detected coming in over the Thames Estuary. No. 66 Squadron Kenley (Spitfires) were vectored to the Thames Estuary as was No. 72 Squadron Croydon (Spitfires) and No. 111 Squadron Hurricanes (Croydon). Most of the action commenced from 0900hrs onwards as the British fighters engaged a mixture of Bf 110s and Bf 109s.

0930hrs: The Bf 109s stuck to their task well, keeping the Hurricanes and Spitfires at bay and allowing a number of the Bf 110s to get the Eastchurch airfield. Fighter Command released a number of squadrons towards the Dover area, but some excellent defensive action by the British fighters stopped most of the Bf 110s from getting through; although the harbour and the barrage balloons came under fire but most of the damage was at Lympne where a number of bombs hit buildings and again the aerodrome was cratered. The balloons at Dover continued to be shot up. No. 111 Squadron, even though they forced the Bf 109s to retreat, did lose two of their pilots, both over the Channel off Folkestone. Eastchurch also became a target and a number of bombs made deep craters in the runway and some stores were damaged.

1230hrs: Radar at Dover and Rye detected a wide formation coming across the Channel for the midday attack. Some 300 enemy aircraft were detected crossing the coast in the vicinity of Folkestone and Beachy Head. This consisted of 50-plus Heinkel He 111s, 30-plus Dornier Do 17s and 200 Bf 109s. Again, they split into groups and headed towards five different targets. A total of fourteen squadrons of Fighter Command were to be placed at readiness. More enemy aircraft are spotted coming in from the Channel close to Brighton and Worthing in Sussex.

All anticipated the positioning of the enemy bombers meant that their plan again was to break into two separate formations, as seemed the usual tactics of the Luftwaffe over the last few days. Air Chief Marshal Keith Park again was to take no chances placing half his squadrons at readiness from Tangmere to Debden, and the other half on standby.

1300hrs: No. 43 Squadron Tangmere (Hurricanes) were ordered up giving protection along the Sussex coast. No. 46 Squadron Stapleford (Hurricanes) were to patrol the Thames Estuary, No. 66 Squadron Kenley (Spitfires) who had already been up once that morning, No. 72 Squadron Croydon (Spitfires) also up for a second time, No. 79 Squadron Biggin Hill (Hurricanes), No. 222 Squadron Hornchurch (Spitfires), No. 249 Squadron North Weald (Hurricanes), No. 234 Squadron Middle Wallop (Spitfires), No. 253 Squadron Kenley (Hurricanes), No. 601 Squadron Tangmere (Hurricanes), No. 602 Squadron Westhampnett (Spitfires) and No. 603 Squadron Hornchurch (Spitfires) were all scrambled for this biggest build-up of the day. No. 11 Group were further reinforced by No. 73 Squadron (Hurricanes) who had been transferred from Church Fenton to Debden, No. 41 Squadron (Spitfires) came down from Catterick and found their new home at Hornchurch. With all personnel fresh and rested, it would not be long before their services were put to good use.

1315hrs: Squadrons were divided as two separate formations and came in from two different parts of the English coast. Heavy action took place over north Kent and, as was usual, in the Thames Estuary with the skies over Kent and Sussex were chaos, vapour trails now hung like heavy white clouds as two-thirds of No. 11 Group battled it out at 20,000 feet. What radar did not pick up was a low-flying formation of Bf 110s that were following the railway line from Hindhead to Guildford until it was too late. This small formation of Bf 110s managed to get through the British defences and were not intercepted until just north of the town of Guildford, which is to the south-west of London. They were met by No. 253 Squadron Kenley (Hurricanes) who had reasonable success, although a couple of Bf 110s did get through, and although the target was the Hawker factory at Brooklands, they by mistake hit the Vickers factory again. Six 500kg high-explosive bombs fell on the machine shops at the Vickers factory, killing 86 personnel and seriously injuring 630 others. Six of the Bf 110s were destroyed prior to the bombing of the Vickers factory, while another nine were destroyed as they turned for home.

1320hrs: Park instructs that a squadron patrol the sector station to the south of London, and also a squadron was to patrol the sector station of North Weald, who was still trying to repair the damage of the previous day. While all this was going on, the crack

Bf 110 Erprobungsgruppe 210 group crossed the coast almost unnoticed and attacked the radar station at Poling, but not before a Spitfire squadron had been instructed to intercept. German aircraft had now crossed all along the south coast, and now Tangmere was brought into the action. Ventnor radar had picked up enemy formations coming in from the Channel.

Patrolling over Tangmere, the 12 Spitfires of No. 234 Squadron led by Australian ace Pat Hughes have spiralled up to 15,000 feet (4,600m) by 1.20 pm. Down below, on the airfield, the Hurricanes of No. 601 Squadron are taking off. At the controls of one is Clive Mayers. Then Hughes spots two groups of German aircraft. About 50 Bf 110s are coming in over the coast while 15 others are already circling over Haslemere lower down. Detailing Red, Yellow and Green Sections to attack the larger formation, Hughes leads Blue Section down after the others. As soon as the Spitfires are sighted, the 110s form their usual defensive circle.

Hughes attacks the leading Messerschmitt head on. His aim is deadly. The 110 rears up and another short burst strikes its fuselage, causing it to erupt in flames. Seconds later the Australian comes in directly behind another 110 and fires briefly twice. The heavy escort fighter crashes and blows up. Suddenly Hughes is surrounded by three Messerschmitts and he notices a fourth slipping in behind. Manoeuvring wildly, he fires three sharp bursts to break them up and causes one to dive away. He pounces after it and empties the remainder of his ammunition. The 110 sinks and turns slowly towards the coast; it cannot get far because both engines are burning.

While all this is happening, No. 601 Squadron intercepts bandits near Worthing. Clive Mayers goes into line astern, following Red 1, who attacks a defensive circle of Bf 110s. Mayers finds a Messerschmitt slightly below him and fires briefly from above and behind. He attacks again from dead astern and sees smoke coming from both engines. He dives underneath and, as he does so, notices Red 1 attacking. He leaves his section leader to deliver the coup de grace and he last sees the Messerschmitt trailing smoke with Red 1 in dogged pursuit.

Looking around, he sees another aircraft flying out to sea. It is a Dornier bomber. Gradually he overhauls it but as he draws abreast, it suddenly turns towards him. Mayers reacts quickly and charges in head on. He presses his firing button and the bomber's glasshouse nose shatters to pieces as he flashes past. As he hauls back on his Hurricane's controls, the crippled German plane rolls over onto its back and dives vertically into the sea.

The German escort fighters have suffered badly and No. 234 Squadron alone claims a record 14 Bf 110s and one Do 17 destroyed for only one damaged Spitfire.

Another raid reaches Rochester, where the Short Brothers factory producing the new four-engine Stirling bombers is damaged.

By nightfall, the Luftwaffe changed from the bombing of Fighter Commands airfields and aircraft producing factories to the bombing of large towns and cities. Night bombing raids were made on Bristol, Cardiff, Swansea, Liverpool, Newcastle and Tilbury Docks. In South Wales, large oil storage tanks received direct hits and the red glow lit up the dark night sky that it was a wonder that they couldn't see it from London. In all, for the day, the RAF had shot down 20 German aircraft which consisted of 6 Bf 109s, 1 Heinkel He 111 and 13 Bf 110s.

Fighter Command lost fifteen valuable aircraft, nine Spitfires and six Hurricanes. Six RAF pilots were killed including Flying Officer Alec Trueman of No. 253 Squadron.

Casualties:

0915hrs: Channel 5m E of Folkestone. Hurricane R4172. No. 111 Squadron Croydon; F/L D.C. Bruce listed as missing. (Crashed into Channel after combat with Bf 109)

0915hrs: Channel 5m E of Folkestone. Hurricane Z2309. No. 111 Squadron Croydon; P/O J. Macinski listed as missing. (Shot down by Bf 109 and pilot baled out but body was never found)

[The above is as recorded, but aircraft excavated at West Stourmouth is believed to be Hurricane Z2309.]

1000hrs: Ashford. Spitfire N3048. No. 66 Squadron Kenley; Sergeant A.D. Smith died of injuries 06.09.40 (Baled out with serious injuries after combat with enemy aircraft)

1000hrs: Banstead. Hurricane V6638. No. 253 Squadron Kenley; F/O A.A.G. Trueman killed. (Shot down during combat action over Kenley aerodrome)

1315hrs: Hawkwell. Hurricane P3052. No. 46 Squadron Stapleford F/O R.P. Plummer died of injuries 14.09.40 (Shot down in flames by Bf 110. Pilot baled out with serious burns)

1330hrs: Maidstone. Spitfire X4278. No. 222 Squadron Hornchurch; P/O J.W. Cutts killed. (Shot down by Bf 109 and aircraft crashed at Sutton Farm)

[Originally listed as missing but body fragments discovered on excavation of crash site. Now listed as KIA]

1335hrs: Yalding. Spitfire K9962. No. 222 Squadron Hornchurch; Sergeant J.W. Ramshaw killed. (Crashed after combat with Bf 109s. Was dead on arrival at West Kent Hospital)

1340hrs: Biggin Hill. Hurricane P3676. No. 79 Squadron Biggin Hill; Sergeant J. Wright died of injuries 05.09.40. (Shot down by Bf 110 over base. Pilot crash landed aircraft at Surbiton)

2130hrs: Kirton-in-Lindsey. Defiant N1628. No. 264 Squadron Kirton-in-Lindsey; F/O D.K.C. O'Malley killed. Sergeant L.A.W. Rasmussen killed. (Aircraft crashed during night landing practice)

Unknown time: RAF Digby. Hurricane V7406. No. 151 Squadron Digby; P/O R. Ambrose killed. (Crashed into a crane during takeoff on ferry flight. A/C burnt out)

Unknown time: 25m S of Bognor. Spitfire R6909. No. 151 Squadron Warmwell; Sergeant J.K. Barker killed. (Possibly shot down by Do 17 over Channel. Body washed up on French coast.)

Here is a letter written by Ian that I received a copy of:

BY IAN TRUEMAN - GRANDSON OF PILOT OFFICER A.A.G. TRUEMAN.

When I was first asked to write something about my visit to the crash site, I wasn't really sure what to say. There were so many feelings and emotions going round inside my head, I thought that perhaps the best thing to do would be to write an account of the entire day.

For several years I have been interested in what happened to my grandfather. This was partly due to the fact that Floyd Williston was writing a book which included a chapter on the life of Alec Trueman and therefore he required information which only the family would have. However, it was also the fact that at that time I was coming up to my 26th birthday, which was to be the same age as my grandfather when he died. As you can imagine, this was a sobering thought to think that at the same age as me, he was engaged in dogfights over the skies of the country he was trying to protect.

Following the initial conversation I had with (a relieved) Colin Lee, several of my friends and neighbours had asked me how I felt. The simple answer was that I did not know how I was going to feel, but I was concerned that the RAF had removed perhaps not all of my grandfather's body. The only thing I knew for sure that it was an opportunity I could not miss and it was something my wife and I had often discussed. Also, with my father and brother both on holiday, I felt it was important to have a member of the family present. I had been to his grave when I was a small child and could still remember the day clearly.

My first feeling was how nice the area was where he had crashed; my second feeling was how strange it was to be recognised by several members of the dig purely from my grandfather's photograph. My third feeling, which remained throughout the day, was how extremely friendly and welcoming the other members of the dig were.

We had just got there in the nick of time, as the group was about to lift out the final part of the aircraft, the propeller unit. Before this though, I was introduced to several people who gave us various parts of the aircraft to look at and showed us books highlighting where within the aircraft they came from. The thought that kept going through my mind was how violent the impact must have been due to the depth of the hole in solid chalk and how much damage there was to the engine; I just hoped that he had died before he hit the ground.

I was asked if I would like to go down the hole before the final piece was removed; I was glad to be asked because I really wanted to. This was one of the most moving experiences of my life, to think that I was as close to where my grandfather had died as perhaps any member of his family had been before. There was so much to say that I ended up saying nothing. The other aspect which made the moment so special was the attitude of the other people who were involved in the dig, the respect and dignity they showed whilst handling the parts of the aeroplane was humbling and dignified all at the same time.

We were also taken upstairs in the house to the window where a photograph had been taken just after the crash. This was a profound moment which I will always remember; the view was almost unchanged apart from the height of the trees. Some of the parts of the aircraft we were given were quite likely to have been touched by my grandfather, which made it very special.

We had many conversations that afternoon and learnt a terrific amount about the history of my grandfather, the day of the crash and about the Hurricane, which according to my grandma, he loved to fly. All too soon, the afternoon had become the early evening and as the hole was being filled in, I felt I had to help. It seemed like the last act I could do knowing that this would be the last time his crash site would ever be dug.

There was of course one last thing we had to do that day, and that was to visit the grave. Colin had meticulously written some directions how to get to Whyteleafe and after saying our goodbyes to all the wonderful people we had met that day, we were on our way. We pulled up outside a small, quiet churchyard. It was obvious where the war graves were, as they were clean and the ground well kept. We placed some flowers on the grave and took some photos, which my grandma had requested.

Again, I was completely speechless; I had no words to say but felt a real sense of belonging and relief that I was at last beside his grave. We both felt saddened when we looked at the other graves and realised that the people buried there were so young and that many came from other parts of the world, as did my grandfather. It made us realize that so many of these young men's graves have probably never been visited by their families, and it saddened us further that we did not live nearer to pay our respects more often.

As we left London, I felt almost numb. It had been such a moving day, yet filled with wonderful memories which I felt privileged to have experienced.

We are expecting our first child soon and it will be the only one in the family at the moment that will carry the Trueman name. We have decided that from now on, we will endeavour to visit the grave once a year, and if this is not possible for any reason, ask one of our newfound friends to place some flowers on our behalf.

All that remains to do is to thank everyone including Terry Parsons for allowing us the opportunity to share such a moving and memorable day which we will treasure for the rest of our lives.

Yours sincerely,
Ian and Jackie Trueman

The Surrey Mirror of 11 November 1999 carried a story about historian Colin Lee's appeal for further information about the crash. He was helping to compile a book to mark the 60th anniversary of the Battle of Britain. Mr Lee, who helped organise the recovery of Pilot Officer Trueman's Hurricane, said: 'I decided to go to the site and approached Ken and Jean Penton, who owned the site in Tudor Close, Banstead, to see if an excavation to recover artefacts from the aircraft would be possible. It was known that the Rolls-Royce Merlin engine was still buried at a depth of seven to eight feet in solid chalk with the propeller unit beyond that.'

With approval from the Ministry of Defence and permission from Ken and Jean Penton, an excavation went ahead, in which various parts of the aircraft were uncovered. Mr Lee told the newspaper the dig was made all the more special by the arrival of Pilot Officer Trueman's grandson, Ian.

Not long after the dig was completed, a Canadian Maple Tree was planted at the site in honour of Pilot Officer Alec Trueman, 'One of the Few'.

Above left: A young Alec Trueman just before he joined the RAF.

Above right: Pilot Officer Alec Trueman and his bride, Ethel, on their wedding day.

The excavation team with Steve Vizard and the artefacts they discovered at the crash site almost sixty years after the tragedy.

Terry hard at work during the second dig at the site of Trueman's Hurricane, which crashed in Tudor Close, Banstead, Surrey, on 4 September 1940. This picture shows Terry unearthing a crank shaft and six pistons.

Terry takes a rare break during the dig for the Hurricane in Tudor Close.

Ian Trueman – grandson of the heroic pilot, Alec – was honoured to have opportunity to recover the remains of his grandfather's aircraft in 1999.

Evidence of the Battle of Britain Hurricane is plain to see as Terry locates part of it protruding from the bottom of the pit.

Ian Trueman assists with the removal of the weighty Merlin engine.

The team at rest during the dig for Pilot Officer Alec Trueman's Hurricane.

The digger and excavation crew in Clapper Lane, Staplehurst, Kent – the place where Hurricane P5185 crashed after being shot down on 1 September 1940. Pilot Officer John 'Curly' Clifton of No. 253 Squadron was wounded by enemy fire over Dungeness, and as the aircraft came down near Staplehurst, an eye witness saw the 21-year-old pilot slumped over the controls.

148

Terry and Ed Francis examine artefacts in a field at Grays Road, Westerham Hill, Kent in the early 1970s – this is the crash site of a Hurricane which was destroyed by the guns of Me 109s during combat on 1 September 1940. The Hurricane had been flown by Flying Officer Leofric Trevor Bryant-Fenn, DFC, of No. 79 Squadron. Bryant-Fenn baled out with a wounded leg and was sent to RAF Hospital Torquay to recuperate. He served with the RAF until 1968 and retired as a group captain.

A photograph taken outside Sevenoaks Hospital in 1940. Left to right: Pilot Officer Jack Davis, AFC, of No. 54 Squadron, Pilot Officer Brian Noble of No. 79 Squadron, Nurse Buick and Pilot Officer Bryant-Fenn.

149

The digger hard at work seeking out the wreckage of Bryant-Fenn's Hurricane.

This under-carriage pump was discovered by Terry during a dig for Bryant-Fenn's Hurricane.

Chapter 10

A LUFTWAFFE 'OLD HAND' IS SHOT DOWN

WHEN Melody first set to work on this book, she decided to tell the story around my ten most memorable digs. Well, every single one of the 900 aircraft wrecks I've unearthed have been special so choosing just a few of 'The Few' has been difficult indeed. What readers should understand is how finding an artefact from any era of history is like pulling a thread on a blanket. Whilst the useful life of an item albeit it an aircraft or an ancient Roman pot met its end all those years ago, for the finder, a whole new adventure of a discovery begins.

Any time I unearthed a piece of fuselage, cracked Perspex, the treasured stick from a cockpit, or a tyre still full of the air from 1940 – indeed anything indicative of the past – then the questions began the moment I scraped the earth from its precious surface: 'Who? Why? What? Where?' and 'When?' The answers and indeed, the search for them are the ingredients for any good story, and realising the Battle of Britain was as historically important to the world stage as the Battle of Waterloo, I have always felt honoured to have been genuinely involved at the start of the archaeological process to establish this fact.

As anyone who knows me will tell you, I often walk away from the many who like to stand around making preposterous statements about digs when they've never experienced one at all. The politicking and rows I've witnessed over the years in regard to the discovery of aircraft wreckage and the remains of aircrew fallen in battle, are sadly another reminder that humanity often prefers to destroy instead of respect.

Historians like to debate about who or what is to blame for aggression and war. I take a philosophical stance and examine the wide situation. What I do know is that there's is nothing truer than the saying: 'We know more about killing than we know about living.' This is a quote by a Second World War US Army General by the name of Omar Bradley. He has a serious point. His infinite words sit high on the wall in the exhibition centre at La Cambe in Normandy – a cemetery full of thousands of German soldiers who died during the Second World War, mostly during the D-Day Landings on 6 June 1944.

Over the years though, I've learned to avoid those folks who dwell in secrets and darkness which satisfy their own tragic sense of self. Believe me when I tell you just how many confessions I've heard over the years from several men who were riddled with guilt for not acting with respect and dignity towards the fallen. They hadn't treated the living too well either, because of some peculiar fear their 'ownership' of the Battle of Britain would be challenged; their personality insulted in some way.

Indeed, when digging up the past becomes an unhealthy obsession, I believe it's time to stop, step back and take a long, hard look at yourself. There have been occasions when I witnessed punches being thrown during a debate over a piece of metal from 1940 and some chose to deride others who challenged them. It's often just when I see and hear too much 'BS' – as the Americans would say – or codswallop spoken by those unwilling to learn and explore genuine reasons for digging, I am suddenly reminded of the good which has come out of my life's work as a wreck hunter – an endeavour which I have always felt was guided by a certain purity of spirit.

As I explained, it was always best to excavate crash sites which you knew did not contain human remains. However, if I ever came across any body parts, I would – like most decent people – stop the dig and we'd take appropriate action by contacting the police and the coroner's office. There were times of course, when I was asked to be on a dig team when the aircrew or pilot was listed as missing and by doing so, I helped make sure the decent thing was done if any body parts were found. In fact, since the Protection of Military Remains Act came into force in 1986, strict rules and regulations have been put in place and everything must be played by the book; licences applied for and justifications for a dig at the ready for the Ministry of Defence to study. There have been occasions, however, when the MoD has not been overly helpful.

Without sounding too worthy, I have a destiny to recover aircraft once flown by those young men of 1940 who served their countries with honour, valour and blind courage, some of whom I saw plunge to their death in 1940 as a boy. Who else was there to do this in the 1960s, when the war was deemed too recent and too horrific to remember?

I am lucky to have had a balanced life, a loving wife, Rose – now much missed – and daughters Mandy and Julie, and an honest day job. I strongly believe that the rich histories of the RAF and Luftwaffe aircrews should never be used as a tool to advance the cause of petty politics. Today, I recognise that there is a worrying amount of morally dubious people in the world.

But out of such potential darkness within humanity, there are always reminders of the positive I have done and the help I have provided by actively honouring the memory of 'The Few'. Such a reminder came when I met two German gentleman who were relatives of a Luftwaffe pilot called Oberleutnant Siegfried Lothar Stronk of the 8./JG 53. They wanted some information from me about his Me 109, which I knew had gone down in Sutherland Ave, Biggin Hill in 1940. It was one of three Me 109s which crashed near the same road during the same time after heavy combat with the RAF.

One of the men I met in 2013 was Herr Florian Stronk, who introduced himself as the great-nephew of Oberleutnant Stronk. Florian said the family had always longed to know more about what had happened to Siegfried, and all his young wife had ever been told by the Nazi authorities during the war was that Siegfried was 'missing in action'.

It was then when I remembered how this young Luftwaffe pilot had been found dead, still seated in the wreckage of his aircraft in 1940. The Me 109, which remained mostly on the surface of its crash site, had been cleared away by the salvage teams but a piece of fuselage into which the wheel would have retracted was found along with a radiator and presented to me by a local resident much later. I loaned these items to a local amateur museum, which was visited in 2013 by Florian Stronk.

I told Florian how in the 1970s, when I investigated the crash, I had been told about the Me 109 flown by his great-uncle by an eyewitness who had run over to the stricken aircraft on 2 October 1940 after it hit a house, slithered down a slope and through a hedge as it glided to an ungainly halt. Many believe Oberleutnant Stronk's Me 109 was hit by anti-aircraft fire. Other historians claim it was shot down by Flight Lieutenant John Boulter of No. 603 Squadron.

The woman who reached the fallen aircraft in 1940 lived in a house close to the spot where the Me 109 came down. I told Florian that the news was distressing, as this eyewitness had informed me that she had found the pilot with a clean shot through the head. But Florian was calm and said there was comfort in knowing his great-uncle had not suffered, as such a direct shot would have killed him outright. He then told me he would tell his family, who would be pleased to finally know that the death of the young pilot so forever in their hearts had been instantaneous.

It's these sorts of poignant meetings with the relatives of 'The Few' which inspire my faith in the knowledge that all the recovery and archaeological work carried out by the genuine early dedicated archaeologists I worked with, including Tony Graves, Ed Francis, Andy Saunders, Steve Vizard, Tony Parslow, Steve Hall, Dick Walker and Mark Kirby, was not, nor ever will be in vain.

As I explained in a previous chapter, one of my personal heroes of the Battle of Britain was Group Captain Johnny 'Kentowski' Kent, DFC*, AFC, Virtuti Militari. It was therefore a momentous occasion in 1982 when I arrived at Burmarsh Halt, Dymchurch, Kent (not far from the Romney, Hythe and Dymchurch Little Railway) to join the team led by Steve Vizard excavating an Me 109E-7 which had come off worst in a dog fight on 2 November 1940 against a Spitfire flown by Canadian ace Johnny Kent – CO of No. 92 Squadron at Biggin Hill.

The Me 109 had been flown by Luftwaffe ace Hauptmann Wilhelm Enßlen of 9./JG 53. This 29-year-old pilot did not survive the combat.

At this point it's best to let Group Captain Kent describe the moments of 8.55 am, 2 November 1940. This excerpt from his excellent memoir, *One of the Few* is reproduced here with the kind permission from his daughter, Alix:

'The rest of the formation dived for the coast and did not attempt to turn and fight, at least all but one. We chased after the fleeing Germans and I caught up with this one and attacked. I found that I had picked an old hand; instead of just running away, he waited until I was very close and then suddenly broke to the right and into the sun. I momentarily lost sight of him but as he continued to turn he moved out of the glare of the sun and a tail chase developed.

As we came round full circle he repeated his manoeuvre but this time I pulled my sights through him and, although losing him under the nose of my aircraft, gave a short burst in the hopes that I might get some tracer near enough to him to frighten him into running for home.

I misjudged my man, however, and he continued his tactics and apparently had no intention of running at all but finally after the fourth or fifth circle I drew my sights through him again, gave a longish burst and was startled when he suddenly appeared from under my nose and we very nearly collided. I still have a very vivid mental picture of him looking up at me as we flashed past not twenty feet apart. I distinctly remember that he had his goggles up on his helmet and his oxygen mask in place.

I also recall the gashes along the side of the Messerschmitt where my bullets had struck and the tail of the aircraft with practically no fabric left on it and a control cable streaming back with a small piece of metal whirling around on the end of it.

It is one of those pictures of a split-second action that remains indelibly imprinted on one's mind. I did not, in the heat of the moment, fully appreciate the significance of all this and was jubilant when I saw that my opponent was reversing his turn, a fatal move in a fight, and gave him one last burst from "fine quarter" into his left side.

A thin trail of grey smoke appeared, and the aircraft rolled quite slowly onto its back and started down. I immediately thought that he was getting away and followed him with throttle wide open, hoping to catch him as he levelled out.

The last time I glanced at the airspeed indicator, it was registering something like 450mph but still the Me 109 outdistanced me and I finally lost it against the ground. While continuing my dive and waiting to see the grey plan-form of it as it pulled out, I was startled to see a vivid red flash and a great cloud of jet-black smoke appear as the machine hit the ground and exploded.

I came down low to see where the aircraft had struck but could see no sign of it, until I noticed some soldiers running across the fields waving to me. Then I saw it. A gaping hole that looked just like a bomb crater and hundreds of little bits scattered around.

A few days later an Intelligence Officer told me that the pilot had been quite a highly decorated major, but it had not been possible to establish his identity. Apparently, I had shot away his controls and he was on the point of baling out when my last burst killed him. This was deduced from the fact that his fighting harness was picked up undone and undamaged and the left half of his tunic was found with six bullet holes in it.'

Johnny Kent (who retired from the RAF in 1956 as a group captain) had shot down a Luftwaffe ace that day. Hauptmann Wilhelm Enßlen

(1911 – 1940) had taken part in the Spanish Civil War in 1936 as a fighter pilot and was one of only twenty-eight men awarded the Spanish Cross in Gold with Swords and Diamonds.

Enßlen was an experienced fighter leader and had played his role in the campaigns in Poland and France and then survived time and time again during the whole of the Battle of Britain, adding to his significant score of claims. That is until he decided to go head to head with Johnny Kent on 2 November 1940.

Although from the cockpit of his Spitfire Johnny Kent hadn't witnessed what exactly had happened when the Me 109 disappeared against the countryside below, Wilhelm Enßlen had apparently abandoned his Messerschmitt and fallen with an unopened parachute or had dropped out of his harness. It is unclear as to the precise order of events that day, although we do know for sure that he fell into the sea at Dymchurch.

Andy Saunders writes:

'Mortuary records reveal Enßlen was "rescued" from the sea, which suggests he was pulled out alive and died later. However, it seems more likely that he fell dead without an open parachute. What is not debatable, however, is that for some unknown reason his body defied identification and he was ultimately buried at Folkestone (New) Cemetery in Hawkinge under the name "A Schenk".

Quite where this name comes from is a mystery, although it is entirely possible that it was a tailor's name or some such in a piece of clothing, or maybe the name of a previous owner or even a manufacturer on his parachute harness for example. Either way, no identity disc was discovered and although personal effects were found they clearly did not help put a name to the man.

A piece of linking evidence, however, was found when enthusiasts excavated the wreck and the fact that the unknown German airman pulled out of the sea just a short distance away had fallen from this aircraft, the discovery of the main aircraft data plate showing it to be a Messerschmitt 109 E-4 with the Werk Nummer 3784 confirmed this to indeed be the aircraft being flown by Hptm. Enßlen when he was lost.

Whilst circumstantial only, and providing insufficient proof that "A. Schenk" was indeed Wilhelm Enßlen, it was nonetheless a most valuable piece of the jigsaw. With all the pieces of the puzzle assembled and presented to the German War Graves Service (a charitable organisation run like the British RNLI) it is heartening that this evidence has now been accepted and a named headstone was apparently due to be erected to this previous "missing" pilot whose remains are laid to rest at Folkestone New Cemetery, (Hawkinge) in plot O, grave number 404 under the inscription A. Schenk. However, when the gravestone was recently checked it had not been changed. The fact "A.Schenk" remains on the stone has been confirmed by the Commonwealth War Graves Commission August 2017.'

On the day of the dig for Enßlen's Me 109 in Dymchurch in 1982 I recall a light sea breeze inspiring our energies to merge and circulate, as artefact after artefact was raised from the sandy soil. The Me 109 had dived in deep at great speed and so when we set to work on its recovery forty-two years later, we had no preconceptions of what we might find. In 1940 an official report had revealed that a piece of one shell gun (20mm) was found, thus indicating the armament had been two shell guns and two MG17 machine guns.

What did we discover that day once the giant digging machine had exposed the wreckage of Hauptman Enßlen's Me 109 buried so very deep beneath the sands of time? Well, for a long time I had in my personal collection the back armour from the cockpit. I do remember that the engine and a lorry full of aircraft was removed from the scene that day. Where exactly it all finished up I am not sure.

In the 1970s and 1980s when I was digging aircraft with Steve Vizard (now managing director of Airframe Assemblies) we'd do three or four crash sites in a weekend! We'd do a Heinkel in the morning, then maybe an Me 109 just off the M2 in Kent, then there'd be a party at Steve's house, then we would jump on a ferry to the Isle of Wight and dig a Heinkel or an Me 110. There was one particular 1940 aircraft on the island that had plummeted fifty-five feet down a well. On a weekend of digs my diary shows we'd then follow that up with an Me 109 in the afternoon! We always did cover a lot over the weekends. They were good days and we were beginning to establish the art of what is now known as 'aviation archaeology'.

A Ju 88 which came down on 16 October 1940 at Shotley foreshore near Harwich, Essex was dug in 1984 by me and a team led by Steve Vizard. Records revealed the aircraft had flown into a balloon barrage during a mine-laying sortie. It came down at 10.20 pm. The Luftwaffe crew, U.Oberleutnant Zur See Stender, Feldwebel Heinz

Guenther, Unteroffizier Hans Martin and Obergefreiter Erhard Irrgang were all killed.

On that dig we found a MG15 machine gun in near-perfect condition. This was something we just had to save from its damp, soggy grave. The team on that memorable dig included the dedicated aviation crash researcher Philippa Hodgkiss. She was up to her eyes in all the mud that day. She's a great lady devoted to the cause. I remember she is happy to fix anything mechanical and the last time we talked, I heard she was still repairing her own motorcycles. In those days and still now it was unusual for women to get involved in aircraft recovery digs. Philippa's own 1984 dig to locate and unearth a Heinkel He 177 bomber and the acknowledgement of its one missing Luftwaffe airman Feldwebel Ernst Graf beneath what is now Lamberhurst Golf Course, is rightly well documented. This aircraft went down on 24 February 1944. Thanks to Philippa a plaque has been placed on the spot in memory of Feldwebel Graf.

I was lucky because my dear wife, Rose, was always interested in the aircraft excavation work and, like me, had a great interest in the RAF of the Second World War. She, too, was a child during the Battle of Britain and had some incredible memories, some of which I shared with you in the first part of this memoir.

In April 1971 I was pictured in the *Hampshire Telegraph* with my friend Ed Francis and other members of the Halstead War Museum crew during the muddy excavation of another Heinkel – this time at Bracklesham Bay, West Wittering in Hampshire. That day on a deserted stretch of beach we had to fight against time as the tide was about to move in and stop all of our efforts. But we never gave up. This operation was organised by Peter Diamond.

The aircraft, a Heinkel He 111 which was coded GI+DM, had been put down by its pilot on 26 August 1940 and it had been with Kampfgeschwader 55. It had been attacked by RAF fighters during a sortie to bomb Portsmouth Docks and was shot down by Sergeant Basil Whall of No. 602 Squadron at 4.30 pm that day.

At first the Heinkel squadron flew over the Channel without meeting opposition but within minutes it was intercepted by RAF squadrons from Nos. 10 and 11 Group. Apparently, the weather was cloudy although there were some bright patches over the south of England. The Luftwaffe had set out to hit several airfields including Biggin Hill, Kenley, Debden, Portsmouth, Warmwell and Hornchurch.

Spitfire pilot Sergeant Whall managed to attack two fighter Me 109s and then got into position to attack the Heinkel GI+DM. With a press of the Spitfire gun button he hit the port engine of the Heinkel.

An excerpt from Sergeant Whall's combat reports reads:

'I dived down onto the bombers, selecting one He 111 on a south-easterly course. I adopted full beam, attacked slightly in front from 1,000 feet with a two second burst and saw the port engine stop, and the aircraft dropped out of formation. I followed this down doing four more attacks with short bursts, all on the beam and saw the He 111's second engine stop and the port engine was in flames. The He 111 landed on the beach at West Wittering. I circled it and saw the Army taking prisoners.'

The pilot, Leutnant Albert Metzger, was captured wounded in the thigh but the flight engineer, Feldwebel Julius Urhahn, the observer, Unteroffizier Rolf Schandner, the radio operator, Unteroffizier Rudi Paas and the gunner, Flieger Rudolf Fessel, had all been killed. The Heinkel was a write-off. Five hundred bullet strikes were found to have hit the aircraft, many of them coming from ground troops who believed surviving crew members might torch the downed aircraft.

In 1971 we found portions of the lower gondola, a port section of a window airframe, a radiator and various fragments of shattered airframe and armour plate. The local newspaper reporter described what we were doing as a 'new scientific pastime – aircraft archaeology'. But we were in fact carrying out a serious business. We were recovering pieces of aircraft to help trace its history so that a complete dossier could be written about its part in the great German war machine of 1940. Of course, if we could we always went in on a dig with details about the RAF activity on the day of the crash and do our best to track down what Luftwaffe records were available to us at the time.

Peter Cornwell and Andy Saunders have since carried out some incredible research on this Heinkel and in 1979 managed to track down the pilot, Leutnant Metzger, who was living in Bonn in West Germany. They went to see him as there was some claim that local soldiers on watch who ran to the crash site in 1940 had shot and killed the Luftwaffe crew and in fact a war crime had been committed.

Leutnant Metzger then put the story straight and explained how his colleagues died after being hit by a spray of bullets from Sergeant Whall's Spitfire. He knew this as he had tried to speak to them after the aircraft had been hit and he was met with utter silence. Leutnant Metzger confirmed he had to struggle with the controls of the Heinkel and the aircraft was falling apart. He aimed for the stretch of beach at West Wittering and landed as a company of soldiers were involved in target practice and turned their guns towards the aircraft. By the time Leutnant Metzger was rescued from the cockpit as sole survivor of Sergeant Whall's attack, he knew his crew were already dead.

Sergeant Basil Whall flew Gladiators from 1939 and by April 1940 he was with No. 263 Squadron in Norway. After destroying several Luftwaffe aircraft at this time, he was awarded the DFM. Sergeant Whall ensured the Gladiator went down in the history books for playing its role with the RAF during the war.

By July 1940 Sergeant Whall was back in the UK and in action with No. 602 Squadron continuing his bravery in the air until 7 October 1940, when his Spitfire X4160 was damaged by a Ju 88. As he attempted a forced landing near Alfriston, Sussex, the aircraft spun and landed badly, inflicting deadly injuries upon him. Sergeant Basil Stewart Patrick Whall, DFM, died aged 22. He is buried in St Mary's Churchyard at Amersham in Buckinghamshire.

Above left: Hauptmann Wilhelm Enßlen. A veteran of the Spanish Civil War, Enßlen was shot down and killed by Johnny Kent of No. 92 Squadron on 2 November 1940. The crash site of Enßlen's Me 109, in the sands of Dymchurch Beach, was investigated in the 1980s.

Above right: Group Captain Johnny Kent, DFC*, AFC – a noble Canadian who led the highest scoring Hurricane Squadron (No. 303) of Polish pilots during the Battle of Britain.

A gun from the Harwich
Heinkel.

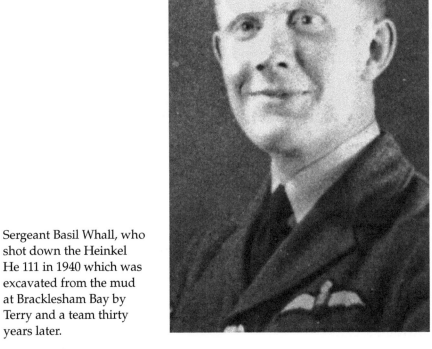

Sergeant Basil Whall, who
shot down the Heinkel
He 111 in 1940 which was
excavated from the mud
at Bracklesham Bay by
Terry and a team thirty
years later.

Race against time for buried plane

A score of men with two winch lorries and a mechanical digger arrive on a deserted stretch of beach and start digging large dark objects out of the sand.

They fight against time, for soon the tide will move in and put an end to their work.

When that happens, it's an unwelcome moment for Peter Dimond of Petersfield, for it is his idea that the men and machinery are there.

The task — to recover as much as possible of a German Heinkel III Bomber shot down on August 23, 1940.

Cranks? Certainly not, says 29-year-old Peter, a self-confessed addict of a new scientific pastime — aircraft archaeology.

"This is a serious business. All the pieces we dug up will help trace the history of this plane and eventually a complete document will be prepared about it."

With the help of about fifteen friends and half-a-dozen

experts from the Halstead War Museum, Kent, the remnants of the plane are carefully loaded up to be taken to the museum.

There a full scale operation begins to clean the parts, and almost immediately inquiries begin.

Statements are taken from eye witnesses of the crash, and all possible information is gleaned about the plane.

"The Royal Air Force supplies details, and Air Ministry and Luftwaffe records are consulted to provide the fullest possible picture," said Peter.

"They want to know details right down to the names of the crew members," he added.

Eventually a comprehensive dossier is built up describing ... lane's his... from t... its dr...

"R... us a l... about... flowr... belo...

A... lesh... co... tw... c...

The planediggers at Brackl... Small pieces of debris are p...

Object of the big dig is a Heinkel bomber similar to this one.

Above and opposite above: Cuttings from the *Hampshire Telegraph* in April 1971 reporting on Terry and the team's excavation of the Bracklesham Bay Heinkel He 111, which had been force landed by its pilot on 26 August 1940.

anical igging

Halstead the rem- ire care- taken to.

operation arts. and inquiries

ken from he crash. formation plane. orce sup- ir Minis- cords are the ful- e," said

know to the w mem-

mprehen- up des-

The planediggers at Bracklesham Bay. A mechanical digger helps to remove tons of sand burying the bomber. Small pieces of debris are piled on one side: they are pieces of the jigsaw experts at a war museum will be trying to fit together.

Members of the team look through the wreckage that was recovered from the crash site of the Bracklesham Bay Heinkel He 111.

163

Chapter 11

SPITFIRES AND HURRICANES

WHENEVER I can, I try and visit an airfield where I can see a Spitfire in flight. Even after all these years I find the whole experience exhilarating. Who doesn't love the sound of the Merlin engine as it speeds this beautiful little fighter through the sky, above and around the clouds? Spinning out loops, victory rolls, stylishly revealing all as supreme commander of the air. Such a sight sends a chill of recognition for times gone by.

I savour the liberty it represents, and I am proud to know and watch such a legend up high where it belongs – in flight and full of purpose. I know the Spitfire more intimately than most. I'd seen them sad and lost, their hearts exposed, longing for me to find them. Crumpled? Yes. Mangled and burned? Yes – and yet still glorious to know and uncover, and picture as they were at the height of their beauty. Show me any piece of a Spitfire and I am sure to recognise what it is, what it was for and where it belonged on the aircraft. I know every inch of one you see, after removing a fair few from the sodden ground.

Nobody can argue when I say a Spitfire is an enduring legend and with that comes a raft of love and respect from this boy of the Battle of Britain. We all need to know Goddesses exist; yes? And like all deities, I think most of them fly in one way or another.

The Spitfire was being manufactured in the thousands during the war. Records show 20,351 to be precise, compared to the seventy or so worldwide flying in 2017. Supermarine Vickers, created by pioneers like Noel Pemberton-Billing, Reginald Mitchell (who designed the Spitfire) and Joe Smith, had its headquarters at Woolston, near Southampton. Its big factories at Castle Bromwich in Birmingham and Southampton were supported by smaller construction plants dotted secretly around Britain.

The development of this elegant little aircraft with its top speeds of 370-plus mph continued throughout the conflict and it proved especially effective as a backup support to the sturdy and faithful Hawker Hurricane during the Battle of Britain. This brings me to point out why at least sixty per cent of my work as an aviation archaeologist has been about recovering Hurricanes. The reason being, there were just more of them about in 1940. (By the end of the war, a little more than 14,000 of this heroic little aircraft designed by Sydney Camm in 1935 had been built.) I probably found and helped recover at least 600 of them from the fields, woods and gardens of the South East.

During the Battle of France, records from ten days in the month of May 1940 show that Hurricane pilots logged 499 kills and 123 probables. (However, German records charting this time of the conflict are not quite so boisterous.) But if British RAF archives are correct then that's going some, with the Hurricane showing just what it is made of in the heat of aerial conflict.

One of the most famous Hurricane pilots has to be Group Captain Peter Wooldridge Townsend, CVO, DSO, DFC* (1914 – 1995), who in 1940 was commanding officer of No. 85 Squadron. On 31 August 1940 Squadron Leader Townsend was shot down and wounded in the left foot during a dogfight with Me 110s over Tonbridge, Kent. A cannon shell ripped through the glycol tank of his Hurricane P3166 and exploded in the cockpit. He baled out and landed at Cranbrook Road, Hawkhurst and as the Hurricane came in, it flipped so that it was upside down and was deemed by the RAF a 'write-off'. The heroic Townsend was admitted to Hawkhurst Cottage Hospital.

Almost thirty years later, on a warm Sunday in August 1969, Ken Anscombe collected me and told me we were going to Bedgebury Forest near Goudhurst, Kent (now known as Bedgebury National Pinetum) as there was 'something very interesting there'. I was delighted to hear from him. I was far more interested in finding Battle of Britain aircraft than listening to hip bands of the day.

Well, when we got to the site of Group Captain Townsend's Hurricane, I told Ken I would be surprised if we found much of it, especially as I had learned from eyewitnesses some months before that souvenir hunters had already raked over the site. But as I searched and dug around, I managed to discover a battery casing still with its cardboard cover on and there were still remnants about, just inches from the surface of the forest floor. Knowing I was hunting for pieces of an aircraft flown by Townsend made all the difference. That was indeed provenance!

I recall how in the late 1960s Bedgebury Forest was still a tree plantation and there were these fire breaks which were roadways between the saplings. I think the first diggers on the site must have somehow got a lorry down there and chucked the whole lot of the Hurricane on it. But I still managed to find a few artefacts – pieces of Perspex, nuts and bolts and fragments of fuselage. Remember, a Hurricane contains a lot of wood and canvas, which over time don't survive as well as metal. I've heard from a lot of Second World War pilots about how it was always best to be in a wooden aircraft if you were going to crash as it absorbed the impact and protected the aircrew far better than metal fuselages ever would.

'Wood is very forgiving,' I was told by Battle of Britain pilot Group Captain Tom Gleave, CBE, (who once came out on a dig for his own crashed Hurricane with me – a wonderful experience I have described beside a poignant photograph in this book). His fellow member of the hallowed 'Few', Peter Townsend, was born in Burma and was one of seven children. Townsend's flying career was to be greatly admired and, as with so many young aviators of the time, so was his sincere bravery in the skies. It's little wonder that by 1947, HRH Princess Margaret had fallen in love with this dashing young aviator – a handsome high-achiever always keen to follow his heart.

By 1952 he obtained a divorce from his first wife (Rosemary Pawle) perhaps to make himself available to wed his royal love. But in high-profile romantic affairs there's not always a happy ending. HM The Queen, as the Church of England's Supreme Governor, allegedly ruled that her sister, Princess Margaret, was not allowed to marry a divorced man. Both HM the Queen and Princess Margaret had known Townsend since 1944 when he was appointed as Equerry to their father, King George VI. From 1952 – 1953 the Battle of Britain ace was royal aide to the newly-crowned young monarch HM Queen Elizabeth II and her mother, Queen Elizabeth, The Queen Mother.

By the summer of 1953 he had been appointed Air Attaché in Brussels and retired from the RAF in 1956. Three years later Townsend married a Belgian woman named Marie-Luce Jamagne and the newlyweds moved to France. His new life as a writer proved fruitful, and his work as aviation consultant on the film *Battle of Britain* (released in 1969) provided authenticity to the script and Guy Hamilton's dramatic directing.

Of course, Townsend's aviation career should not be buried or forgotten beneath the schmaltz of his love life involving HRH Princess Margaret and the emotional declarations made within the walls of

Windsor Castle which have become embedded in popular folklore. It's important to remember social values of the time were different to those of today and yet historians will always want to set themselves up as judge and jury about any socially notable situation which I'd argue isn't the right attitude at all.

In 1940 during his RAF service Townsend claimed three He 111s destroyed on 22 February and 8 April, and on 10 April he damaged another. He was awarded the DFC (gazetted 30 April 1940). On 23 May he was posted to Debden to command No. 85 Squadron. On 11 July reports came in that he had been shot down into the sea three miles off Southwold during an attack on a Do 17, in Hurricane P2716. He was rescued by *Cap Finisterre*, which took him to Harwich. The Do 17 did not get off lightly and was reported as 'damaged'. Townsend received a 'mention' in Despatches (gazetted on 11 July 1940).

On 11 August he destroyed a Do 17 and damaged an Me 110 and on 18 August he destroyed two Me 109s and an Me 110, on 26 August he shared in the destruction of two Do 17s, on 28 and 29 August he destroyed two Me 109s, on 30 August he damaged an Me 110 and on 31 August he probably destroyed an Me 109. It was this day the Luftwaffe stopped his chances of any more combat for a while as an Me 110 scored a direct hit on his Hurricane, P3166, which crashed at Bedgebury Park, near Badgers Oak, Goudhurst.

Townsend was awarded a 'Bar' to the DFC (gazetted 6 September 1940) and rejoined No. 85 Squadron at Church Fenton from sick leave on 21 September. After the Battle of Britain No. 85 Squadron went over to night fighting. From then on and until February 1944 when he joined the royal household, Group Captain Peter Townsend continued to fly successfully into combat against the enemy Luftwaffe.

I will never forget one day in the 1960s when I was walking along Biggin Hill High Street and suddenly this fancy sports car pulled up alongside of me. The driver leant over and asked: 'Can you tell me the way to London?' – and it was him – Group Captain Peter Townsend!

I would have recognised him anywhere, as by then he'd appeared in many a national newspaper, and I'd seen his face in my books about the RAF. (During his time as CO of No. 85 Squadron in 1940 he had been based at Croydon.) Anyway, I pointed him the right direction and supplied him with quite a detailed route and map and he thanked me profusely and sped off. Afterwards I just had to laugh. I thought to myself, 'How on earth did you fly a Hurricane across the skies of the South East and yet managed to get lost driving a car to London?!' It was a shame I didn't have the foresight to jump in that car with him and join him for a chat during the journey – a trip which no doubt would have proved remarkably insightful.

I was to be deeply honoured in the early autumn of 2015 when I met HRH Prince Michael of Kent – a royal friend of Group Captain Townsend. Prince Michael was visiting a local museum at the time – a place to which I had loaned a small collection of artefacts from Group Captain Townsend's Hurricane that I found back in 1969. The Prince stopped and looked at the items and told the assembled party he had known Peter Townsend quite well. I only wish I'd had more of a chance to talk to HRH about the dig, as I believe he would have liked to hear more from a pioneer of aviation archaeology who had spent more than fifty genuine years of his life preserving the memory of 'The Few'.

Finding and recovering aircraft involved in one of the bloodiest aerial conflicts the world has ever known continues to dominate my thoughts. Everything it stands and stood for is at stake and archaeologically it must be respected and taken as seriously as any Roman ruin or Egyptian tomb ever was. And, therefore, speaking of historical importance, I must return to the Spitfire and conclude how many have I recovered. A hundred or so according to my diary.

What I will never forget is the gallantry of the United States Air Force who came to help us in 1982 when we located the engine of Spitfire R6779 flown by a Canadian Pilot Officer – George Henry Corbett – who was shot down and killed on 8 October 1940.

When we located the site and got to the marshes at Upchurch near Chatham, Kent, we at first approached the RAF for help removing the engine which weighed several tonnes. We needed it lifted out as it was so deep in the mud. There was no way we could haul it up with the machinery we had. Our request was turned down so we contacted the USAF next, who said cheerily, 'No problem,' and immediately sent in a 'Jolly Green Giant' helicopter.

Well, not only did these guys remove the engine for us, they got the propeller out, too – a massive artefact which weighs a ton! When the 'Jolly Green Giant' arrived, they told us to stay out of the hole. They put one American airman down in the mud because there was a 200mph down-draft and he managed to strap the massive engine up and hoist the strap to a hook dangling from the helicopter. Within a minute or two they had put the mighty old Merlin engine on the road and waved us goodbye with a 'Cheerio lads!'

They were fantastic and completely understood why we had to get the helicopter to help us. The saltings in that area are little islands and we needed a helicopter – any heavy vehicle would sink for sure. An individual called Dave Smith turned up soon afterwards and told me it had taken him fourteen years to find that engine. I was pleased to tell him we'd found it in half an hour! That day I was in the excavation team with Steve Vizard and a team from the Tangmere Museum in West Sussex, where the engine and prop are now on display.

It is amazing when I look back on that day, as without the assistance of that helicopter and its crew, this incredible artefact of the Battle of Britain would still be deep down in the mud flats of Upchurch.

When I first began to look into the crash site of Pilot Officer Corbett of No. 66 Squadron I was struck by the affection with which he is held by the villagers of Upchurch and of course his family in Canada. On the day of his death, No. 66 Squadron was based at RAF Gravesend.

The last time I looked, his grave in the village church of St Mary was in good condition and someone had placed flowers by the headstone.

Pilot Officer Corbett had British parents who in 1914 moved to Canada, where he was born in 1919. They then moved to Oak Bay, British Columbia and as a boy, George was avidly interested in aircraft. During a family break in England he applied to join the de Havilland School of Aeronautical Design in Hatfield and got in. By 1937 he had joined the RAFVR.

When war was declared on 3 September 1939 the young pilot was visiting his family back in British Columbia. Within a week he was back in Britain and had been posted to No. 66 Squadron to fly Spitfires from RAF Coltishall, Norfolk.

An article by Major William March, written on the 75th Anniversary of the Battle of Britain in 2015, reads:

'Although P/O Corbett participated in a number of combat patrols, his first true combat experience came on 9 September 1940. After already damaging an Me 109, he was positioning his aircraft for a rear attack on a bomber when he was bounced by three German fighters. With the cockpit filling with smoke and the controls jammed, he found himself in a severely damaged, uncontrolled aircraft plummeting toward the ground in a tight spiral dive. At 12,000 feet (3,658 metres), he bailed out, suffering a slight injury in the process.

Corbett quickly returned to the fray, and on 27 September he and his squadron mates intercepted German bombers attacking London. In the midst of heavy British defensive fire from anti-aircraft guns below, he got a quick burst into one bomber before breaking off the attack and leaving the damaged enemy aircraft to other RAF fighters. He then selected a lone Junkers 88 as his next target, closed to within yards of the German aircraft, and opened fired. The enemy aircraft fell away, its port engine burning fiercely, but the smoke was so thick that Corbett had to break off the attack.

He had little time to enjoy his victory because his Spitfire was damaged by friendly fire when an artillery shell burst nearby, destroying one elevator and riddling the fuselage and starboard wing with shrapnel. He skilfully executed a forced landing in the London district of Orpington, emerging from his damaged but repairable Spitfire with a new-found respect for anti-aircraft gunners and a Junkers 88 claimed as destroyed. Two London bobbies who came to his assistance had witnessed the combat, and confirmed Corbett's claim.

More combat followed, but this young man who had survived being shot down twice would not be so lucky the third time. On 8 October 1940 Pilot Officer Corbett, who was wearing a new watch sent to him by his parents as a 21st birthday gift, was surprised by a large number of Messerschmitt 109s. In a slashing attack, Corbett and No. 66 Squadron pilot pal 23-year-old Sergeant Rufus Ward were shot down near Bayford Marches, Upchurch; neither pilot survived. Sergeant Ward's Spitfire N3043 crashed in Valley View Road, Borstal, near Rochester.

P/O Corbett's mother, Mabel, received a letter from her son which tried to comfort his family's fears that made light of his two earlier brushes with death, and explained the importance of what he was part of. Corbett wrote, "Having got out OK, my confidence has tremendously increased and I want you to be confident also. The Jerries are a long way from getting supremacy in the air, and until they get it, there'll be no invasion."'

The memories of eyewitnesses have always played a major role when it came to pinpointing crash sites. Reverend William Joseph Wright was at his St. Margaret of Antioch Church nearby when he saw the dogfight in the skies which led to the death of Pilot Officer Corbett. It was Reverend Wright who stood horrified at the sight of the young pilot and his Spitfire tearing down into the earth. He ran over to the smoking, abused wreckage, hoping to provide assistance. But it was clear, due to the bullet damage around the cockpit, that George Corbett had been killed instantly before the crash. Reverend Wright offered prayers and a blessing, and stayed with the body of the young pilot until he was recovered. His parachute was used as a shroud.

Back in Pilot Officer Corbett's home town of Oak Bay, Canada and, in a cruel twist of fate his mother, Mabel, having only just read her son's optimistic letter of days before, received an official notice to inform her he had in fact been killed. This heroic young man was among so many whose sacrifice had truly touched people on two continents.

In Canada, his family commissioned a stained-glass window in St. Mary the Virgin Anglican church in Oak Bay. The window depicts Pilot Officer Corbett in his RAF uniform. He wears a life preserver, clutches a flying helmet and earphones, and gazes upward at an image depicting the Ascension, when, the Bible teaches, Jesus rose to Heaven following his crucifixion. Amid a number of impressive stained-glass windows, this one stands out because it is the most modern and because it is the only window dedicated to a member of the local community. On the Sunday closest to Battle of Britain Day (15 September), a single rose is placed beneath Pilot Officer Corbett's window.

Far away, in St. Mary the Virgin churchyard at Upchurch, Kent, where Pilot Officer Corbett is buried, members of the local community regularly tend to the grave of the young Canadian who gave his life for our liberty. One resident said: 'I walked through the churchyard yesterday and I saw another resident standing beside the grave talking to this young hero of the Battle of Britain. This person explained how he visited the grave often... just for a chat. "Please don't think I am mad," he said, "I just enjoy my visits."'

In 1981 a rededication service was held in Upchurch, at which members of the Corbett family attended a ceremony with the RAF. Special guest that day was Dunkirk and Battle of Britain pilot, Wing Commander Robert Stanford Tuck, DSO, DFC**.

My link to Pilot Officer Corbett doesn't stop at Upchurch, as on 9 September 1940 he baled out of Spitfire N3049, which was seen by eyewitnesses to crash into a field at Cowden, near Sevenoaks, Kent. The young pilot escaped with minor injuries but the Spitfire smashed through the earth and until this day, that's where it remains. I joined Steve Vizard in the 1980s to look for the crash site. Well, we searched for hours, first with a metal detector, going over every inch but found nothing. Sometimes it happens like that. That Spitfire is still on my list to find one day.

One summer around 1976 I received a call about a Spitfire which on 27 November 1940 crashed and sunk in the mud at Blacketts Marshes in Essex. The wreck had been reported by a local person who told me how to locate the aircraft which was flown at the time of its demise by Pilot Officer Peter Chesters of No. 74 Squadron.

While the Battle of Britain officially came to an end on 31 October 1940, it's important to point out the Luftwaffe didn't just disappear. Attacks on Kent, Sussex, Hampshire and Surrey airfields and factories just grew less frequent as they started fully focusing on London and the major cities, further justifying the importance of the RAF's role to try and keep the Germans out of British skies altogether at all costs.

When Pilot Officer Chesters in Spitfire P7306 flew into trouble on 27 November, he was over the Isle of Sheppey at 25,000 feet to investigate anti-aircraft bursts. Suddenly he spotted a pair of Me 109s heading towards the south.

No. 74 Squadron led by Squadron Leader Sailor Malan stormed after the German fighter aircraft and within fifty yards took them on. One Me 109 fell apart and scattered in pieces into the sea and the other Me 109 was reported to be on fire. It was during this deadly skirmish over Chatham, that Pilot Officer Chesters' Spitfire P7306 was hit, badly damaging his controls. Despite suffering wounds and burns to his leg, the 21-year-old pilot remained with the crippled Spitfire until he was clear of the built-up areas beneath him. Finally, he was able to jump clear and float down via parachute only to land in thick mud at Conyer Creek, Faversham, Kent. At this point the weight of his clothing and a thick Mae West life-jacket caused him to start sinking. It was thanks to a local resident named Bob Hodges, who ran over to rescue Pilot Officer Chesters and pull him from the lethal and merciless swamp, that he survived.

The story is well known among Battle of Britain historians of how a letter 'from the people of Conyer' was sent to No. 74 Squadron about the young pilot who had saved their village. Pilot Officer Chesters was presented with the letter as he recuperated in hospital. The community thanked the young aviator for steering the crippled Spitfire away from their homes. The aircraft was reported as plummeting into the Essex marshes at 700mph – no homes or local factory would have withstood the impact of such rapidly descending metal ball of flames.

Not long after reading the letter, Pilot Officer Chesters, touched by the villagers' gratitude, sent Bob Hodges a watch bearing the inscription, 'R. Hodges. With grateful appreciation, Pilot Officer Chesters, 27.11.40.'

By this time Chesters, with his baby face and youthful energies, had become something of a character in the squadron. On 27 October

1940 he shot down an Me 109, which left its Luftwaffe pilot Feldwebel Schieverhofer no option but to force-land at Penshurst, Kent. Chesters was flying as Yellow 4 in Spitfire P7494 at the time. His combat report states:

'The enemy aircraft which I attacked was diving down to the clouds and I followed him. He saw me and tried to get on my tail, I managed to turn inside him and put a burst into his engine causing it to stop. I jockeyed him earthwards, and he landed on Penshurst Aerodrome with his wheels in the "up" position. I fired two three-second bursts at 150 yards. As I did not know my position and was short of petrol, I landed on the same aerodrome. This engagement took place at 3000ft.'

Almost sixty years later, Chesters' friend, Wing Commander John Freeborn, DFC, revealed the following:

'After shooting down the Me 109 at Penshurst, Peter landed beside the aircraft and dragged the German pilot from his cockpit, who promptly spat in Peter's face! A fistfight started with Peter and the Luftwaffe pilot swearing at each other in German. It was only broken up by the arrival of a police officer, soldier and someone from the ARP. Peter managed to pull off the Iron Cross from the pilot's jacket as a souvenir but was made to return it by the policeman. Peter demanded a trophy and took the first aid kit from the cockpit of the 109, which he kept in his Spitfire from then on.'

What an extraordinary tale for the archives. The Me 109E (Werk Nummer 3525) was from 3/JG52 flown by Feldwebel Lothar Schieverhofer, who was reported as missing at first, later being confirmed as a prisoner of war.

Sadly, the boisterous young Chesters from Thorpe Bay, Essex, who enjoyed taking part in his fair share of pranks among his RAF acquaintances and had confidently achieved several notable victories in aerial combat, died within a few months of the Conyer incident.

On 10 April 1941 he was in one of twelve Spitfires ordered to patrol the Folkestone area of Kent. Pilot Officer Chesters was at the controls of Spitfire P7854 when a number of Me 109s were seen escorting bombers on their way to strike Canterbury. No. 74 Squadron dived on them and Pilot Officer Chesters engaged an Me 109E (5670) from the 2nd Staffel of Jagdgeswader 51, ('Black 8') piloted by Feldwebel Friedrich Moeller.

The feisty Chesters shot it down and the Me 109 crashed at Frost Farm, St Nicholas at Wade, Kent. Locals found Feldwebel Moeller dead at the scene.

Pilot Officer Peter Chesters' exhilaration over this victory was not to last long, however, as within minutes of his opponent's demise he attempted a forbidden victory roll in celebration, but misjudged the height of his Spitfire and crashed horribly into the parade ground at Manston. He was killed instantly.

More than thirty years later, as I accompanied the big digging machine on its journey towards Blacketts Marshes to find Pilot Officer Chesters' Spitfire that went down on 27 November 1940, I had no knowledge about his adventures. All I knew was that the pilot had baled out and it was going to be 'pretty straight-forward' to dig!

Well how wrong can a person be? The digger went down the huge hole it had dug as we searched for the Merlin engine and got stuck. When parts of the wreckage did come out, they left the mud quite quickly with a sucking noise like bad teeth being pulled! We dug down to about fifteen feet and got the wreckage out with just the engine left down in the crater we'd made.

As we started to pull up the mighty old Merlin, the digger started to slide into the hole so the operator had to stop the engine and put the arm on the machine right out to stop the whole digger going right down into the abyss! Then it was well and truly stuck, and we just couldn't get it out. The operator tried everything... No, still wedged firm. So we got another digger out there the next day to pull him out and he had no success either. So eventually we got this massive D8 bulldozer, a huge piece of machinery which hooked on the diggers and managed to pull them out one at a time.

The sticky dramas surrounding this Spitfire dig made me wonder if the spirit of Pilot Officer Chesters was having a joke at our expense! I can hardly be blamed for thinking this in hindsight, having since read about his lively character and the stories about his antics from his friends who survived the war.

Meanwhile, we had to leave that Merlin engine in the end. The hole was full of what at first we thought was water but turned out to be gallons of highly flammable fuel which had leaked out from the aircraft. I remember one person wanted me to get back down the hole to fill a petrol can for him so he could say he had some Battle of Britain aviation fuel! Everyone was told to stop smoking and not to light any matches. By this time, I had a complete lorry-load of wreckage to haul away.

The Merlin engine which was choked up with mud, grass and the like was later taken away by a member of staff from the local garage who came along and somehow removed it and took it to his premises, where he had it on show for decades. When he became ill, he presented it to a museum.

So where did all the aircraft wreckage itself go? Well, this is the question I have asked myself about many digging experiences over the years. For Pilot Officer Chesters' Spitfire, I had a 7-tonne lorry loaded from front to back, piled 5-foot high with wreckage and artefacts. I drove it off after the dig and took it to a yard in Gravesend belonging to one of the men on the digging team. This man is no longer with us so I am unable to quiz him about the finds from that Spitfire. I do know, however, that there was another person around at the time who wanted to build a sculpture and create a memorial of Battle of Britain aircraft. He wanted all the pieces of recovered aircraft he could lay his hands on to melt them down. I know he had a lot of stuff. I can't think where else it could be.

I never heard any more about this project. Shame, as I thought it was a good idea at the time. But the sad fact remains: there were a lot of original Battle of Britain Spitfire bits that just disappeared without a trace.

Pilot Officer George Henry Corbett, who was shot down and killed on 8 October 1940.

175

Two of the team examine the damp and sodden marshes of Upchurch in Kent in which the engine of a Spitfire flown by Pilot Officer George Corbett had been buried for almost forty years.

Above: The engine hangs from the rope before being gently placed on dry land.

Left: The mud-caked Merlin which was pulled out of the marshland by a USAF 'Jolly Green Giant' helicopter.

Terry, just visible on the right, watches the helicopter moving in to assist with the recovery of the engine.

Despite appallingly wet and atrociously muddy conditions, the team achieve their aim and the Merlin which powered a legendary Spitfire during the Battle of Britain was hauled back into the daylight.

Feldwebel Lothar
Schieverhofer.

Group captain Peter Townsend dismounts from his Hurricane.

Above and below: The hunt is on for the remains of an Me 109 which crashed at Frost Farm, St Nicholas-at-Wade near Rochester, Kent on 10 April 1941. The pilot who was found dead at the scene at the time was Feldwebel Friedrich Moeller of Jagdegeschwader 51.

Chapter 12

MUD, GLORIOUS MUD

WHILE most of us discuss the weather as general chit-chat, the subject became a major issue for us aircraft archaeologists of the early days. Especially when we knew we were up against storms, snow blizzards, ice, rising tides and lashing rain.

Some might argue our dedication in terrible conditions to the job of finding the stricken aircraft flown by our heroes was verging on lunacy but I believe it made the experience all the more rewarding. To know we'd battled the elements, scored a victory and completed our mission – against the odds. The weather was NOT going to stop us. That was a fact.

Indeed, one look at the photographs of us at Portsmouth Harbour on a winter's day in the late 1970s show that despite our rain-soaked faces and anguished expressions, there was a glint of determination in everyone's eyes.

It was always exciting to hunt for a Luftwaffe aircraft, as contrary to wartime propaganda, there were far more British aircraft that went into the ground. My diver acquaintance Brian Oliver once told me he'd seen a great deal of stricken Luftwaffe aircraft sitting on the bottom of British waters, especially Heinkel He 111s and Dornier Do 17s. Luftwaffe crews of the war always attempted a smooth ditch into the sea if their aircraft was in trouble in the hope they would be picked up and rescued. Quite rightly none of them fancied burning to death.

It is important to point out that I treat the Luftwaffe crash sites with the same respect as I do those of the RAF. The Luftwaffe were carrying out their orders, too and more than 2,000 German aircrew were killed in action in 1940 alone. The figure for RAF aircrews of that brutal year stands at a little more than 500.

It was my friend Andy Saunders, who I'd coached on his first-ever dig, who asked me to join him on a particularly memorable adventure – the search for a Junkers Ju 88A-1 (4078) which had gone down in the harbour on Monday, 12 August at 12.10 pm.

The aircraft of 8./KG51 failed to return from operations over South East England having had its tail shot off by anti-aircraft fire from a French gunnery-training ship by the name of *Courbet*. Seriously damaged, this Ju 88 broke up and its crew of Oberleutnant Otto Stärk, Unteroffizier Heinz Droese, and Oberleutnant Eberhard Wildermuth successfully baled out and were taken prisoner. Reports reveal their comrade Offizier Konrad Rösch was noted as missing.

Almost forty years later the dig for that Ju 88 was wild! The rain was lashing down in buckets and was hitting my face so hard I could hardly see. As the photographs show, the excavation was tough as the weather beat against us for most of the day. The dig itself was like fishing in a way. The big dredging machine was on the end of the pier and lowered down this giant clamp which consisted of two huge metal buckets each side.

Without this machine and its amazing driver we'd never have reached any part of that aircraft. It managed to locate and gently bring up to the shore some lovely artefacts, including bomb racks, as seen in the 2nd image at the end of this chapter, and a propeller assembly.

The crew, which consisted of Andy Saunders, Chris Bennett, Malcolm Pettit, Nigel Parker, Steve Vizard, Stevie Hall and myself, were thrilled to find a pedal control lever, parachute silk and shroud lines, which had been sitting on the bottom of the harbour until we came along to rescue these important artefacts from their watery grave.

I remember, Andy went out alone in low tide in a small boat and found a piece of a cockpit, a pair of binoculars, a compass and a flare pistol. I believe these artefacts later went on display at Tangmere Aviation Museum.

Another difficult excavation was a wet, sodden, knee-deep mud-squelching hunt just off Bee Ness Jetty on the Isle of Grain in Kent for Spitfire R6642, which had been shot down on 15 October 1940 by Me 109s.

The pilot was amazing 22-year-old John Lund, an Oxford history scholar and a former member of the University Air Squadron. Lund had proved a courageous fighter pilot and joined No. 611 Squadron on 23 June 1940. Within days he shared in the destruction of a Do 17 and another on 21 August.

It was while serving with No. 92 Squadron at Biggin Hill that Pilot Officer Lund encountered the might of the Me 109s on 15 October and had no option but to bale out of his Spitfire, which went down into the waters off Bee Ness Jetty. Lund was picked up from the choppy waters of the River Medway by HMS *Nysan* and went on to damage an Me 109 on 1 December 1940.

Sadly, in October 1941, having survived the brutalities of the Battle of Britain, he was shot down by Fw 190s as he was returning from special operations in Northern France. His aircraft went down over the Channel into the sea and he was reported as missing.

Finding a Spitfire once flown by this hero became imperative to many of us archaeologists, including Steve Vizard, who is seen in the photographs wading through deep, heavy mud on his way to the crash site at Bee Ness Jetty.

We retrieved some incredible pieces of the aircraft from this muddy excavation, including the plate from the Merlin engine which now forms a special part of my own small collection. It still makes me proud to think I helped recover an artefact which represented a time when, as Churchill said: 'Never before in the field of human conflict has so much been owed by so many to so few.'

More often than not at harsh crash sites like Portsmouth Harbour and Bee Ness Jetty we needed the help of heavy machinery, which was exactly the case when we went out to find and excavate Hurricane V6601, which was flown by Cambridge scholar, and pre-war aviator and businessman Flying Officer James Alan MacDonald Henderson.

As a hero of No. 257 Squadron, Flying Officer Henderson was in combat over the Essex marshes on 31 August 1940, when having already destroyed two Me 110s, his own Hurricane had a direct hit in the petrol tank. Realising this had robbed the aircraft of all power, he baled out, suffering from burns and other serious injuries. A quick rescue meant a speedy journey to Brightlingsea Naval Hospital, where he stayed until 10 September, followed by further convalescence at RAF Hospital Torbay.

His doting wife was American socialite Louise Lyman, who he had married in 1937.

Sadly in 1940, having recovered physically from his injuries, medics decided Flying Officer Henderson was not fit to fly operationally and he was posted to Canada, where he served with Ferry Command. Rising to the rank of Flight Lieutenant, he was released from the RAF in 1946 and later died at the age of 78.

Digging his Battle of Britain Hurricane from the boggy marshland just outside Clacton-on-Sea, Essex, was a massive challenge, as it involved some serious specialist machinery. I recall how the digger crew and us archaeologists had to place great mats over the mud, which enabled the machinery to move forward and reach the exact area of the site where the majority of the aircraft wreckage could be found deep beneath the surface.

There was a lot of logistical planning with this dig, especially as the conditions were so adverse. We were so lucky, as there was an individual out in the marshes with a digger, carrying out some drainage work and he was more than happy to help us. Eventually we pinpointed the exact location, which was by a great mound of rocks by the sea defence.

My friend Richard Walker had organised this one, and from a great deep pit created by the heavy plant, we managed to find some incredible artefacts. It made me realise that no two digs were ever the same and as ever it was a huge learning experience each time we came across an item.

I still have the gun mounts I found that came from this beautiful Hurricane and once we had winched up the incredible Merlin engine from the mud, it was cleaned up and for many years it was in the care of Gordon Ramsey in his private collection.

As I have mentioned, respect was owed at all times to all aircrews, including that of the Luftwaffe who had died carrying out the orders of their bombastic leader, Hermann Goering. It was a warm day in late spring in the late 1970s when I arrived at a sloping field in Rotherfield, East Sussex with Steve Vizard, Pat Burgess, Andy Saunders, Mark Kirby, Steve Hale, Peter Diamond and an eyewitness who saw the crash.

We had been reliably informed that this was the place where highly decorated Luftwaffe ace Gruppenkommandeur Walter Rubensdörffer (posthumously awarded the Knight's Cross of the Iron Cross) and his radio operator Obergefreiter Ludwig Kretzer had been killed as their badly shot up and burning Me 110 crashed to the ground. Of course, we had no idea what might be left of the aircraft in that field.

Rubensdörffer and Kretzer, of Erprobungsgruppe 210, died on 15 August 1940, having mistakenly bombed Croydon Airfield instead of the intended target Kenley Aerodrome. On this date, KG1 and KG2 of the Luftwaffe spread across the skies of South East England like clusters of black locusts dropping tonnes of bombs on Kent, Sussex and the Isle of Wight, including Hawkinge Airfield, Maidstone, Dover,

Rye, Portland and CHL radar systems. The RAF scrambled ardently into action and Nos. 111 and 32 Squadron in Hawker Hurricanes met their foe.

Former Spanish Civil War Condor pilot Gruppenkommandeur Rubensdörffer was already a hero of the Luftwaffe and had led many successful raids. On August 15, however, he faced a big decision, which ended catastrophically. As he flew towards London that summer's evening around 6.30 pm, he knew he had missed an important rendezvous with his Me 109 escort from JG 52 over France. Should he carry on without essential backup, and assist the Dornier aircrews who had flown on ahead, or should he abandon his orders to attack Kenley Aerodrome?

The 30-year-old Swiss-born Rubensdörffer, ever loyal to his men, flew on towards his target but attempted to confuse the RAF by making a wide sweep over Sevenoaks which would bring him high up over Kenley from the north. Just a minute before 7.00 pm the bombs from his Me 110 were dropped, but he'd missed Kenley by some distance, as it was the buildings of Croydon Airfield which took the hit. But with his Erprobungsgruppe 210 known for its penchant for destroying buildings as well as runways, sixty-eight people were killed including six servicemen and 192 were injured. Croydon Airfield was a mess of black smoke and hell, and had taken the hit he meant for Kenley. Ironically, they were in fact defying Hitler's orders by attacking airfields too close to London. Mistakes were made by the Dornier group, too, who hit West Malling in Kent instead of Biggin Hill.

Rubensdörffer and Kretzer, having made their own blunder, were then set on by No. 111 Squadron led by long-serving RAF pilot Squadron Leader John Marlow Thompson. By 15 August 1940 Thompson had already experienced the might of the Luftwaffe and had in the January of that year destroyed an Me 110, shared in the destruction of an Hs 126 and then shot down an He 111. It was at this time his Hurricane L1733 was hit and he crash landed in a field. He was fortunate enough to be helped by British soldiers and got a ship back to England from Boulogne. He was then given command of No. 111 Squadron on 24 January 1940.

Leading Battle of Britain historian and committee member of the London Battle of Britain Memorial Edward McManus writes: 'Under Thompson's command the feats of No. 111 Squadron against heavy odds were quite spectacular. This had much to do with his own philosophy of taking the enemy head on. Sometimes a whole flight would attack in line abreast, guns blazing. One of its pilots, Flying

Officer Henry Michael Ferriss, shot down eight German aircraft in three sorties, a feat which can seldom have been equalled.' Sadly, on 16 August 1940 Ferriss was killed after colliding head on with a Dornier 17. His Hurricane crashed at Sheephurst Farm, Marden near Tonbridge, Kent and the Do 17 crashed at Moatlands, Benchley, Paddock Wood.

As Squadron Leader Thompson and his pilots rounded on the Luftwaffe invaders on 15 August, they were joined by No. 32 Squadron from Biggin Hill. The Germans made desperate attempts to fly into cloud cover and head south but Thompson gave chase and within a minute or so, his guns scored a direct hit on Rubensdörffer and Kretzer's Me 110 over Rotherfield. Thompson recalled seeing a trail of fire in the evening sky as the aircraft carrying some of Germany's finest aircrew plummeted towards the countryside of Rotherfield. Initially, both men were buried in Tunbridge Wells but they were later reburied with honours at Cannock Chase Military Cemetery.

Thompson, who was awarded the DFC for his outstanding bravery throughout the Battle of Britain, served a long and successful career in the RAF and retired in 1966 with the rank of air commodore and was made a CBE.

By the end of such a heavy day of battle, 15 August 1940 proved a big turning point for RAF Fighter Command Air Chief Marshal Hugh Dowding. For he now realised the Germans could not detect any major failings or weaknesses in Britain's air defences and was amazed by the wasted energies the Luftwaffe had expended on small and arguably insignificant airfields. Dowding noted that day how nearly fifty German aircraft had been destroyed during raids on areas which had no real importance in the realms of defence.

Almost forty years later, when we arrived at the place the Rubensdörffer Me 110 went down, we did find some interesting artefacts, including a lot of cannon shells by the hedge – in fact they were all over the field. We had known beforehand we would never get a digger there on that slope, so we ploughed on the best we could with metal detectors and shovels. I know a pistol and a penknife were among the items recovered.

There were many small fragments of the aircraft scattered far and wide that day. We found what we could and realised the impact of the crash. Combined with the fire caused by Thompson's furious Hurricane guns, it meant destruction all around. We were lucky to find what we did, since they were significant and important artefacts of the Battle of Britain.

Terry defies the wet conditions during the Ju 88 dig in Portsmouth Harbour.

Some of the artefacts recovered from the crash site in Portsmouth Harbour.

A piece of the compass once used by the crew of the stricken Ju 88.

A data plate on a large section of the Ju 88 excavated from Portsmouth Harbour in the late 1970s.

Members of the team begin to sort through the artefacts recovered in Portsmouth Harbour.

Locating the crash site of Pilot Officer John Lund's Spitfire in grim conditions near the Bee Ness Jetty on the Isle of Grain in Kent.

Down in the depths of the mud, members of the excavation team, including Steve Vizard, (left) unearth a piece of Lund's Spitfire.

Above: Pilot Officer John Lund.

Right: A data plate from the wreckage of Spitfire R6642, Pilot Officer John Lund's aircraft, which was shot down on 15 October 1940.

The search for the remains of Flying Officer James Henderson's Hurricane, which went down near the Clacton sea defences during the Battle of Britain.

189

James Henderson and his bride, Louise Lyman.

Part of the gun mounts from Hurricane V6601, which was being flown by Cambridge scholar and pre-war aviator and businessman Flying Officer James Alan MacDonald Henderson when it was shot down over the Essex marshes on 31 August 1940.

Above: Terry, on the right with his back to the camera, investigating the crash site of the Me 110 flown by Gruppenkommandeur Walter Rubensdörffer. A recipient of the Knight's Cross of the Iron Cross, his aircraft was shot down on 15 August 1940. The crew, including Rubensdörffer, were all killed. The hunt for remains of the aircraft took place in the late 1970s.

Right: Gruppenkommandeur Walter Rubensdörffer.

Chapter 13

THE SUNDRIDGE DORNIER

ON 7 September 1940 the Luftwaffe launched a massive bombing raid on the South East and left London's docklands to burn and smoulder. Indeed, the East End was a scene of devastation after He 111s and Ju 88s had dropped raft upon raft of deadly explosives, including hundreds of incendiaries and delayed action bombs.

All this happened in the sunlight of a late afternoon in early autumn. RAF fighter pilots in Hurricanes and Spitfires flew like darts among the great marauding Luftwaffe in a desperate attempt to drive off such a relentless foe. However, no one on the ruined streets heard the fierce aerial battles overhead, as loud bells rang out from the emergency vehicles on their way towards the smoke and chaos of a city under siege.

Earlier that day and within hours of Hitler's famous rant to the German people about how he was on his way to England, the Luftwaffe discovered to their relief they had a head start on the RAF and began arriving in their hundreds unchallenged. Where was the RAF? It seems Fighter Command at Bentley Priory had made the defence of the airfields a top priority that day until a quick change in strategy by Air Chief Marshal Hugh Dowding and Air Vice Marshal Keith Park. By 4.00 pm they had scrambled eleven squadrons and put other neighbouring nervous aircrews at the mercy of the bell to scramble.

The German invasion of bombers and their Me 109 fighter escorts had turned the skies of South East England dark with terror. They had mostly arrived unchallenged until No. 43 Squadron flew in and attacked twenty-five Dornier Do 17s near the coast of Folkestone. Along the Thames Estuary No. 73 Squadron met twenty-five Luftwaffe bombers escorted by Me 110s and the Spitfires of No. 609 Squadron intercepted enemy bombers south-west of London.

Pilots including John Curchin of No. 609 chased a Dornier and shot it down within seconds and then within the same minute aimed their guns at an Me 109 which then, shattered by bullets, broke into pieces and crashed into the Thames Estuary.

For Australian Flight Lieutenant Paterson 'Pat' Clarence Hughes, leading No. 234 Squadron's Blue Section in his Spitfire X4009, the sight of the enemy had become a familiar and often deadly challenge. Such responsibility then led to incredible displays of bravery and skill – attributes which ran in the blood of young aircrews who had little choice but to live for the day. There was no time for them to question their actions. The Luftwaffe must be stopped. Hitler must be stopped. The fight for liberty was top priority. Everything else which once constituted a normal life had to wait. A peaceful future would be a blessing and an ideal they dared to hope for.

On 7 September 1940, No. 234 Squadron ran into sixty Luftwaffe aircraft close to Folkestone, Kent. Do 17s and Me 109s on their way home found themselves being dived on and relentlessly attacked from above by Spitfires and Hurricanes. Flight Lieutenant Hughes was instructed by Squadron Leader John 'Spike' O'Brien, DFC, to go after the fleeing bombers. Hughes, ever keen to carry out his trademark courage, headed straight into the enemy formation and told his wingmen to follow close by.

What happened next has been the cause of some debate among eyewitnesses of the time but there is little doubt the recently married 23-year-old Flight Lieutenant Paterson Clarence Hughes made a successful attack on a beaten up and straggling Do 17 and riddled the aircraft with bullets from his Spitfire guns. Within seconds of his attack, enormous pieces of the Luftwaffe bomber flew off and when a wing collapsed, it was seen spinning wildly towards the ground.

On board that Do 17Z (2596) of Stab KH 76, coded FI+BA, were Leutnant Gottfried Schneider, Oberfeldwebel Karl Schneider, Feldwebel Erich Rosche and Unteroffizier Walter Rupprecht. Their mission was to take aerial photographs but they had previously come under fire from Spitfire pilot Ellis Aries of No. 602 Squadron and Flying Officer George Peters of No. 79 Squadron.

When they met with the guns of Flight Lieutenant Pat Hughes, their bomber instantly spiralled down and crashed horribly into a small stream which ran into the River Darent at Sundridge, Sevenoaks. The aircraft had narrowly missed a waterworks station nearby. The wireless operator, Erich Rosche, baled out in time and was taken PoW.

The rest of the crew were dead. The tail fin of the Do 17 landed some yards away and artefacts were removed from the wreckage at the time, including a leather flying helmet which was taken from Rosche after his capture.

But what happened to Flight Lieutenant Hughes – a pilot from Cooma, New South Wales who had become a hero of No. 234 Squadron?

It is believed by many that his Spitfire X4009 somehow collided with the ailing Luftwaffe bomber as it fell to pieces and a wing from his own aircraft flew off, which caused it to plummet out of control and crash at Sundridge, too. Flight Lieutenant Hughes managed to bale out but was soon found dead among the flowers of a back garden nearby. His parachute was unopened, and his faithful dog, Butch, who often flew with him is believed to have died with him that day as well.

Flight Lieutenant Pat Hughes, DFC, had been an experienced aviator who had realised a boyhood dream and joined the Royal Australian Air Force in 1935. Wearing his dark blue RAAF uniform, he then travelled to the UK in 1937 to join forces with the RAF and trained to fly light bombers.

On 30 October 1939, the youngest of five brothers from a boisterous Australian family of twelve was posted to No. 234 Squadron as flight commander and by June 1940 'Pat' was stationed at St Eval, Cornwall, having married Kathleen Brodrick from Hull.

As Battle of Britain historian and Memorial archivist Edward McManus reveals:

'Pat was credited with sharing 234's first victory during the Battle, a Ju 88 he shot down near Land's End on 8 July and on the 27th he damaged another and shared in damaging another on the 28th. In August 1940 the Squadron moved to Middle Wallop. During the next few weeks his tactic of getting in close and getting out quickly ensured that he was always where the fighting was fiercest. On 15 August Hughes destroyed an Me 110 and shared another, destroyed two Me 109s on the 16th, two more on the 18th, two more on the 26th, three Me 110s on 4 September, two Me 109s on the 5th and another probable on the 6th.

(Hughes received a 'bar' to his DFC for his part in the shooting down at Marden, Kent of Franz von Werra's Me 109 on 5 September 1940. Von Werra was famous for his miraculous escape from a Canadian PoW camp. A film was made about him in 1957 and called *The One That Got Away*. On 25 October 1941 von

Werra's aircraft suffered engine failure and he disappeared along with it over the sea near Vlissingen.)

It was on 7 September 1940 that the squadron intercepted a large daylight raid on London, comprised of 60 Do 17s plus their Me 109 escorts. Pat was leading his section and dived straight towards the raiders. Within a minute or two his Spitfire, X4009, was seen spinning down with part of a wing missing and it fell in a field at Sundridge, Kent. Pat's body, parachute unopened, fell in the back garden of a bungalow 100 yards away near Dry Hill Lane. The resident was a William Norman who ran to a neighbour to ask for help as "there is a body of a young man on the lawn of the back garden".

From eyewitness reports there is no doubt that his Spitfire was in collision with a Do17 that fell in the same area. Some eyewitnesses on the ground were convinced that they saw Pat deliberately ram the Dornier having used up his ammunition. Another unresolved mystery is that it was common knowledge on the squadron that Pat's constant companion, a terrier called "Butch", flew with him in action. The dog was never seen again after that day and it is widely believed that he died with his master.'

Flight Lieutenant Pat Hughes, DFC*, was buried in St James Churchyard, Sutton, Hull, close to his wife's home. A week after her husband's funeral Kathleen discovered she was pregnant, and a miscarriage four months later revealed a son who, like his father, left this world far, far too soon.

The memory of Flight Lieutenant Hughes lives on thanks to many who have not only written books about the 32 Australian 'Few' who fought in the Battle of Britain, but also to the residents of Sundridge, near Sevenoaks. For many years the graves of the dead Dornier crew were also tended regularly at the village churchyard until they were exhumed and reburied at Cannock Chase Cemetery.

In 2000, Wing Commander Bob Doe, DFC, who also served with No. 234 Squadron and knew Hughes well, said: 'Everyone talks about the wrong people... The self-publicists. Now, who has ever heard of Pat Hughes? He saved our squadron, and he shot down a lot more than others I could name. But he died you see. That was a blow.'

Bob Doe (1920 – 2010), who survived the hell of 7 September 1940, shot down an He 111. Their Squadron Leader 'Spike' O'Brien was killed over Orpington, Kent shortly after he ordered Hughes to chase the straggling Do 17. No. 234 Squadron had lost not only Hughes but O'Brien that day – two of its finest.

Today, Pat Hughes is remembered as one of three top-scoring Australian aces of the Second World War and his name is recorded on the notable War Memorial in Canberra. His sister Muriel Tongue placed a memorial tablet to him at Christ's Church, Kiama, and in England at Westminster Abbey his name is rightfully listed in the Roll of Honour.

In 1968 Ken Anscombe decided to look around the area of the Spitfire crash site at Dark's Farm, Bessels Green with a metal detector. There he discovered some fragments of aluminium and knew he had unearthed the point of impact.

Once he then gained permission to actually dig the site, he found more artefacts including an information plate from the tail fin. Serial numbers helped identify and confirm he had indeed discovered the remains of X4009, flown by Australian top gun – Flight Lieutenant Pat Hughes, DFC.

The dig helped confirm the truth of what had happened to the aircraft, and it indicated it had not been Hughes' intention to ram the Dornier. I thought about this and realised he had too much to live for so he might well have misjudged his attack on the bomber and maybe a piece of it hit his own Spitfire? The Dornier certainly did not blow up and destroy Hughes' Spitfire with it as some suggest.

Local reports of the time reveal that there were attempts to help any survivors of the Luftwaffe crew and free them from the wreckage. A guard was placed around the aircraft until the bodies were taken away.

In 2005 in Sundridge, Kent, a plaque was placed on a wall by Dessie Hall near the garden where Flight Lieutenant Hughes fell to his death. Three years later, in 2008, Flight Lieutenant Hughes' great friend from No. 234 Squadron – Wing Commander Doe, DFC – made a speech and unveiled a new memorial funded and organised by curator and aviation artist Geoff Nutkins of Shoreham Aviation Museum. The tribute marking the courage and honour of the Australian pilot who came to Britain's aid when she called, now sits proudly along the A25 road, close to where he fell.

I recall, this ceremony had particular resonance for me, as I had instigated the excavation of the Do 17Z destroyed by Flight Lieutenant Hughes. As soon as I visited the site with an initial look around with the metal detector, I wrote to the waterworks company which owned the land and received written permission to dig.

When the aircraft crashed in 1940, one or two of the locals took a look among the wreckage and some maps were retrieved from the cockpit. They were covered in oil, but were still important artefacts. One of the men who had these maps later gave them to my friend Ed Francis, who then passed them on to another collector.

It was the summer of 1974 when I began to unearth the Do 17. I found a propeller, a machine gun, a tool kit, cylinder heads, exhaust rings, and Dornier data plates. Much of it was embedded beneath some major waterworks pipes. The port rudder and fin had landed in Chipstead and for years it was stored in a builder's yard.

Local Ken Ellis, who was a boy at the time of the crash, told me: 'During the war we'd peep through the cracks in the door and were thrilled to see that tail fin, its swastika seeming to our minds to be almost luminous. Years later I asked the builder what became of it, and to my pleasure he took me home and gave it to me much damaged (by his two sons, he said).'

It took two visits to the site to remove more artefacts, and still to this day there's a possibility of uncovering more and I plan to dig it again with Geoff Nutkins of Shoreham Aircraft Museum. The problem is with the positioning of course, as in 1949 a huge water pipe supplying homes in the area was placed over the top of the wreckage and the cockpit is nigh on impossible to reach.

However, on the second dig in 1974, with the help of a JCB digger I managed to get an engine out with the gearing mechanism still attached to it and I got it home and cleaned it up. I kept this important evidence of the Battle of Britain in my garage some way away from my home in Oxted. When I grew tired of walking to and from the garage, I decided to get it back home, and as I trundled along the road with it in an old sack barrow, suddenly the whole load collapsed! The sack barrow wheel had broken, and I was left on the pavement with the engine and a red face!

When I eventually got some help and it arrived home, it attracted the interest of Andy Saunders, who then ran the aviation museum at Tangmere in West Sussex. We decided it would be beneficial for it to go on show, so this important piece of a Luftwaffe bomber went to live there. Later on it found a home in another museum.

Today one of my prized possessions is a large piece of that Do 17Z fuselage. On it, and boldly indicative of battle, is a pair of bullet holes caused by the guns of Flight Lieutenant Pat Hughes' Spitfire on that fateful day of 7 September 1940.

Above: The excavation team at the site of the Dornier Do 17Z wreckage in Sundridge.

Left: Deep down in the mud at Sundridge, Terry helps unearth one of the propellers from the Do 17Z shot down on 7 September 1940 by Flight Lieutenant Pat Hughes.

Flight Lieutenant Pat Hughes.

Remains of a mangled engine from the Do 17Z that crashed at Sundridge. Only one crew member, wireless operator Erich Rosche, survived after baling out; the aircraft lost its wing and part of its tail as it spiralled to the ground.

Left: Pat Hughes and his beloved dog, Butch, as a puppy.

Below: A group photograph of personnel from No. 234 Squadron. Pat Hughes is sitting on the left in the front row.

A piece of the Dornier Do 17Z that was shot down by Flight Lieutenant Pat Hughes on 7 September 1940. The aircraft crashed by a small stream which ran into the River Darent at Sundridge, Sevenoaks. Note the two bullet holes.

Above left: The excavation of another Do 17 crash site underway. In this picture Terry can be seen assisting the digger operator. The aircraft in question, a Dornier 17Z-3, crashed at Leysdown on the Isle of Sheppey on 20 August 1940.

Above right: The Leysdown dig continues. Within minutes of this picture being taken, the first pieces of the wreckage were uncovered. The Do 17 fell to the guns of Hurricanes flown by Squadron Leader Joseph Kayll, DSO, DFC, and, possibly Pilot Officer Cecil Young, both of No. 615 Squadron from Kenley.

201

Chapter 14

FLYING HEROES AND THE GIANT TEAPOT

IN the summer of 1984 I helped organise a dig of a Heinkel He 111 near Station Road, Withyham, East Sussex. We got to the site the day before we were due to start excavating and after some food we spent a peaceful night sleeping in a barn on some hay bales – that was until the early morning, when a farmer came in and started up a tractor and we all choked from the fumes! It's an interesting way to be woken up for sure. The Heinkel had been shot down by Sergeant Pilots JC Copeland and Sampson of No. 151 Squadron in a Defiant night fighter at 3.30 am on 11 May 1941.

During another dig for a Heinkel in the 1980s I met a witness to the crash, who told me how he and his wife were looking at the Luftwaffe bomber giant from their window as it headed towards their house, in flames. The man told his wife to move away and as she turned, a bullet came through the window and embedded itself in the wall. When I met him during the dig, he gave me that bullet and talked to me about the near miss experienced by his wife. He was certain that bullet would have killed her, no question. He also gave me half of a white horse ornament which was split in half that day by another Heinkel bullet that peppered their home.

Over the recent decades and despite the sad stories which surrounded most of my digs, I have had reason to smile at some of the more light-hearted moments. These include how on 28 September 1940, when V7497 crashed and burned on a little piece of land at Chartway Street, East Sutton near Maidstone, Kent, several villagers ran over to a nearby shed to find an old man working in there. He asked them, 'Whassup?!' and they told him, 'There's a Hurricane in pieces right next to you!' He didn't know, hadn't heard a thing and was surprised to see the mess just feet away from his shed door!

This Hurricane had been flown by Pilot Officer Everett Rogers of No. 501 Squadron and was shot down by Me 109s over Deal, Kent that day. Pilot Officer Everett, who was later awarded a DFC, baled out and was unhurt.

Then there were the diggers I knew, who gave no thought to any danger on a site which had unexploded bombs and artillery. There was one individual who was busy hacking away with a pickaxe at the mud clinging to a round of machine gun bullets he'd found among the wreck of a Dornier. I let him know what I thought about that idea and asked him if he cared about keeping his hand! I got to know what was dangerous and what was not. I have carried certain German bombs on my shoulders because I knew they weren't charged. Then in the 1980s we began calling in the Territorial Army experts who had special detectors to locate any bombs, which would then be gently dug up and taken away to the corner of a field to be detonated. There's been many a time I held my hands over my ears at the blast and watched from afar as tiny pieces of metal shot into the sky, formed an arc and scattered far and wide.

One day a friend ran over to me at a dig to tell me he could hear a hissing sound coming from the wreckage. He was scared it was a bomb waiting to go off. So I trotted over to this Ju 88 wreckage to listen for myself, only to find it was the air coming out of a tyre which was causing all the hullabaloo! Then the argy-bargy began to get the tyre out of the hole and keep it as inflated as possible because it was genuine German air from 1940!

In an earlier chapter, I mentioned my ambitions to recover certain aircraft which I know for sure are still out there. Of course there are thousands still to be found and all of them crashed during the Battle of Britain. I have dug hundreds of them for 60-plus years and yet the search will never be over and I hope in the future a new generation of archaeologists will take up the struggle to find them and work with English Heritage.

These days I like to take stock of artefacts and keep a check on what might turn up out there. One passion is to find a bizarre old 'mascot' once held dear by aircrews of both world wars. I am keen to find the giant wooden teapot measuring four feet high which at first 'served' with the pilots and mechanics of the Royal Flying Corps (later Royal Air Force) at Biggin Hill.

In 1918 it often appeared at the airfield as if by magic courtesy of the jokers among the resident No. 141 Squadron, who took part in moonlight raids to remove it from outside the Teapot Gardens cafe in the town. Ironically, the squadron's motto 'Caedimus Noctu' translates as 'We Slay by Night'!

When the pranksters of No. 141 Squadron weren't larking about taking possession of their favourite giant comedy mascot, they were flying Bristol F.2 Fighters to fend off attacks carried out by Zeppelins and Gotha heavy bombers.

An old photograph shows the cheeky 'fly boys' with the teapot outside the Women's Institute Hall in Biggin Hill. Among them is the famous Lieutenant Hardit Singh Malik, CIE, OBE, of No. 141 Squadron who was the first Indian pilot to fly with the RFC and Royal Air Force. He claimed six victories and served over the Western Front with a famous Canadian, Commander Major William Barker, VC.

At Biggin Hill and during the days of the high-spirited teapot raids of 1918, Malik was known as 'The Flying Hobgoblin' because of his unusual helmet made to fit over his turban. He was one of two Indian pilots out of four to survive the war and went on to become the Indian Ambassador to France.

The life of the old teapot was equally as adventurous, as it was often stolen then returned days later in the dark of night, only to disappear again and mysteriously arrive or 'come home' to its fans at the airfield – much to the annoyance of its real owners.

Now I am keen to find out what happened to this famous old artefact. I know the moonlight raids on the old teapot became a tradition among the aircrews. It was regularly acquired by squadron pranksters during the Second World War as well. I expect pilot aces like Group Captain Brian Kingcome, DSO, DFC*, who led No. 42 Squadron during the Battle of Britain knew about the old teapot! Indeed, it had become something of a tradition among all of the various squadrons stationed at Biggin Hill to secretly remove it from its perch and return it in the dark of night.

I recall it as a child and a young man, when it was situated next to the grand Highclere House (now demolished) to promote the local cafe along the main road through the town at the Westerham end. You couldn't miss it standing out there. As a boy, I often wondered why it kept disappearing then reappearing again! Above the door of Highclere House there was another sign which read, 'Ye Olde Teapot. Weekends, Apartments, Board and Residence'.

Owing to the rare history of the teapot with the aircrews of both world wars, I would dearly love to find out what happened to it. It would be a dream come true to locate it again. Perhaps there's someone out there with a few clues as to its whereabouts. I would appreciate hearing from anyone with any memories about it during its days around the airfield.

I last saw the historic teapot in the 1960s. It had happily survived its many illicit sojourns from the cafe to the airfield. I bet it could tell a tale or two. In fact, it all sounds like a Roald Dahl story – 'The Flying Heroes and the Giant Teapot'!

I do know that a group of engineering apprentices who were based nearby at Chislehurst were known to have continued the tradition of 'borrowing' it from the cafe in 1961. One of the lads was Stan Weeks, whose father had served with the RAF at Biggin Hill during the Second World War. Stan's father had told him about the practical jokes carried out at the airfield and the tale of the giant teapot stuck in his memory.

One night in 1961, it seems Stan and his friends decided it would be fun to unbolt the teapot from its perch and make off with it – temporarily of course! They took a few jokey snaps of it atop Stan's motorbike and then returned it, apologising profusely to its angry owner at the cafe! Stan explained he had wanted to associate himself with the teapot which had such an incredible history and connection to the flying heroes of two world wars.

I did hear tale the teapot was last seen at the airfield in the 1960s but it suddenly just disappeared. Exactly where it went remains yet another wartime mystery that I would love to solve.

And of course, almost every month or so a unique artefact from an aircraft of the Second World War comes to my attention via acquaintances in the vintage aviation world. In the summer of 2019 I met a chap by chance who as a boy in 1940 lived close by to the Dornier 17 crash site at Sundridge. He kindly gave me two items

The cheeky 'fly boys' of the First World War with the famous teapot outside the Women's Institute Hall in Biggin Hill. Among them is the famous Lieutenant Hardit Singh Malik CIE, OBE of No. 141 Squadron.

he'd found at the site which he had kept for almost eighty years. A few machine gun bullets and a piece of fuselage from this aircraft shot down by Australian top gun Pat Hughes now sit among the pieces in my carefully chosen collection, with each one representing my life's work to honour the memory of those aircrew who took part in such legendary and historic battles in the skies over Britain and Europe during the Second World War.

These artefacts were presented to Terry by a local resident who had picked them up at a crash site during the Battle of Britain. They came from the wreckage of Hauptmann Lamberty's Do 17Z-2, which crashed at Leaves Green, near Biggin Hill, on 18 August 1940.

A close-up of the wreckage of the 1942 Hurricane crash.

A dig underway in Devon in the 1970s at the crash site of a Fleet Air Arm Fairey Fulmar. The aircraft in question, BP813, was being flown by Sub-lieutenant John Heyworth Huggan when it crashed on 19 May 1942. Also on board was 19-year-old Air Mechanic 2nd Class John William Longson. The Fulmar was seen spinning into the ground three miles north-west of Torquay, killing both men.

Part of the control column of Fairey Fulmar BP813 that was recovered at the time of the dig.

A dig underway at Winchelsea, near Rye in East Sussex, at the crash site of a photo-reconnaissance Spitfire, X4784, which went down on 24 April 1942. The pilot who was killed that day was Pilot Officer Charles Bertram 'Bertie' Barber of No. 140 Squadron.

207

Acknowledgements

THERE have been some smashing people to whom I owe a whole heap of thanks for their support and interest during the writing of this book which aims to serve as a tribute to all those men and women of the Battle of Britain and The Blitz.

Firstly, there is Terry Parsons of course, for so vividly collecting his memories together from six decades, who allowed me to consult his diaries and notes about the hundreds of stricken aircraft he has recovered from the earth.

It was the forward-thinking team at Frontline Books who gave me the opportunity to record Terry's memories and achievements as one of Britain's leading pioneers in the field of community aviation archaeology, and blend them in with my commentary on the social history of the war.

And to the legendary Battle of Britain pilots I've had the honour to meet and talk to over the years, including Wing Commander Paul Farnes, DFM, Wing Commander Tom Neil, DFC*, AFC, AE, Flight Lieutenant Bill Green, Squadron Leader Tony Pickering, Squadron Leader Geoffrey Wellum, DFC, and Sergeant Ken Wilkinson – ever thanks for such rare, genuine and authentic inspiration and encouragement to battle on despite the odds!

Also, the star who is historian Edward McManus for his steady compilation of such an important and available archive of information about the men of the Battle of Britain at www.bbm.org.

Dr Julian Brock has provided sterling support and his considerable organisational skills once again.

Thanks as always to Henry and Hattie cats and my family. Also, the great teams at Bentley Priory Museum, The Battle of Britain Memorial at Capel-le-Ferne, Shoreham Aircraft Museum, and of course not forgetting – John and Pat Coles for access to the 'Herbert Black Memorial Tree' site. Plus Nigel Price and John Ash at *Britain at War* magazine, and colleagues at Waterstones bookshops. And of course, the late Sergeant Pilot Neville Croucher – may he rest in peace – Hurricane pilot of No. 289 Squadron, and the amazing 'Spitfire Girl', ATA First Officer Mary Wilkins Ellis – never forgotten.

Terry would like to dedicate this book to the memory of his devoted wife Rose Parsons, and family. Also, it serves as a salute to his hero – the late, great Battle of Britain ace – Group Captain Johnny Kent DFC, AFC, Virtuti Militari (1914 – 1985). Terry joins me in a massive thanks to – Phillipe and Adrienne Lecoeuvre, The Guinea Pig Club, Angela Lodge, The Battle of Britain Memorial Trustees at Capel-le-Ferne, Kent. Not forgetting – Andy Saunders, Alix Kent, Dr Helen Doe, Steve Vizard, Dr Vince Holyoak, Lewis Deal MBE, Geoff Nutkins, Ed Francis, Tony and Pat Graves, Mark Kirby, Dick Lukehurst, Harry Wynch, Adrian Crossnan, Gordon Ramsey, Tony Webb, and the late Tony Parslow.

Finally, much heartfelt appreciation goes out to Dr Bernhard Klebe and his amazing medical team. And to all those community organisations and history societies who book me for talks and lectures; it's been marvellous to meet you all. Ever thanks.

Bibliography

The Battle of Britain Memorial Trust: *Men of the Battle of Britain* (Frontline/Pen & Sword Books, 2015)

Connelly, Mark: *We Can Take It!: Britain and the Memory of the Second World War* (Routledge, 2004)

Gleave, Tom: *I Had a Row with a German* (*RAF Casualty*) (Macmillan & Co Ltd, 1943)

Kent, Johnny; Kent, Alexandra: *One of the Few* (History Press, 2016, first edition, 1971)

Mason, Francis: *Battle Over Britain* (McWhirter Twins Ltd, 1969)

Newton, Dennis: *A Spitfire Pilot's Story: Pat Hughes, Battle of Britain Top Gun* (Amberley, 2016)

Ogley, Bob: *Biggin on the Bump: The Most Famous Fighter Station in the World* (Froglets Publications, 1990)

Ogley, Bob: *Ghosts of Biggin Hill* (Froglets Publications, 2001)

Ramsey, Winston: *The Battle of Britain, Then and Now* (After the Battle, 1987)

Saunders, Andy: *Finding the Foe* (Grub Street, 2010)

Saunders, Andy: *Finding the Few* (Grub Street, 2013)

Steinhilper, Ulrich; Osborne, Peter: *Spitfire on my Tail* (Independent Books, 2009)

Willis, John: *Churchill's Few: The Battle of Britain Remembered* (Guild Books, 1985)

Index

Diamond, Peter, 73, 74, 158, 183
Dornier Do 17 excavations, *see*:
  Gincocks Farm
  Leysdown, Isle of Sheppey
  Schneider, Gottfried
Droese, Heinz, 181
Dymchurch, Kent, 154

Edenbridge, Kent, 107
Elmley, Isle of Sheppey, xiv, 55
English Heritage, xii, xiv
Enßlen, Wilhelm, 154, 155, 156, 157, 160

Fairey Fulmar excavation site:
  see Huggan, John Heyworth
Fessel, Rudolf, 159
Flimwell, East Sussex, 38
Fokes, Ronald, 48
Foreman, Melody, 104
Francis, Ed, 8, 52, 53, 149, 154, 158

Gaunt, Geoffrey, 79
Geisswinkler, Karl, 47, 48
Gelferin, D.R.K., 43, 44
Gincocks Farm, Hurst Green, 40
Gleave, Tom, 35, 36, 49, 166
Goudhurst Road, Horsmonden, 38
Graves, Tony, 7, 34, 41, 85, 94, 106, 107, 109, 154
Grays Road, Westerham Hill, 149
Grice, Dick, 14, 23
Gruszka, Franciszek, 83, 84, 96
Guenther, Heinz, 158

Haase, Julius, 39
Hall, Steve, 8, 154, 181, 183
Halstead War Museum, 32, 33, 40, 44, 52, 53, 158
Happy Valley, Old Coulsdon, 39, 50

Hawker Hurricane Society, 136
Heinkel He 111 excavations, *see*:
  Metzger, Albert
  Stender, Wilhelm
  Withyham, East Sussex
Henderson, James Alan MacDonald, 182, 190
Hodgkiss, Philippa, 8, 158
Holm Fen, Cambridgeshire, xiv
Holyoak, Vince, xii, xiv, xv
Homer, Michael, 119, 120
Hothfield Park, Kent, 97
Huggan, John Heyworth, 207
Hughes, Patrick Clarence, 139, 193, 194, 195, 196, 199, 200, 206
Hurricane excavations, *see*:
  Allgood, Harold
  Beresford, Hugh
  Black, Herbert
  Bryant-Fenn, Leofric Trevor
  Buchanan-Wollaston, Arthur
  Carver, Kenneth
  Clifton, John
  Gleave, Tom
  Homer, Michael
  Kozlowski, Franciszek
  Henderson, James Alan MacDonald
  McKay, Donald Alistair Stewart
  Newton, Harry Snow
  Olding, Harold
  Pearson, Geoffrey Wilberforce
  Pickering, Tony
  Pisarek, Marian
  Ravenhill, Malcolm
  Rogers, Everett
  Stansfeld, Noel Karl
  Trueman, Alec Albert Gray
  van den Hove d'Ertsenrijck, Albert Emmanuel Alex
  Townsend, Peter Wooldridge

RAF Faygate No.49 Maintenance Unit, 6, 7, 9, 10
Ramsey, Gordon, 8, 85, 86, 98, 99, 183
Ramsey, Winston, 55, 85, 98
Ravenhill, Malcolm, 60, 64
Rogers, Everett, 203
Rösch, Konrad, 181
Rosche, Erich, 193, 194
Rotherfield, East Sussex, 183
Rübensdörffer, Walter, 183, 184, 185, 191
Rupprecht, Walter, 193, 194, 199

Saunders, Andy, 5, 7, 73, 74, 96, 123, 154, 159, 181, 183, 197
Schandner, Rolf, 159
Schenk, A, 156, 157
Schieverhöfer, Lothar, 67, 68, 173, 178
Schneider, Gottfried, 193
Schneider, Karl, 193
Schöpfel, Gerhard, 92, 120
Shotley, Harwich, 157
Shuart Farm, St Nicholas at Wade, 73
Skinner, Bill, 71, 76
Spitfire excavations, *see*:
    Barber, Charles Bertram
    Chesters, Peter
    Corbett, George Henry
    Cutts, John Wintringham
    Gaunt, Geoffrey
    Gruszka, Franciszek
    Lund, John
Stansfeld, Noel Karl, 51 *et seq*, 61, 62
Stärk, Otto, 181

Steinhilper, Ulrich, 65 *et seq*
Stender, Wilhelm, 157
Stronk, Siegrfried Lothar, 153
Sundridge, Kent, 193
Sutherland Avenue, Biggin Hill, 153

Tamblyn, Hugh, 42
Teapot (Biggin Hill), 18, 203, 204, 205
The Grange, Tatsfield, 21
Torquay, 207
Townsend, Peter Wooldridge, 111, 112, 165, 166, 167, 168, 178
Trueman, Alec Albert Gray, 135, 136, 140, 141, 144
Tudor Close, Banstead, 135

Upchurch, Chatham, 168
Urhahn, Julius, 159

van den Hove d'Ertsenrijck, Albert Emmanuel Alex, 122 *et seq*
Vizard, Steve, 7, 74, 123, 154, 157, 171, 181, 182, 183

Walker, Dick, 154, 183
Webb, Tony, 109
Wellum, Geoffrey, 15, 24
Westbere, Kent, 82
Whall, Basil Stewart Patrick, 158, 159, 160, 161
Wildermuth, Eberhard, 181
Winchelsea, East Sussex, 207
Withyham, East Sussex, 202
Worcester Park, Cheam, 41, 49